EX LIBRIS
Lynne Rudder Baker
Philosopher
1944 - 2017

On the Plurality of Actual Worlds

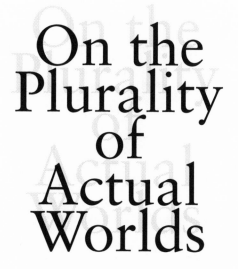

On the
Plurality
of
Actual
Worlds

Andrew L. Blais

UNIVERSITY OF MASSACHUSETTS PRESS   Amherst

Copyright © 1997 by
Andrew L. Blais
All rights reserved
Printed in the United States of America
LC 96-51454
ISBN 1-55849-072-8

Designed by Sally Nichols
Set in Sabon by dix!
Printed and bound by Braun-Brumfield, Inc.
Library of Congress Cataloging-in-Publication Data

Blais, Andrew L., 1954–
On the plurality of actual worlds / Andrew L. Blais.
p.   cm.
Includes bibliographical references and index.
ISBN 1-55849-072-8 (cloth : alk. paper)
1. Pluralism.   2. Relativity.   I. Title.
BD394.B45   1997
115—dc21   96-51454
                                            CIP

British Library Cataloguing in Publication data are available.

To Andrew Van Blais: anarchist, metaphysician, son

Contents

Introduction

Even if a metaphor cannot be the basis of a serious philosophical argument, a metaphor may certainly introduce such an argument. Accordingly, consider the following metaphor from Otto Neurath:

> *There is no way of taking conclusively established pure protocol sentences as the starting point of the sciences.* No *tabula rasa* exists. We are like sailors who must rebuild their ship on the open sea, never able to dismantle it in dry-dock and to reconstruct it there out of the best materials. Only the metaphysical elements can be allowed to vanish without trace. Vague linguistic conglomerations always remain in one way or another as components of the ship. If vagueness is diminished at one point, it may well be increased at another.[1]

Here, Neurath likens our beliefs, or the sentences we take to be true, to a ship on the open sea. When Neurath's ship needs repairs, dry-dock is not an option, and so it is necessary for repairs to proceed on a plank-by-plank basis. Similarly, when our system of beliefs needs repairs, that is, when it is discovered to contain false or vague beliefs, there is no epistemic position equivalent to dry-dock, and so it is necessary for our epistemic repairs to proceed on a belief-by-belief basis. One of his central points is that it is, consequently, impossible for us to replace all of our beliefs at one time.

Neurath's metaphor leaves open a diachronic or historical question: Could the fragmentary reconstruction of our beliefs result in a time when they had all been replaced? It also leaves open a synchronic or anthropological question: Could there be beings whose beliefs were completely different from ours? The anthropological question may be reducible to the historical question: If there were beings whose beliefs were entirely different from ours, could the fragmentary reconstruction of our beliefs result in a time when we had theirs? These questions raise the pivotal issue of the conditions under which one belief system may be said to be the same or different from another. In a way that aptly continues Neurath's metaphor, and also discloses this issue, Thomas Hobbes writes:

> [I]f . . . for example, that ship of Theseus, concerning the difference whereof made by continual reparation in taking out the old planks and putting in new, the sophisters of Athens were wont to dispute, were, after all the planks were changed, the same numerical ship it was at the beginning; and if some man had kept the old planks as they were taken out, and by putting them afterwards together in the same ship order, had again made a ship of them, this, without doubt, had also been the same numerical ship with that which was at the beginning; and so there would have been two ships numerically the same, which is absurd.[2]

Hobbes makes a quite literal point here that makes it possible to extend Neurath's metaphor. First, consider the literal point. Were identity transitive, and were the replacement of a single plank to fail to yield a new and different ship, then the original ship of Theseus would be the same as the reconstructed ship of Theseus. However, were we to put the old planks together, there would be the old worn ship, there would be the shiny new ship, and one would be two, which is absurd. One important lesson here is that to replace all planks is to bring about a new and different ship. Or, more generally, one lesson is that to replace every part of an object is to bring about a new and different object.

Second, to see how this point of Hobbes' thought-experiment makes it possible to extend Neurath's metaphor, suppose that the object in question is the congeries of our beliefs. One way to get two ships of belief is to begin with one ship, and then to replace all of its planks. But, can all the planks in a ship of belief be replaced? More literally, one way to get two belief systems is to begin with one, and then to replace all of its parts. Neurath has shown, however, that it is impossible to replace all our beliefs at one time, but it does not follow from this that it is impossible to replace all of our beliefs. If we cannot replace all our beliefs at one time, it is an open question whether there are other conditions under which there could be two belief systems, and whether these conditions can be realized. Is it, for example, possible to replace all our beliefs over an extended period of time? Powerful reasons have been pressed for thinking that at least some parts of a belief system cannot be replaced, and so the answer must be negative.

Donald Davidson has argued that not all of our beliefs can be replaced. One way in which he has made this point is by focusing on what he takes to be the dominant metaphor of conceptual relativism, and by then pointing out how this metaphor reveals its incoherence. Davidson writes:

> The dominant metaphor of conceptual relativism, that of differing points of view, seems to betray an underlying paradox. Different points of view makes sense, but only if there is a common co-ordinate system on which to plot them; yet the existence of a common system belies the claim of dramatic incomparability.[3]

As Davidson understands the conceptual relativist, she believes that there are essentially incomparable belief systems, and that they are incomparable in a way that is importantly similar to the way that points of view are incomparable. Davidson maintains that since any two points of view must be locatable within a common coordinate system, they must be comparable. So, either there is a significant way in which conceptual frameworks are not similar to points of view, or conceptual frameworks must be comparable. In other words, either the dominant metaphor is falsified, or the claim of essential incomparability is falsified. Supposing that the metaphor is a good one, it follows that belief systems, or conceptual schemes, are essentially comparable. If belief systems must be comparable, some of our beliefs cannot be replaced, else there would be no basis for comparison. Consequently, whereas Neurath's idea seems to have been that we cannot replace all of our beliefs at one time, Davidson's idea is that we cannot replace all of our beliefs.

Much of the force of Davidson's argument depends upon the adequacy of his premise that the dominant metaphor of conceptual relativism is that of the point of view. It is evident, I think, that it is not, since it does belie the conceptual relativist's claim that some conceptual schemes are essentially incomparable. Ironically, a better metaphor might be that of the coordinate system. Given the mere possibility of nonabsolute space, different coordinate systems do not need a common space within which they have absolute location. Indeed, the idea of a space within which coordinate systems have location is somewhat confused, since it is in terms of coordinate systems that location is defined. So, not only do different coordinate systems make sense, but it is not necessary for there to be a common space within which they have location. So, the better metaphor for the alternative conceptual schemes of conceptual relativism may well be that of alternative coordinate systems. The pivotal question is whether there is reason to doubt the claim that different coordinate systems can be essentially incomparable, which would mean that this metaphor also belies the claim that different conceptual schemes can be essentially incomparable. The answer would be affirmative, if there were a way to transform, or translate, any location in any one coordinate system into any location in any other system. This is the essential idea of Davidson's criticism of conceptual relativism.

In his argument, Davidson surreptitiously separates two questions. (1) Can there be two conceptual schemes? (2) What ontology does the scheme idea presuppose? Davidson himself writes: "Reality itself is relative to a scheme: what counts as real in one system may not in another."[4] If this thesis is right, and there are many conceptual schemes, then there are many realities. It might seem obvious that this thesis is the weak link in the chain of reasoning that supports the conclusion that there are many realities, but curiously, Davidson's strategy is not to work on breaking this link. Instead, he aims to assail the very idea of a conceptual scheme. In doing this, however, he isolates the scheme idea from the ontological background that gives it sense. Like the magician whose trick depends on his ability to focus our attention on something other than the legerdemain, the persuasive force of Davidson's argument depends on his ability to focus our attention on something other than the ontological background of the scheme idea. However, in disregarding this ontology, Davidson criticizes a shadow. The critical evaluation of his argument, not to mention other antirelativist arguments, presupposes an account of this ontology. Although this volume contains my response to Davidson's argument, this response is incidental. In Christopher Marlowe's *Doctor Faustus,* after Mephostophilis has appeared, Faustus inquires, "Did not my conjuring raise thee?" Mephostophilis answers, "That was the cause, but yet *per accidens.*"[5] Davidson's argument was the cause of the appearance of my account of this ontology, but yet *per accidens.* My aim here is to articulate and defend the ontology which is presupposed by the thesis that there are alternative conceptual schemes, and which has been ignored by Davidson. In short, this ontology can be expressed as the literal thesis that there are many actual worlds.

This work divides into five chapters. The goal of chapter 1 is to introduce the thesis that there are many actual worlds by introducing the thesis to which it is opposed, to wit, the thesis that there is just one world that has just one complete and true description. By getting clear on this contrary idea, I hope to make clear some of the tasks that the articulation and defense of my idea must accomplish. In other words, I begin to explain the ontology presupposed by the idea of an alternative conceptual scheme by explaining the ontology to which it is opposed. I will also display a reading of Protagoras that I think illustrates the idea that I aim to develop. I also argue that the objection that my idea is self-refuting fails. In chapter 2, I will discuss the work of Whorf and Quine, and in chapter 3, will turn to the work of Goodman and Putnam. Not only does the work of these four thinkers illustrate various elements of the ontology that I articulate, but each poses a number of questions to which I think the explanation of my idea must provide answers. In chapter 4, I explore a number of the basic ideas that I will use to make sense of the thesis that there are many actual worlds, for example, the idea that an object is what a manifold of objective representations represents, and the idea that a world is the sum total of what exists in a time. I do this by appropriating the metaphysical inversion, which Kant, in his *Critique of Pure Reason,* called his Copernican Revolution, and by appropriating the central insight of Robert Paul Wolff's essay *"Narrative Time,"* namely, that the structure of time is constituted by purposes.[6] In chapter 5, I turn from the exposition and defense of my thesis to use it to explain a case, described by Foucault, in which representation dependent objects are experienced as if they are representation independent.

Since the argument of the first four chapters that follow is quite complicated, it may serve my readers well, if I include the following summary.

1. There are many representing beings. [Premise]

2. The set of representing beings partitions into many nonempty classes. [Premise]

3. For each such class of representing beings, there is a set of purposes, and each set of purposes is incompatible with every other such set. [Premise]

4. For each class of representing beings, there is an ideal sum of representations that has an asymmetric structure that is imposed by the set of purposes that is associated with the class of representing beings in question. [Premise]

5. There is no ideal sum of representations that includes or subsumes all the ideal sums of representations that are associated with the various classes of representing beings. [3,4]

6. There are many ideal sums of representations. [2,4,5]

7. For each ideal sum of representations, there is an actual world. [Premise]

8. There are many actual worlds. [6,7]

9. There are many truths. [6,8]

This is, however, only a summary, and it requires expansion and explanation. To this task, I now turn.

I
The Worlds of Protagoras
Problems and Questions

In this work, two theses are under consideration. (1) There are many actual worlds, and (2) there are many truths. The latter should not be taken to mean that there are many truths in the sense that *snow is white* and *7 + 5 = 12* are many truths, namely, two truths. What, then, does it mean? To explain the answer to this question, I will temporarily place aside these two theses, and I will consider an alternative account of truth and what it is to be a world. Simply put, this alternative is that there is just one actual world. It consists of a number of representation independent objects that have, moreover, just one complete and correct representation, where a correct representation is one that represents, or corresponds to, objects as they independently and really are.

Hilary Putnam has succinctly summarized this alternative:

> [1] [T]he world consists of a fixed totality of mind-independent objects. . . . [2] [T]here is exactly one true and complete description of the way the world is. . . . [3] [T]ruth involves some sort of correspondence.[1]

In Putnam's terms, the truth, if one exists, is the unique, true, and complete description of the way the world is. The truth is, in other words, all the true sentences. A truth is just one of the many true sentences, for example, *snow is white* or $7 + 5 = 12$, which may be seen, therefore, as parts of the complete and true description. Context suffices, I think, to disambiguate. However, there is another source of ambiguity, since the ideas of *the world*, and *a true sentence* are themselves unclear. In the context of the alternative, or realist, account under consideration here, these ideas can be partly clarified by showing how Putnam's three theses form an integrated account of what it is to be *a world* and *a truth*.

Putnam's first thesis is that independently of every actual representation, and independently of our capacity to represent, there is the order of things, or objects, that possess various properties, that is, there is the world. Note well that an important part of what this means is that these properties are also independent of both our capacity to represent, and how they may be actually represented. In other words, objects are distinct by virtue of the properties or characteristics that they possess, or fail to possess, independently of whatever concepts or predicates we happen to possess.

Now, Putnam's second thesis is that the world, that is, the representation independent order of representation independent objects, has just one true and complete description. As I said above, such a description is the truth, but what is it for a description to be true? Moreover, why is there just one such description? that is, why is there just one truth? These questions cannot be answered in the absence of a specific conception of what it is to be a true sentence, description or representation. Although problematic, the required conception is provided by Putnam's third thesis.

To put Putnam's third thesis somewhat crudely, true sentences are true because they correspond to the facts. The problem, which makes this formulation crude, is that the idea of a sentence corresponding to the facts and the idea of a true sentence are equally enigmatic. There may be no problem with understanding this in cases such as its being true that the cat is at the door, since the required fact would seem to be just the cat's being at the door, and this seems both simple and easy to understand. But, there are cases that are not so intelligible. For example, were it true that *Socrates is not at the door*, to what fact would this true sentence correspond? It is tempting to postulate negative facts, but these are odd posits: not only isn't Socrates at the door, but Plato isn't there either, and moreover the round square isn't there, and so on. Moreover, it seems that nothing distinguishes the fact that Socrates isn't at the door from the fact that Plato isn't at the door, not to mention that fact that the round square isn't there. But, if facts can't be distinguished, why not say that there is just one fact?[2]

Putnam does not offer us much aid here, but Michael Devitt, who has presented an abundance of assenting behavior in the presence of theses such as Putnam's, provides, or attempts to provide, a more refined account of what it is to be a true sentence, that is, an account that does not explain the enigmatic by means of the enigmatic. He writes:

> Consider a true sentence with a very simple structure: the predication 'a is F'. This sentence is true in virtue of the fact that there exists an object which 'a' *designates* and which is among the objects 'F' *applies* to. So this sentence is true because it has a predicational structure containing words standing in *certain referential relations* to parts of reality, and because of the way that reality is. Provided structure, relations and reality are objective then the sentence is correspondence true.[3]

Devitt's explanation relies on the notions of *designation, application,* and *certain referential relations,* but these need explanation as much as the notion of a true sentence. More specifically, these notions need to be explained because if one maintains that the objects of which the world consists are representation independent, and that truth is correspondence, then one faces, as Putnam argues, two deep enigmas.

The first enigma is that given Putnam's three theses, that is, given realism, any representation could be false, even if it is ideal. So, for example, it could be that every sentient being is a brain in a vat. Putnam argues that this—to wit, skepticism—is impossible, and for this reason, he rejects these theses.[4] The second enigma also turns on the premise that Putnam's three realist theses entail that even an ideal representation could be false. Putnam argues that if consistency is a necessary condition for being an ideal representation, it is, for model theoretic reasons, incoherent to say that an ideal representation could be false, and so realism ought to be rejected.[5] Since at least the former problem will arise again in what follows, I will not go any further into the details. My point is that they reveal the need to provide a fuller account of the referential notions—designation, and so on—that are presupposed by Devitt's account of truth.

To provisionally circumvent this cluster of puzzles, and to return to the topic of the place of a unique truth in the ontology described by Putnam's three theses, I will replace Devitt's account of what it is to be a true sentence with an image, which I will entitle *the string theory of truth*. Here, strings are place-holders, and to be rid of them, it is necessary to construct an ontological apparatus that can explain the relation between representation and world.[6] Although I will return to this topic below, I will now present an argument that Putnam's three theses, in relative abstraction from any particular account of reference, entail that there is just one truth. Recall that my overall aim here is to make sense of the idea of *truth,* as in *there are many truths,* by making sense of the idea of *the truth.*

Here is an image that explains what it is for a sentence to be true, and that coheres, I think, with the intuition articulated in the above quote from Devitt. Take an object and take a name; let the latter be *a*. Now take some string, tie one end of the string to the name, and tie the other end to the object. Now, take a property and take a predicate; let the latter be *is a F*. Now, take some more string, tie one end of the *string* to the predicate, and tie the other end to the set of all the objects that have the property. (Ignore the problem of how one ties a string to a set.) Then, *a is a F* is true just when the object tied to *a* is an element of the set tied to *is a F*.[7] For example, if we let the name be *Fido*, and we let the predicate be *is a dog*, then *Fido is a dog* is true just when the object tied to *Fido* is an element of the set tied to *is a dog*. This is an essential part of the idea of the complete and true description of the world, and what it means to say that there is just one such description. Given this account, and given that there is just one world of representation independent objects that have, and are distinguished by, representation independent properties, there can only be one truth. In other words, if the world is unique, and truth is, in the sense just explained, correspondence, then there is just one true and complete description of the way the world is. The following thought experiment shows this by showing how such a description could be constructed, if it were possible to construct it.

With respect to the question of whether realism, or metaphysical realism, entails that there is just one truth, Putnam writes:

> [A]ssume . . . [that] . . . there is a definite set *I* of individuals of which
> the world consists. . . . And there is a definite set of all properties and
> relations . . . , call it *P*. Consider an ideal language with a name for
> each member of *I* and a predicate for each member of *P*. . . . Such an
> ideal language . . . is unique . . . and the theory of the world . . . the
> set of true sentences . . . is . . . unique.[8]

The idea seems to be this. To construct the one, true and complete
description of the way the world is: for every object, take a name, take
some string, tie one end of the string to the object, and tie the other
end to the name. Do this so that no name is tied to two objects, and
that no object is tied to two names. Moreover, for every property, take
a predicate, tie one end of the string to the set of all the objects that
have the property, and tie the other end to the predicate. Do this in
such a manner that no predicate is tied to two such sets, and that no
set is tied to two predicates. These two tasks done, here is how the
unique truth can be constructed. For any name, *n*, and for any predicate, *is P*, add *n is P* to the description of the world just in case the
object tied to *n* is an element of the set tied to *is P*. For example, let the
name be *Fido*, and let the predicate be *is a dog*, add *Fido is a dog* to
the description of the world just in case the object tied to *Fido* is an
element of the set tied to *is a dog*. When every combination of name
and predicate has been considered, the resultant list of true sentences
will be the one true and complete description of the way the world is,
that is, it will be *the truth*.

It is quite obvious that no finite being is capable of constructing
the complete description of the way the actual world is, but this is
irrelevant to my purposes. In this regard, recall that my aim has been
to explain the meaning of two theses: (1) there are many actual worlds,
and (2) there are many truths. Hitherto, my strategy has been to explain the relevant conceptions of *world* and *truth* by explaining a
realist account of them, but the realist explanation only serves as a
beginning. According to the realist, there is just one actual world, truth
is correspondence, and so there is just one truth. According to the
relativist, there are many truths because there are many actual worlds.
Moreover, a truth is what it is within the context of Putnam's three
theses, that is, truth is correspondence—except that there are many
truths, because there are many totalities of objects to be described. The

basic idea is that there are many actual worlds, and although each is, in a sense yet to be articulated, representation dependent, there is exactly one true and complete description of the way each world is. So, there are many truths.

The theses that there are many actual worlds, and that there are many truths raise the obvious questions—perhaps I should say doubts —about whether anything goes, or whether anything may be believed. On the one hand, although there are limits to what can be believed by a finite mind, within these limits, it seems that there is nothing that cannot be believed. On the other hand, this question has another sense, namely, whether believing something is sufficient for its being true. On one reading, this is Devitt's question: "What is the reality that *constrains* us, and prevents us saying absolutely anything?"[9] If there isn't a unique, representation independent and belief constraining world, why isn't saying something equivalent to its being so? In terms of my two theses, is believing something sufficient for the existence of an actual world where it is true?

It is not obvious what it means to say that belief is constrained by the world, not to mention any one of a plurality of actual worlds. To say that the world constrains belief is not to say that the world makes us believe what is true, and it is not to say that the world makes us believe what we happen to believe, although the latter may be the case. To say that belief is constrained by the world is, I think, to say that not every belief is true. In other words, to believe something is not *ipso facto* to believe something true. Thus, there is an ambiguity in Devitt's question. It is trivially true that there are physical constraints on what can be said or believed, but there are also social and political constraints, to wit, pointedly ostending objects, for example, pistols. Devitt may well have intended the latter, but I will bracket this reading here. Within the limits of physical constraints, there does not seem to be anything about the world that constrains or prevents us from saying or believing what we please. Devitt's question seems to be motivated by the realization that many people seem to believe quite spooky things, and the desire to find something about the world that will stop them. In other words, his question seems to be motivated by the absurd desire for the world in itself to police what we say or believe. At most, however, Devitt could show that there are constraints on saying and believing in this quite limited sense: to say or believe something is not *ipso facto* to say or believe something true. It might be that this is all that Devitt intends, but I do not think that this—that is, Devitt's thesis that belief is not sufficient for truth—conflicts with the two theses under consideration here. In other words, I maintain that the following three theses are compatible: (1) there are many actual worlds, (2) there are many truths, and (3) belief is not sufficient for truth. Moreover, an essential part of my task is to explicate the first and the second in such a way that the third is assured, and thereby preserve an important realist intuition.

The realist conception of world and truth that I have been discussing is, I think, mainly motivated by the fact that its unique, representation independent actual world is taken to be belief constraining. In other words, realism is principally motivated by the idea that it seems to yield the highly desired result that belief is not sufficient for truth.[10] For example, suppose that Socrates believes that Fido is a dog, but the object tied to *Fido* is not an element of the set tied to *is a dog*. It follows from the above account of realism that *Fido is a Dog* is not true, and so in this case, belief is not sufficient for truth. The point is general: belief or assertion is not sufficient for truth. Now, what I hope to do is to make sense of the thesis that there are many belief or assertion constraining worlds. I hope to make sense of the thesis that there are many actual worlds, and for each, to believe something is not *ipso facto* to believe something true.

Clearly, the above requires exposition, and it raises all sorts of questions, for example: Must there be many actual worlds in order for there to be many truths? It seems obvious that there is just one actual world, and it seems obvious that truth is correspondence. Moreover, although it takes a bit of work to articulate the inference, it seems obvious that it follows that there is just one truth. Consequently, it might also seem obvious that no case can be made for the theses that there are many actual worlds, and there are many truths. However, Hartry Field has argued that even if there is just one representation independent actual world, no complete and true description could be unique. His premise is the apparent triviality that

> [t]he concepts we use in describing the world are not inevitable: beings other than our selves might use predicates whose extensions differ from anything easily definable *at all* in our language.[11]

The idea, I surmise, is this. Were there to be collections of predicates that had extensions different from those of our present repertoire of predicates, they would yield different true and complete descriptions of the way the world is, and thus there would be more than one truth. Not only isn't Field's multiplicity of truths the multiplicity that I seek to explicate, but more importantly, Field fails, I think, to reconcile the uniqueness and representation independence of the objects of the world with the plurality of truths.

To see this more clearly, suppose, with Field, that there might be two sets of predicates, and suppose that no predicate from one set has the same extension as any predicate from the other. Since the extension of a predicate is the set of objects to which it applies, for each set of predicates, there would be the union of their extensions. Or, if a predicate involves more than one argument, let its extension be the set of objects that are elements of the n-tuples to which it applies. Given that there are two sets of predicates, it is possible to ask whether the union of the extensions of one set is the same as the union of the extensions of the other set. Here is an essential difference between Field's multiplicity of truths and the one I hope to more fully explicate. When I say that there are many truths, part of what I mean is that there are many disjoint sets of objects, and that for each, there is a complete and true description of its elements, which is just one of many truths. When Field says that there are many truths, part of what he means is that the above described sets of objects are the same. Field's suggestion is that we might use alternative predicates to differently describe the world of representation independent objects, but then there is still the one and only actual world that is allegedly described differently, and not many actual worlds that have different descriptions.

I maintain that Field's suggestion cannot yield a multiplicity of truths. If there were just one actual world that consisted of representation independent objects, there could only be one truth, and it would be the one, true, and complete description of *these* objects. Suppose that the objects that populate the world according to Field are representation independent, as they are within the context of Putnam's three theses. Such objects would be distinct from one another by virtue of the properties that they possess, or fail to possess, independently of whatever concepts or predicates we happen to possess. The complete description of all the representation independent properties that all the representation independent objects possess would be *the truth*. There is, therefore, a quite determinate relationship between predicates, their extensions, and the representation independent properties of objects, on the one hand, and the number of truths, on the other. It is irrelevant to object that were we to use different names and different predicates, we might be inclined to say that there are different objects. If the names and predicates we use do not match up with the world's representation independent objects and properties, a description that employs them cannot be a truth in the sense explained above. Names and predicates that do not reflect the world's objects and properties cannot be part of a description of the way the one representation independent world of objects is. So, Field's suggestion does not yield a multiplicity of truths.[12]

If there are to be alternative truths, the application of alternative predicates to alternative grammatical subjects must be related to the possession of alternative properties by alternative objects, which constitute the ontologies of alternative worlds.[13] Given the intuitive power of the ideas that there is just one actual world, and that truth is correspondence, how could it be that there are many truths? My answer is that there are many actual worlds, and so there are many truths; namely, there is one truth, that is, one complete and true description, for each actual world. In other words, if there are many actual worlds, each of which consists of a distinct order of objects, then there are, in the sense explained above, many truths, that is, there is one complete and true description for each actual world. Therefore, it should be clear that my task is to explicate what it is to be a world in a way that makes it possible to show that there are many actual worlds.

There is a problem with this way of putting things, however. My aim is to make sense of the thesis that there is some plurality of worlds, and that each has a maximally complete and true description. But this is misleading, because it fails to include an essential component of the final view of this essay, namely, that making sense of my two theses requires a certain ontological inversion. But I get ahead of myself. The pictures presented in this section are sufficient to begin to explain the conception of world and truth to be more fully delineated in what follows. I mean here to warn my readers that the contents of this section are not final. To paraphrase Wittgenstein, these contents are rungs to be climbed up and beyond—my reader must, so to speak, throw away the ladder after he has climbed it.[14]

The problem here is to make sense of the theses that there are many actual worlds, and that there are many truths. I find a clue to the solution of this problem in the doctrines that Plato imputes to Protagoras. In his *Theaetetus,* Plato reports that Protagoras maintained that "a man is the measure of all things: of those which are, that they are, and of those which are not, that they are not."[15] On my reading of Plato's text, this contains the seeds of a coherent alternative to the idea that there is a unique belief constraining world in itself that is the same for all observers and all thinkers, yet it does not require the rejection of the idea of a belief constraining world. On my interpretation, Protagoras urges us to think that there are many belief constraining worlds, and that there are many truths. This is an idea fraught with difficulties, but I find, as I have just said, a clue to its explication, and their solution in the Protagorean doctrines.

The idea of belief constraint is not discarded by Protagoras. This is a key element in his thought, not to mention any viable explanation of the thesis that there are many actual worlds and truths, but belief is not always constrained in the same direction. As I see it, this is essential. So it is wrong to say that his view is that anything goes, or that nothing is objective. He maintains that more than one thing goes, and that there are many objectivities. Moreover, he explains this in terms of the idea that there are many actual worlds. Clearly, there are at least three relevant questions that need to be answered:

1. What is it to be an actual world?
2. How can there be many belief constraining actual worlds?
3. How can there be many truths?[16]

The text of Plato's dialogue *suggests* that the Protagorean thesis that man is the measure can be developed into an account of what it is to be an actual world, and into an argument that employs this account to show both that there are many actual, belief constraining worlds, and consequently that there are many truths. In short, the text of Plato's dialogue suggests answers to these three questions. Since it is, in this case and at this stage, clear that a plurality of actual worlds entails a plurality of truths, worlds come first.

Protagoras maintained that the world of Socrates is, for example, the aggregate of whatever appears to him, and since perception is the principal mode of appearance, his world is the aggregate of what he perceives.[17] This leaves open the question about whether this means that his world is the aggregate of (i) what he does perceive, (ii) what he does and can perceive, or (iii) what he does and can perceive plus whatever may be connected by rules to what he does and can perceive. It is reflection upon these sorts of questions that leads to an essentially different version of the thesis that there are many actual worlds and truths. The Protagorean vision is just one rung on a ladder. Be this as it may, an account of truth obviously corresponds to this ontology.

The assertion that *the wind is cold* is true for Socrates just when the wind that appears to Socrates is cold, or the wind perceived by Socrates is cold. This can be put in the idiom of the string theory of truth. Consider the general idea first. Take an object that appears to Socrates, that is, take an object that Socrates perceives. Take a name, or some expression. Now take some string, tie one end of the string to the expression, and tie the other end to the object. Now take a property, take a predicate, take some more string, tie one end of the string to the predicate, and tie the other end to the set of all the objects that both appear to Socrates and that have the property. If a is the name or expression, and *is F* is the predicate, then *a is F* is true for Socrates just when the object tied to a is an element of the set tied to *is F*. In the case of the present example, if we let the expression be *the wind,* and we let the predicate be *is cold,* then *The wind is cold* is true for Socrates just when the object tied to *the wind* is an element of the set tied to *is cold.* Similarly, the assertion that *the wind is warm* is true for Theaetetus just when the wind that appears to Theaetetus is warm, or the wind that Theaetetus perceives is warm. The string theory of truth applies similarly.

Moreover, if the wind that appears to Socrates is cold, the assertion that the wind is not cold is not sufficient for it to be true for him. Similarly, if the wind that appears to Theaetetus is not warm, the assertion that the wind is warm is not sufficient for his assertion to be true for him. So, one consequence of Protagoras' ontology, which is a desired consequence, is that there are many belief constraining worlds. The aggregate of whatever appears to someone, or the aggregate of what someone perceives, is her world. Such a world constrains belief or assertion, that is, with respect to such a world, saying that some object has some property is not sufficient for that object to have the property in question. In other words, to assert something is not *ipso facto* to assert something true. There can be many truths, because there are many belief constraining winds, that is, one that appears to Socrates, and one that appears to Theaetetus, and so assertion is constrained, but not always in the same way. More generally, for any subject, *s*, to assert or believe something is not *ipso facto* to assert or believe something that is true for *s*. With this, Protagoras constructs an alternative to the views that *there is just one truth,* and, rather interestingly, although given the aim of this work, perhaps not as importantly, that *there is no truth*.

More generally, according to Protagoras, the aggregate of what is perceived by an individual, or the aggregate of what appears to an individual, is her world. Since there are many individuals, there are many worlds. Clearly, such a world is not a merely possible world. Such a world is just one of many actual worlds. For each Protagorean world, there is a total description, and so there is a truth. It is important to note that the relevant notion of relative truth is that of a correspondence between what is said and a segment of a world, to wit, what is said is true just when it corresponds to, or correctly describes, some segment of a world. So this is a correspondence theory of truth as described above. The contentious question concerns the number of worlds to which what is said can correspond. The difficulty lies in showing that there are many belief constraining worlds, but once this is given, it is obvious that there are many truths. This requires that a proposition, or sentence, or statement, et cetera, be true for an individual just when it describes what she perceives, or it describes what appears to her. A truth, or total truth, would just be a totality of propositions, sentences, or statements, et cetera, that describe someone's world.

It is, of course, quite difficult to understand the status of the Protagorean account of the plurality of actual worlds and truths, since it does not appear to be about what is perceived by any individual. This account seems to tell us what individuals are like independently of how they are perceived by any individual, but Protagoras has no place for such propositions in his scheme of man measured things. His picture is that of a multiplicity of individuals, each of whom is conscious of a certain field of things, but there are different things in different fields. A world is, in this picture, just the sum total of what appears, and can appear, in a field. Thus, there are different worlds, and, on the assumption that truth is correspondence between what is said and some segment of a world, there are many truths. To represent a world, to have the truth, is to represent what is in one of these fields, to give a complete description of the field. It might be that no one could produce such a description, but that is what a truth, a total truth, would be. What about the Protagorean picture? According to it, all pictures depict the contents of a field. Since the Protagorean picture aims to depict all the fields, it cannot depict the contents of any particular field. This seems incoherent, but it is not a serious objection to the Protagorean picture, or so I argue.

In his *Theaetetus*, Plato has Socrates raise this sort of objection against the Protagorean thesis that man is measure all things:

> [I]t [the Protagorean thesis] involves this very subtle implication. Protagoras agrees that everyone has in his [sic] judgements the things which are. In doing that, he's surely conceding that the opinion of those who make opposing judgements about his own opinion—that is, their opinion that what he thinks is false—is true. . . . So if he admits that their opinion is true—that is, the opinion of those who believe that what he thinks is false—he would seem to be conceding that his own opinion is false.[18]

This refutation begins with the assumption that the Protagorean thesis implies that "everyone has in his judgements the things which are."[19] This is, however, ambiguous between (i) when one judges truly, one judges about the things which are in one's world, and (ii) whatever one judges is *ipso facto* true. As I reconstruct Protagoras, he meant the former: everyone who judges truly judges about the things which are in her world. As Plato reads him, Protagoras meant the latter: whatever one judges is *ipso facto* true. In addition to Plato, as recent an interpreter as M. F. Burnyeat reads Protagoras in this manner:

> No one lives in a world in which his [sic] *mere belief* in a proposition is either a sufficient or a necessary condition for its truth (in that world). But that everyone lives in such a world is precisely what the Measure doctrine asserts. . . . Protagoras alleges we all . . . live in a world in which their *mere belief* in a proposition is a sufficient and necessary condition for its truth (in that world).[20]

Plato predicates his subtle refutation of the Protagorean thesis on this uncharitable reading. It begins with the obvious consequence that whatever Plato judges is *ipso facto* true. Since Plato judges that the Protagorean view is false, it follows that it is true that the Protagorean view is false. So, the Protagorean view is false. It seems that Plato's refutation shows that the Protagorean thesis entails its own negation, that is, that it is self-refuting.

Burnyeat also predicates his account of the subtle refutation on this uncharitable reading. On his reading, Protagoras offers us a picture of a multiplicity of individuals, each of which is conscious of a certain field of things. In this picture, a world is just the sum total of what appears, and perhaps what can appear, in a field. The pivotal point is that for each field, the *mere belief* in a proposition is both a sufficient and a necessary condition for its truth. Now, given the assumption that Plato merely believes that the field of what appears to him is not such that the mere belief in a proposition is both sufficient and necessary for its truth, it follows that the field of what appears to Plato is a counterexample to the Protagorean picture. So, once again it seems that the Protagorean thesis entails its own negation, that is that it is self-refuting. The pivotal problem with these subtle refutations is that had Protagoras asserted that whatever one judges is *ipso facto* true, he would have been inane, not a relativist. On a more charitable reading, Protagoras meant that everyone who judges truly judges about the things which are in her world, and there are many worlds, et cetera. It is not obvious that this version of the Protagorean thesis is self-refuting, but what I have to say about this, and the question of whether relativism is self-refuting in general, concerns the analysis of how self-refutation arguments work.

Plato presents the essence of the famous objection that relativism is self-refuting.[21] I will here only briefly indicate why I think this objection fails. In general, this objection has the following form. Some version of relativism, *R,* will be said to entail either its own negation or a contradiction, and then we are urged to reject *R*. Since a proposition entails its own negation just when it entails a contradiction, and the result is the same, namely, the proposition in question is necessarily false, I will only discuss the former case, which is more intuitive to me.

What is self-refutation? This is an important question. Although the term is often used, it is rarely explained. Some writers suggest that it is best explicated by laying out its form. For example, John Passmore suggests that: "Formally, the proposition p is absolutely self-refuting, if to assert p is equivalent to asserting both p *and not-p*."[22] This is confusing for a number of reasons. Asserting is something that persons do. Here, a *formal* account would be an account of the *logical* structure of self-refuting propositions. It would not matter that someone does or does not assert them, or at least this is what an antirelativist should say. A formal account of *modus ponens* would be an account of the logical structure of a particular sort of argument, and it would not matter that someone does or does not assert an argument with this structure. Moreover, it is mysterious what it could mean to say that asserting p is equivalent to asserting p *and not-p*. Does this mean that, where p is self-refuting, every speaker who intends to assert p finds herself actually, although accidentally, asserting, in the manner of a slip of the tongue, p *and not-p*? If this is a formal account, why mention assertion? So, if we drop the part about asserting, we are left with this: p is self-refuting, if p is equivalent to both p *and not-p*.

Although this may be a matter of the subjectivity of simplicity, this version is overly complicated. I think it more simple to say that p is self-refuting, if p implies $\sim p$. Nothing is at stake here, since the two versions are logically equivalent. Note, moreover, that by this criterion, when p is self-refuting, since it is a truth of logic that:

$$[p \supset \sim p] \supset [p \supset (q \ \& \ \sim q)],$$

p also entails a contradiction. On this account, therefore, a case of self-refutation is the same as a case of contradiction. This is so even if one adopts the analysis of self-refutation recently offered by F. C. White, who writes:

> Self-refuting propositions have three essential characteristics. [1] They are false. [2] They falsify or contribute to falsifying themselves. [3] They falsify themselves through self-reference.[23]

When White says that self-refuting propositions "falsify or contribute to falsifying themselves," this amounts, I think, to the claim that when p is self-refuting, if p is true, then p is false. In other words, when p is self-refuting, p implies $\sim p$. So, a proposition, p, is self-refuting just when (1) p is false, (2) p implies $\sim p$, and (3) p refers to p. These three features are exemplified in what may well be the paradigm of the self-refuting proposition: every general statement is false. As Putnam has put this point:

> A 'self-refuting supposition' is one whose truth implies its own falsity. For example, consider the thesis that all general statements are false. This is a general statement. So if it is true, then it must be false. [Because it refers to itself by virtue of quantifying over itself.] Hence, it is false.[24]

The pivotal condition is (3), which is where I suspect the objection from self-refutation fails.

Whatever version of relativism is considered, let it be R, the self-refutation argument will have the following structure, where p is a variable ranging over propositions:

$$[R] \quad \forall p(\ldots p \ldots).$$

The self-refutation argument proceeds. The variable, p, is said to range over R, and it is allegedly shown that when p takes R as a value, it is easy to show that R implies its own negation, or to deduce a contradiction. The conclusion is that R is incoherent, or, what is more to the point in this context, R is self-refuting. Are relativists without a response to this? They could say the following: Do not let p take R as a value.

Is this ad hoc? I think that it is not. Consider an analogous case in the world of those who think that there is one unique world, who think that truth is getting it uniquely right, who countenance both a form of bivalence and Tarski's Convention T. Consider the following proposition, A:

[A] A is not true.

Is A true or not true? It is easy to show that A is true just when A is not true, and this is logically equivalent to a contradiction. We are never asked to conclude that the nonrelativist conception of truth is contradictory or self-refuting. This contradiction does not provide the kind of pressure required to establish the essential incoherence of this sort of conception of truth, but what about the contradiction?

There are many stories about this. One might say that the specification of A is viciously circular (Russell), or propose a hierarchy of languages and truth predicates (Tarski), or say that since A is not grounded, it lacks truth value (Kripke).[25] It does not matter whether or which of these is the uniquely correct one story. Because the point is that an antirelativist, or someone who wants to preserve a nonrelativist idea of truth, is permitted to amend a rule of her logic, if it should yield an inference that she is unwilling to accept. As Goodman once said: "A rule is amended if it yields an inference we are unwilling to accept; an inference is rejected if it violates a rule we are unwilling to amend."[26] Is *this* ad hoc? If we deny so in the antirelativist's case, we should deny so in the case of a relativist. From the relativist's point of view, the choice is between allowing and disallowing p to take R as a value. What could be wrong with the following line of reasoning? Premise: If we allow division by zero, we can show that one equals zero. The proof is obvious.

1. Begin with the obvious: $1 = 1$.

2. From (1), and by subtracting 1 from both sides, we get: $1 - 1 = 0$.

3. From (2), and by multiplying both sides by $1/(1 - 1)$ [which requires division by 0, because $1 - 1 = 0$, but since a point is being made, this is allowed] we get: $(1 - 1) \times 1/(1 - 1) = 0 \times 1/(1 - 1)$.

4. From (3), and since $a \times 1/a = 1$, and $0 \times a = 0$, we finally get the result that: $1 = 0$. Q.E.D.

Conclusion: Don't allow division by zero. Here, a rule is amended because it yields a conclusion that we are unwilling to accept. The rule is something like: for all a and b, there is a c such that $a \div b = c$, and the amendment is that b cannot equal zero. Now suppose the relativists allow p to take R as a value, and suppose that the antirelativists are correct when they claim that under this condition, R entails either its own negation, or a contradiction. It is obvious that the prudent policy is for the relativist to bar p from taking R as a value.[27] Here is the argument for the prudence of this policy. Premise: If we allow p to take R as a value, R entails the negation of R, and a contradiction.

Conclusion: Do not allow p to take R as a value. So, with this way out, the argument from self-refutation is not a sufficient critique of relativism, Protagorean, conceptual, or otherwise. This response is the same as the doctor's response to the patient who says, "It hurts when I do this!" The doctor says, "Don't do that!" When the antirelativist says, "Incoherence is the result of applying relativism to itself!," the relativist should say "Don't apply relativism to itself." This is a well-known response to the problem of propositions such as "This proposition is not true." It seems to me that any solution to the so-called liar paradox is, in some way, a solution to the paradox of relative truth, that is, it would be, so to speak, a solution to the relativist liar paradox. No one says that realism, or antirelativism, is self-refuting because there is no universally accepted solution to the liar paradox. There is, therefore, no reason to say it of relativism.

Above, I said that whatever version of relativism is considered, it will have the structure of R, but this fails to do justice to relativism. Indeed, it would be an abstract relativist who would assent to R. Those who proffer the argument from self-refutation rarely, if ever, attempt to figure out just what case the relativist might be making. White is one example.[28] They assume that the relativist thinks something witless like *everything is relative,* and then with equal wit they go on to prove that this is self-refuting or incoherent. But then it cannot be claimed that the argument is based on a deep, or even moderately brief, analysis of the relativist's position. For example, it can't be claimed that the argument is based on a deep, or even moderate, analysis of the writings of Whorf, Quine, Kuhn, or Feyerabend. It is not based on an analysis at all. This may be a stronger response to the objection that relativism is self-refuting. Thus, there are two responses to this. (1) The self-refutation argument must be directed at a developed version of relativism. (2) The paradoxes of relative truth can be resolved by developing a logical apparatus that is analogous to those that have been proposed to resolve the paradoxes of nonrelative truth. The development of the required logical apparatus presupposes, however, a given account of relativism, that is, of the theses that there are many actual worlds and there are many truths. So, first comes the philosophical work, and then comes the logic. Here, I will only attend to the former, and I will leave the development of the technical logical apparatus aside as beyond the scope of this work. This said, I will now return to the task of elucidating the analysis, or the ontology, that makes sense of the relativist's notion of multiple actual worlds and multiple truths.

The above version of Protagoreanism provides us with a story wherein we can see three things: (1) what an actual world is, (2) how it is possible for there to be and that there are many actual worlds, and (3) how it is possible for there to be and that there are many total truths. I have no idea how one could prove that any version of relativism must provide such a story. It has assumed many forms. To make these ideas more clear, I shall examine how they function in the thought of a number of thinkers. It might be that none of these thinkers would accept either the epitaph, or epithet, *relativist,* so I limit my investigation to the role that these three themes play in their writings. Here, my aim is ancient: To elucidate certain themes by showing how I see them developed, or able to be developed, in the thought of my predecessors. My final cause is, of course, to thereby articulate my own version of the development of these themes.

II
Updating Protagoras
Whorf and Quine

The writings of Benjamin Lee Whorf contain elements that suggest an account of what it is to be a world that shows how it is possible for there to be, and that there are many actual worlds, and so many truths. I will begin with them. If there were a plurality of actual worlds, there would be, I think, a plurality of truths, namely, there would be one truth, that is, one complete description, for each actual world. So, I will mostly focus on what I think suggests an account of how there can be a plurality of actual worlds.

As I have read Whorf, the premise of this account is that "language produces an organization of experience."[1] This premise is not difficult to accept. Whorf provides us with many examples, although they seem to have been directed to linguists, anthropologists, and those who happen to be well acquainted with a variety of disparate languages. The most famous among Whorf's examples is, of course, Hopi. Suppose, as Whorf asserts, that "the Hopi language contains no reference to 'time'."[2] Without a temporal vocabulary, for example, how could one then describe change? This question is not about the conditions under which it would then be possible to describe change, but it is about what such a description would be like. If one does not think that the very idea of describing change without a temporal vocabulary is incoherent, then one might suspect that something must be omitted from a Hopi description of change, but Whorf assures us that "the Hopi language is capable of . . . describing correctly, in a pragmatic or operational sense, all observable phenomena of the universe."[3]

Whorf alleges that someone who describes change with the aid of a temporal vocabulary experiences change differently from someone who describes it with an atemporal vocabulary. The point of the above question is to get one to see that his claim is correct. In Hopi, Whorf asserts:

> [T]here are no verbs corresponding to our "come" and "go" that mean simple and abstract motion, our purely kinematic concept. The words in this case translated "come" refer to the process of eventuating without calling it motion—they are "eventuates to here" *(pew'i)* or "eventuates from it" *(angqö)* or "arrived" *(pitu, pl. öki)* which refers only to the terminal manifestation, the actual arrival at a given point, not to the motion preceding it.[4]

As strange as it may seem, in using Hopi to describe the motion of an object from one location to another, one does not say that after the passage of some time, and after some preceding motion, the object finally arrived here. Moreover, I am not clear on what one does say. This lack of clarity is not an objection to Whorf's example, however, since the point of the example is, I think, that anyone who experienced the object of the Hopi description would have an essentially different experience from someone who experienced the object of the corresponding English description. Such examples often strike many of us as quite alien. So, although the fact of their strangeness, or distance may itself be one of the best examples, or one of the most obvious consequences, of the linguistic ordering of experience, I will describe and consider another illustration of Whorf's premise.

For us, there can be at least two experiences of the following:

1. If the mouse is on the house, the mouse is dizzy, and the mouse is on the house, so the mouse is dizzy.

2. If the mouse is on the house, the mouse is dizzy, and the mouse is not dizzy, so the mouse is not on the house.

3. If the mouse is on the house, the mouse is dizzy, and the mouse is not on the house, so the mouse is not dizzy.

4. If the mouse is on the house, the mouse is dizzy, and the mouse is dizzy, so the mouse is on the house.

Someone whose vocabulary includes, or whose language has a syntax that can capture, *modus ponens, modus tollens,* the fallacy of denying the antecedent, and the fallacy of affirming the consequent will have one experience of this. Someone who lacks this vocabulary, and whose language lacks the relevant syntax, will have a quite different experience. The former will experience this as four variations on a theme, and the latter will experience it as a chaos. This is only an example, however. The pivotal question is whether the premise that language orders experience can be developed into an account of actual world multiplicity.

Not only does Whorf assert that language orders, or arranges experience, but he also asserts the stronger thesis that the result of this is a world order. He writes that "language . . . is a classification and arrangement of the stream of sensory experience which results in a world-order."[5] Although one sometimes experiences the world, and experience is one of the many things that comprise the world, it is important to be clear that experience is essentially different from the world, and so the world order is essentially other than the order of experience. Hence, it is unclear how the linguistic ordering of experience could be related to the order of the world, and it is also unclear, perhaps more so, how it could be that the world itself is ordered by language. Yet Whorf asserts both that "languages dissect nature in many ways," and that "we dissect nature along lines laid down by our native languages."[6] The difficulty, as Devitt points out, is that

> we can make good sense of talk of our [language?] imposing on, organizing and cutting up experience. But this is not to say that we construct the world; it is our experience of the world, not the world itself, that we [by means of our language?] are imposing on, organizing and cutting up.[7]

Note well that Devitt concedes that there is good sense to be made of Whorf's talk of our *language* imposing on, cutting up, organizing, and ordering our experience of the world. But, it is a very different thing to claim that language imposes on, cuts up, and orders the world itself, which would seem to be cut up, and ordered in its own language independent way, and this is the very difficulty at hand.

Whorf goes even further, however. He asserts that "different languages differently 'segment' the *same* situation or experience."[8] Not only do different languages differently order the experiences of their speakers, but in some manner, different languages differently order the same world. So, if there are many languages, and there is a distinct world order for each language, then there are many world orders. It might seem that this is very near to affirming that there are many actual worlds, since it might seem plausible to say that there is one actual world for each world order. Yet this does not quite yield the conclusion that there are many actual worlds. Note well that it is the *same* situation, or world, that is differently segmented, or dissected, by different languages, but there is an obvious difficulty with this. As Roger Trigg has observed:

> There are clearly many ways of classifying and grouping together objects in the world. The fact that different languages may do it differently does not of itself suggest that they are referring to different states of affairs or "different worlds."[9]

The difficulty is that there seems to be just one nature, or actual world, that is differently dissected by different languages, but this only needs to mean that different languages have different resources for picking out and describing different preexisting patterns among preexistent language-independent objects. So, the conclusion that there are many actual worlds is quite distant, if it is even possible to reach it, from Whorf's premise. (It might be instructive to recall the reason that Field's suggestion does not work: if the world consists of representation-independent objects, there can only be one truth, and it would be the one, true, and complete description of these objects.) Thus, once again the pivotal question arises about how, and, perhaps more importantly, whether the premise that language orders experience can be developed in an account of actual world multiplicity.

Whorf's suggestion is that language orders experience. Not only is this merely intuitive and inexact, its relation to the conclusion that there are many actual worlds is unclear, but I have only claimed that it is suggestive. Something more is needed. I would add an alternative to the idea that the world is some sort of sum of experience independent objects. It is unclear whether Whorf could imagine such a thing. As I have noted, he seems to have thought that there is just one world, and that different languages have different resources for picking out and describing different preexisting patterns among preexistent and linguistically independent objects. However, Whorf himself maintains that there is a significant difference between the thesis that "Sentences are unlike because they tell about unlike facts," and the thesis that "Facts are unlike to speakers whose language background provides for unlike formulation of them." [10] This suggests the distinction between the thesis that a true sentence is one that describes a fact, and the thesis that a fact is what some true sentence describes. Despite the obscurity of the Whorfian texts, the metaphysically significant point is that to get the conclusion that there are many worlds from Whorf's suggestion that *language shapes experience,* it is, I think, necessary to add something like the premise that *a world is the ideal sum of the objects of an ideal sum of linguistically shaped experiences.*

As I have interpreted Protagoras above, he maintained the analogous premise that the world of Socrates is the aggregate of whatever appears to him, and since perception is the principal mode of appearance, his world is the aggregate of what he perceives. To arrive at the conclusion that there are many worlds from Whorf's premise that language shapes experience, it is necessary to add an additional premise such as the premise that the world of the Hopi is the aggregate of whatever appears to them. Moreover, since linguistically shaped experience is the principal mode of appearance, their world is the aggregate of the objects of their linguistically shaped experiences.

Whorf seems to have believed a number of trivialities. He seems to have maintained that experience is ordered by language, and that different languages differently order experience. As I noted above, these are not difficult assumptions. However, Whorf has also indicated that he believed that there is just one world, and that different languages have different resources for picking out and describing different preexisting patterns among preexistent and language-independent objects. Such assertions seem to be supported by either reflection on common experience, or most people's natural ontological attitude. [11] So the difficult task lies in showing how, and that, these trivialities support a monstrosity, namely, the thesis that there are many actual worlds. It is clear that it is necessary to make a case for the theses that the world is shaped by language, that different languages order the world differently, and that there are many actual worlds. The case can be made, given the reconception of a world as an ideal sum of the objects of a manifold of linguistically shaped experiences. Then, not only are worlds linguistically shaped, but for each language, there is an ideal sum of objects of linguistically shaped experiences. So, for each language, there is a world. Now, were there to be many languages, there would also be many worlds. It seems obvious that there are many languages, though this is not an uncontested thesis, so it should be obvious that there are many worlds. Moreover, if each of these worlds had a complete description, there would be many truths. As has been pointed out above, however, there are a number of problems with all of this, but their solutions rest on this reconception.[12]

The first problem is that Whorf says that the world is ordered by language because experience is ordered by language, but there seems to be a logical gap between these theses. The solution to this problem is that the idea that there is a gap here presupposes that the world is an ideal sum of experience independent objects. If a world were the ideal sum of the objects of an ideal sum of linguistically shaped experiences, there would be no gap.

The second problem is that the only reason for saying that different languages order the world differently would seem to be that the world is ordered by language. However, the best reason for the latter is that experience is ordered by language, but this brings us back to the alleged first problem. Thus, the solution to this supposed problem is, I think, that if a world is the ideal sum of the objects of an ideal sum of linguistically shaped experiences, it too disappears.

The third problem is that there doesn't seem to be any reason to say that *different languages differently order the world*. On the one hand, if there were such a reason, part of the best candidate would seem to be that *the world is ordered by language,* which is alleged to be itself dubiously supported by the premise that *language orders experience*. But, this sort of difficulty is, once again, partly allayed by the solution to the first problem: a world must be conceived as an ideal sum of objects of linguistically shaped experiences. On the other hand, it might be alleged that the claim that *different languages differently order the world* is only plausible if it is interpreted as meaning that different languages have different resources for picking out and describing different preexisting patterns among linguistically independent objects. But, on this interpretation, it should be clear that this claim lends no support to the monstrosity that there are many actual worlds, and there is, therefore, no support for denying the seeming triviality that there is just one actual world. However, if a world were an ideal sum of objects of linguistically shaped experiences, there would be another interpretation of the thesis that the world is differently ordered by different languages. Moreover, on this reading, this thesis would support the monstrosity, and it would thereby provide a reason to deny the triviality.

Does Whorf offer us even a hint that he understood that a reconception of what it is to be a world is required to pass from the thesis that experience is ordered by language to the thesis that there are many worlds? The situation is ambiguous. On the one hand, as far as I can tell, Whorf never even imagined that the world might be something other than the collection of linguistically independent objects. On the other hand, it seems to be well known that one of his most powerful motivations was his desire to reconcile the scientific world picture with the religious world picture. John B. Carroll tells us that "Whorf's interest in linguistics stemmed from one in religion." [13] George Lakoff adds:

> Whorf's objectivism came from two sources: he was a fundamentalist Christian, and he was trained as a chemical engineer at MIT in the 1910s. His interest in linguistics arose from the discrepancy between his two sources of objective truth: science and the Bible. [14]

Emily A. Schultz claims that "Whorf's personal struggle to resolve the competing claims of science and religion led him to focus on the study of language as a likely source of insight." [15] What could the insight possibly be? and how could it be related to the thesis that there are many actual worlds?

Whorf might have thought something like the following: if the world of science were the ideal sum of the objects of those experiences shaped by scientific language, and the religious world were similarly the ideal sum of the objects of those experiences shaped by religious language, and these languages were sufficiently different, then there would be two worlds, and the claims of science would not be able to conflict with the claims of religion. As noted above, however, Whorf does not, as far as I know, ever suggest that he possessed the reconception of what it is to be a world required for this type of resolution.[16]

To Whorf's work, therefore, it is necessary to add (1) an account of what it is to be an actual world, (2) an account of the multiplicity of actual worlds, and (3) an account of the multiplicity of truths. Moreover, none of his work even approaches (4) the question of the ontological status of these many actual worlds. So, Whorf cannot answer my four questions: (1) What is it to be an actual world? (2) Why are there many actual worlds? (3) What is the ontological status of these actual worlds? (4) Why are there many truths? There is no reason that he should be able to answer them, however, since he had other concerns. His works are important to the explication of my theses, because they contain the premise that experience is shaped by language, and when this premise is added to a sufficiently revolutionary reconception of what it is to be a world, his work becomes a model of how such questions might be answered. This is important, since having such a model brings us closer to my aim of explicating and defending my two theses. Thus, his work is neither irrelevant to mine, nor does it do my work for me.

There are a number of reasons why Whorf's work does not do mine. First, and perhaps most importantly, he didn't explain how language shapes experience. Second, he didn't have a clue that a world might be conceived as something other than a collection of preexistent and language-independent objects. So he had no idea that a world might be conceived as an ideal totality of the objects of linguistically shaped experiences. Third, consequently, he did not have a clue that it might be necessary to explain the idea of an ideal totality of objects. Fourth, even if a world is conceived as an ideal sum of the objects of linguistically shaped experiences, it is not clear how subjective experiences could be distinguished from objective experiences. A world cannot be all of the objects of linguistically shaped experiences, since this would include the objects of linguistically shaped experiences that are, or would be considered, illusory. In short, it is not clear what Whorfian principles would exclude the objects of illusory experiences from a world.

Fifth, Whorf's argument, as I have reconstructed it, seems to move at the wrong level. This argument assumes that a difference among worlds is due to an empirical difference. I do not think that this is right: there are different worlds not because there are different schemes of empirical concepts, but because there are different schemes of a priori concepts. The sort of linguistic variation necessary to derive an account of the plurality of actual worlds is not the variation of divergent vocabularies. This is why the infamous multiplicity of Eskimo words for snow is totally irrelevant: world multiplicity is, to borrow some Kantian terminology, due to a multiplicity of categories, not a multiplicity of empirical concepts.[17] Why think that there are many alternative sets of categories? But I get ahead of myself.

Sixth, Whorf's writings suggest that if there are many experience shaping languages, and something is a part of a world just when it can be the object of a linguistically shaped experience, then there are many worlds, and so many truths. This suggestion presupposes the existence of languages that are different to the point of being capable of differently shaping experience, but this is deeply enigmatic. How different must such languages be? One possible answer, which has been articulated by Davidson, is that such languages must be different to the point of untranslatability. There is reason to believe, however, that an untranslatable language could not be discovered. This would undermine the legitimacy of the anthropological and linguistic investigations that motivate the premise that there are languages that differently shape experience, that is, the premise of one possible argument for the plurality of actual worlds. Donald Davidson illustrated this reason well, when he wrote that:

> Whorf, wanting to demonstrate that Hopi incorporates a metaphysics so alien to ours that Hopi and English cannot, as he puts it, "be calibrated," uses English to convey the contents of sample Hopi sentences.[18]

Upon the discovery of an untranslatable language, one would want to report to one's fellows that there are natives who speak a language that cannot be translated into our language, and *this* is what they say. This cannot be: if *this* is part of one's own language, one has translated what is untranslatable; if *this* is part of the native's language, one has failed to report what the natives say.

This is the argument that Davidson describes as "a very short line indeed."[19] Its premise is that nothing . . . could count as evidence that some form of activity could not be interpreted in [or translated into] our language that was not at the same time evidence that that form of activity was not speech behavior.[20]

Its conclusion is that

we probably ought to hold that a form of activity that cannot be interpreted as language in our language [or cannot be translated into our language] is not speech behavior.[21]

I think that the idea is this. On the one hand, translation is the best evidence that something is language. The translation of extraterrestrial signals would be, for example, the best evidence that they are language. On the other hand, repeated failure to translate something is the best evidence that it is untranslatable. It is trivially true that the repeated failure to translate extraterrestrial signals is the best evidence that they are not translatable. Perhaps it should be said that a failure to translate extraterrestrial sounds—in the form of electromagnetic radiation, or something of this sort—is the best reason one could give for saying that they are untranslatable, since to call them signals is to suggest that they are language. In either case, since translation and failure to translate are mutually exclusive, the best reason that one could give for saying that something is language and the best reason that one could give for saying that something is untranslatable are mutually exclusive.

Here's the difficulty. Whorf's thesis is that different languages differently shape experience. Davidson suggests that to make sense of this, such languages must be different to the point of being untranslatable, but this requires that there be something that is both a language and untranslatable. Question: What evidence could support the thesis that this requirement is satisfied? Answer: None. Evidence that some sounds or marks are language, namely, their translation, is obviously evidence inimical to their being untranslatable. To show that they are language is to show that it is translatable. Furthermore, evidence that some sounds or marks are untranslatable, namely, repeated failure to translate it, is evidence inimical to their being a language. To show that something is untranslatable is to show that it is not language. There cannot be, therefore, evidence that something is an untranslatable language. So, no anthropologist, no linguist, no historian, and no social scientist could ever persuade us to believe that there are untranslatable languages. Therefore, no evidence could support Whorf's thesis that different languages differently shape experience. Languages cannot be so different that they differently shape experience, and experiences cannot be shaped differently by different languages. This undermines Whorf's thesis that different languages differently shape experience, and it thereby undermines any attempt to employ his thesis to make sense of my thesis that there are many actual worlds and truths.

Davidson's argument is strikingly similar to Hume's argument against miracles. If there is a miracle, then there is a violation of the laws of nature. If we are to have evidence that there is a violation of a law of nature, then we must have evidence that something is both a law of nature of nature and yet violated. Evidence that something is violated is also evidence that it is not a law of nature. Thus, there can never be evidence that something is a violated law of nature, that is, nothing could be the evidence that shows there has been a miracle.[22] Similarly, an alternative experience would be associated with a language that cannot be translated into our language. Evidence that there is an alternative experience is, therefore, evidence that there is something that is both untranslatable and yet a language. Evidence that something is untranslatable is also evidence that it is not a language. Thus, there can never be evidence for an alternative experience.

Whorf's work only contains a hint of an account of the theses that there are many actual worlds, and that there are many truths. Moreover, this hint needs to be supplemented with an account of what it is to be a world. The work of Willard Van Orman Quine also contains such a hint, but it requires far less supplementation. When it is developed, we are provided with a more or less explicit account of what it is to be a world, and it suggests how there might be many worlds. Unlike Protagoras and Whorf, however, it would not be correct to represent Quine as first arguing that there are many worlds, and then arguing that each has a complete and true description, and so there are many truths. For Quine, or at least as I have construed his words, there are many worlds because there are many truths. So, in discussing Quine's views, it is not possible to begin by exclusively focusing on the issue of the quiddity and plurality of worlds, and then to turn to the issue of the plurality of truths as something that follows naturally from this focus. In the case of Quine, what it is to be a world, the plurality of worlds, and the plurality of truths are three closely related issues. In short, in the following discussion of Quine's views, I cannot focus on the issue of the quiddity and plurality of worlds, and assume that the plurality of truths falls out of the result. With this caveat in mind, what is Quine's hint?

In his essay "On What There Is," Quine articulates what he takes to be *the* ontological question: "What is there?"[23] He distinguishes this question from the question about what sentences, in general, say there is. The former is a question about ontology; the latter is a question about ontological commitment. According to Quine, the answer to this second question is that to be is to be the value of a [bound] variable.[24] In less felicitous words, what sentences say there is is what there must be in order for them to be true. As Quine once put the point:

> [A] theory [that is, a set of sentences] is committed to those and only those entities to which the bound variables of the theory must be capable of referring in order that the affirmations made in the theory be true.[25]

This does not answer Quine's first question about what there is, since it fails to say which sentences are true, but it doesn't follow that it is irrelevant to his first question.

Quine's central ontological insight is that if we possessed a list of all of the true sentences, we would have an answer to his question: What is there? The answer would be: that to which the bound variables of these sentences must be capable of referring in order for them to be true is what there is. In essence, so to speak, Quine maintains that science provides us with a list of true sentences, and he concludes, in "Two Dogmas of Empiricism," that: "Ontological questions . . . are on a par with questions of natural science."[26] Here, Quine adopts a thesis that is similar to Charles Sanders Peirce's thesis that what there is is what inquiry guided by the scientific method will tell us there is. Or, as Peirce himself put this point:

> The opinion which is fated to be ultimately agreed to by all who [scientifically] investigate, is what we mean by the truth, and the object represented in this opinion is the real. That is the way I would explain reality.[27]

I note that Quine does not accept exactly this thesis. He rejects it because he thinks that it rests on the dubious notion of an infinite process of inquiry that employs an ideal version of the scientific method. Moreover, he thinks that it rests on a wrongheaded application of the concept of a limit to theories, which is, as he notes, defined for numbers, but not for theories. From my perspective, the most important reason that Quine gives for rejecting Peirce's thesis is that it presupposes that the result of applying the scientific method forever would be unique, but I get ahead of myself.

Quine's view is that the entities to which the bound variables of all the true sentences must be capable of referring in order for them to be true is what there is. However, it is important to note that Quine's view presupposes an ontological inversion, and this inversion is also presupposed by Peirce's thesis. On the realist view of world and truth delineated above, the concept of truth is explicated in terms of the concept of reality. According to Peirce and Quine, however, the concept of reality is explicated in terms of the concept of truth. Their view is that reality is what all the true representations represent, and the practice of science determines which representations are true. The idea is really quite simple. Since what there must be in order for true theories to be true is what there is, and the practice of science determines which theories are true, its practice determines what there is.

In other words, to the question about what theories say there is, that is, the question about ontological commitment, Quine answers that to be is to be the value of a bound variable. To the question about what there is, that is, the ontological question, he answers that to be is to be the value of a bound variable of a true theory. Note that there is an idea here that is common to Protagoras, Whorf, and Quine, namely, the idea that there is an order of representations, and what they represent is what there is. For Protagoras, the representations in question are some individual's perceptions, and for Whorf, they are linguistically shaped experiences. These are their versions of the previously mentioned ontological inversion. For Quine, the ontology determining representations are true theories. This invites an obvious question: Which theories are true? To this question, Quine defers to natural science. His conclusion is that natural science answers the question about what there is, but can its answer be unique? and is its answer unique? As I anticipated above, Quine answers such pivotal questions negatively.

In *Word and Object,* Quine writes that "in general the simplest possible theory *to a given purpose* need not be unique."[28] Simplicity aside, one instance of this is the algebraic fact that for any finite set of data, *D,* that assumes the form of points in a plane, there need not be just one theory that assumes the form of a polynomial that will generate *D.* It is well known that for any such set of points, there are indefinitely many polynomials that will generate it. For example, if we disregard units such as mass or seconds, we may let:

$$D = \{<0,2>, <1,3>, <2,4>, <3,5>\}.$$

Here are three of indefinitely many polynomials that will generate *D*:

$$(1)\ y = x^5 - 4x^4 - x^3 + 16x^2 - 11x + 2$$

$$(2)\ y = x^4 - 6x^3 + 11x^2 - 5x + 2$$

$$(3)\ y = x + 2$$

In this example, the theories take the form of polynomials, and the evidence or data takes the form of points in a plane coordinate system.[29] Theories and evidence come in many forms, however. The more general point is that for any body of evidence, *E,* there are indefinitely many theories that imply or generate *E*. So, more than one total theory can account for all the possible evidence.

Quine has expressed this point in several ways. In *Word and Object,* he puts this point in the following manner:

> [w]e have no reason to suppose that man's surface irritations even unto eternity [that is, all the possible data] admit of any one systematization [that is, total theory] that is scientifically better or simpler than all possible others. It seems likelier . . . that countless alternative theories would be tied for first place.[30]

In his reply to Chomsky in *Words and Objections,* he asserted that: "The totality of possible observations of nature, made and unmade, is compatible with physical theories that are incompatible with one another."[31] In "On the Reasons for Indeterminacy of Translation," we are told the following:

Theory can still vary though all possible observations be fixed. Physical theories can be at odds with each other and yet compatible with all possible data. . . . In a word, they can be logically incompatible and empirically equivalent.[32]

In addition, in "On Empirically Equivalent Systems of the World," Quine asserts that

[i]f all observable events can be accounted for in one comprehensive scientific theory—one system of the world, to echo Duhem's echo of Newton—then we may expect that they can all be accounted for equally in another, conflicting system of the world.[33]

Thus, sometimes Quine asserts that there are countless alternative theories that can systematize, or account for all the possible evidence, and sometimes he asserts that if there is one theory that can account for all this evidence, then there is at least one more theory that can do the same. In either case, the point is that: "Scientific method is the way to truth, but it affords even in principle no unique definition of truth."[34] In one version of "Empirical Content," Quine also expressed this point in the following manner:

[L]et us suppose that . . . two [theory] formulations are in fact empirically equivalent even though they are not known to be; and let us suppose that all the implied observational categoricals are in fact true, although, again, not known to be. Nothing more, surely, can be required for the truth of either theory formulation. Are they both true? I say yes.[35]

According to Quine, what there is is what true theory says there is, and science is supposed to provide true theory. However, science does not provide *the* true theory; it provides, or is, in principle, capable of providing an array of true theories. Thus, there cannot be a unique answer to the ontological question: what is there? So, what there is is not unique. If an actual world is all of what there is, this means that there are many actual worlds.

In fairness to both my readers and Quine, I must acknowledge that he claims that "it is a confusion to suppose that we can stand aloof and recognize all the alternative ontologies as true in their several ways, all the envisaged worlds as real."[36] Such a supposition confuses, he maintains, truth with evidential support, but recall that he also maintains that two theories can be both logically incompatible and empirically equivalent and empirically complete. Further, nothing more than empirical adequacy and completeness can be required for their truth. As Quine himself has asserted, "whatever evidence there is for science is sensory evidence."[37] There is a real conflict here. If all evidence is empirical evidence, and an empirically adequate and complete total theory is true, and there are, in principle, many empirically adequate and empirically complete total theories, then there are many true total theories. Moreover, if a world is the object of a true total theory, there are many worlds.

Quine suggests that the way out of this difficulty is to find a way of making two theories one. The method is obvious.

> When a sentence is affirmed in one of *two empirically equivalent theories* and denied in the other, the incompatibility is resoluble simply by reconstruing some theoretical term in that sentence as a pair of distinct homonyms [note that the incompatibility of empirically equivalent theories must be due to their theoretical content]. . . . Once the *two empirically equivalent systems of the world* have been rendered logically compatible, they can be treated as *a single big tandem theory* consisting perhaps of two largely independent lobes and a shared logic.[38]

This will not work, however. Quine's claim is that theories can be logically incompatible and empirically equivalent, but such theories are meant to be total or global. As Roger F. Gibson Jr., has pointed out, "when Quine is talking about underdetermination, he is doing so only in connection with global world theories and not in connection with any lesser theories."[39] Thus, it must not be forgotten that the claim is that more than one total theory can account for all the possible data or evidence. Thus, there are, I think, three flaws with Quine's method of making two theories one.

First, a total theory cannot be made part of a larger tandem theory. No theory is larger than a total theory. Second, suppose, per contra, that there could be a larger tandem theory that subsumes two total theories. Still, for any larger, that is, totalizing, tandem theory, there must be another total theory with which it is logically incompatible yet empirically equivalent. Thus, Quine would seem to be stuck with the unsightly spectacle of an infinite regress of totalizing theories. Third, if the reconstrual of the theoretical terms of two conflicting theories were to yield a larger, or totalizing, tandem theory that consisted of at least two independent lobes, then since each lesser theory would be both empirically adequate and empirically complete, every phenomenon would have at least two explanations. If for every totalizing tandem theory, there is another total theory with which it is logically incompatible yet empirically equivalent, then Quine would also seem to be stuck with the really quite odd idea that every phenomenon has infinitely many explanations. Be this as it may, let me note that I have not read Quine in order to get him right. I have read him to help myself understand my own ideas. Here, I have tried to be fair to Quine by conceding that my use of his views rests on a certain amount of twisting, and by showing where I have twisted them.

Questions of Quinean exegesis aside, since there would be a complete description of each world, there would be many truths. Quine himself suggests this:

> Where it makes sense to apply 'true' is to a sentence couched in the terms of a given theory and seen from within the theory, complete with its posited reality. . . . To say that the statement "Brutus killed Caesar" is true, or that "The atomic weight of sodium is 23" is true, is in effect simply to say that Brutus killed Caesar, or that the atomic weight of sodium is 23.[40]

Thus, Quine may also be taken to have provided an account of how there can be many total truths. As I have indicated, I know that Quine would reject this as akin to perdition. He asks, "Have we now so lowered our sights as to settle for a relativistic doctrine of truth—rating the statements of each theory as true for that theory, and brooking no criticism?"[41] Like Huck, he immediately retorts, "Not so."[42] Why not? Quine answers, "we continue to take seriously our own particular aggregate science, our own particular world-theory or loose total fabric of quasi-theories, whatever it may be."[43] Quine admits that there could be an alternative to our best current theory, and that both theories could satisfy any imaginable theoretical constraints equally well, for example, both theories could be equally simple, consistent, et cetera. Why then should we prefer our present theory and its ontology? Why should we take them seriously? Quine answers, albeit a bit vaguely, that "we own and use our beliefs of the moment . . . until by what is vaguely called scientific method we change them here and there for the better."[44] This answer is, I think, that any theory that could do the work that we desire our present theory to do isn't now available to do that work. So, we are, proffers Quine, justified in taking both our scientific practice and our present theory with its ontology seriously.

Quine's views are not without their problems, not to mention the myriad of exegetic problems associated with the task of appropriating them for sake of showing that there is a multiplicity of actual worlds. Rather than delve any further into these problems, I shall focus on the task of showing that an essential fragment of his views fits with, or implies this multiplicity.

On the one hand, Quine adamantly maintains that there is only one world and one truth, and being caught in the web of scientific belief, he also maintains that the former is the world of physics, and that the latter is its description. On the other hand, Quine suggests a view of ontological commitment and ontology that I think implies that there are many worlds, namely, the view that what true representations represent is what there is. His view that there is just the world of science is not inevitable, however, if what there is is what some manifold of true representations represents, and there are many distinct manifolds of true representations. This raises an obvious and pivotal question: How could it be that there are many disparate manifolds of true representations? A clue to an answer lies in Quine's remark that "in general the simplest possible theory *to a given purpose* need not be unique."[45] The element of purposiveness introduces another kind of underdetermination. Let me explain.

Suppose that both our purposes and the set of all possible data are fixed. Suppose that there is at least one total theory that implies all the possible data, that is, suppose that there is at least one empirically complete theory. Then, according to Quine, there is an array of equisimple, empirically complete, empirically equivalent, and yet incompatible theories. Add to this the premise that nothing more than empirical completeness could be required for the truth of a theory, and it follows that there is an array of true theories. Moreover, it follows that there is also an array of domains of objects that are required for them to be true. If each such theoretically ordered domain is a world, there is an array of actual worlds. Moreover, since each such world has a complete description, there are many truths. This is the familiar kind of underdetermination. Quine tells us that it can be overcome, however. According to him, our present theory is to be preferred because only it is available to do the work that we desire done, but this work is determined by our purposes. In other words, relative to our purposes, there is a determinate matrix of work to be done, and so there is a preferred theory, namely, the theory that gets it done. Moreover, there is a preferred ontology, namely, the domain of objects that are required for the preferred theory to be true. At this stage, this too should be familiar, but there is, I think, an additional kind of underdetermination, which is introduced by the very purposiveness that Quine thinks eliminates underdetermination.

Were our purposes to conflict, we would conflict over the work we want to see done, and so there would be no way to identify, and so no justification for preferring, present theory. There can be no preferred theory in the face of conflicting purposes, and since our purposes clearly conflict, there can be no preferred theory. This has, I think, astounding consequences. Quine tells us that relative to each set of purposes, there are many empirically complete and equivalent yet incompatible theories, but relative to a given set of purposes, there is one preferable theory. However, there are many sets of purposes. This much seems clear. For each set, there is both a plurality of theoretical options, and there is one option that is preferable to all the others. Thus, for each set of purposes, there is an empirically complete theoretical option that is, on the empiricist principles that Quine proffers, true. Thus, since it is clear that there are many sets of purposes, there are many empirically complete theoretical options that are true, that is, true on empiricist grounds. For each such theory, there is a domain of objects that is required for them to be true. If each theoretically ordered domain is a world, there are many actual worlds. Moreover, if each such world has a complete description, there are many truths. There is, therefore, an essential fragment of Quine's views that, in conjunction with the truism that there are many purposes, implies that there are many worlds and many truths. So, his view that there is just the world of physics is not inevitable.

Quine's work, unlike that of Whorf, does not require the addition of an account of what it is to be a world. So, he is able to answer the question: What is it to be a world? However, he thinks that there is just one world, and it is the world of science. Moreover, he desires to eradicate any element in his views that leaves open the possibility of a multiplicity of worlds and truths. He at least wants to make it difficult, if not impossible, for anyone to use his views to argue that there are many worlds and truths. So, he has no concern for the questions: Why are there many worlds? and Why are there many truths? I have argued that contrary to Quine's desires, an essential element of his ontological views provides the foundation on which answers to these very questions may be built. This foundation can be extrapolated from his tacit acceptance of the ontological inversion that is presupposed by Peirce's thesis, that is, from the presupposition that reality is what all the true representations represent. In turn, this presupposition must be supplemented with an analysis of the role of purposiveness in theory selection. However, Quine's work only contains a hint of an explication of the ontological status of a world. So, although Quine can tell a very complicated story about what it is to be a world, the issue of the ontological status of a world does not explicitly arise for him, and so he does not explicitly offer an answer to this question: What is the ontological status of the plurality of actual worlds? There is no reason why he should be able to offer such answers, however, since he, like Whorf, had other concerns.

Quine's aim has been to give an account of science from the perspective of science; my aim is to give an account of the multiplicity of actual worlds. Everything that exists, or might exist, from the perspective of science is just one of many actual worlds, and so science has no special place for me. I have not read Quine in order to get him right. I have read him to help myself understand my own ideas. My reading of Quine has been guided by the assumption that his views on the plurality of scientific worlds could serve as a model for articulating my views on the plurality of actual worlds. Thus, like the work of Whorf, the work of Quine is relevant to mine, but it does not do mine.

There are a number of reasons why Quine's work does not do mine. First, Quine's ontological insight is that what all the true representations represent is what there is, but he presupposes that every representation is a sentence. So his ontological insight only has a very narrow range of application, namely, to a world, or worlds, that have a sentential structure. As I have noted, I am working within the confines of this presupposition, but it should also be noted that it keeps a quite wide range of possibilities from sight. Second, Quine can only imagine the world of science. He thinks that whatever room there is for a plurality of worlds lies in the space of science, and even then he thinks that there is really no such room.

Third, Quine maintains that to be is, in short, to be the value of a bound variable of a true theory, and that since the practice of science determines which theories are true, its practice determines what there is. There is an important ambiguity here. On the one hand, this only needs to mean that the practice of science leads to the discovery of which theories are true, and to the discovery of what there is independently of theory. In this case, to determine is to discover what is the case independently of all actual and possible representations, but this makes nonsense of the ontological inversion that I have attempted to show lies at the heart of Quine's central ontological insight. On the other hand, Quine's claim can be taken to mean that the practice of science is what makes true theories true, and that this practice is what makes there be what there is. In this case, to make seems to be to create from nothing, but it is a truly monstrous thing to say that the practice of science begins with nothing, and then creates what there is. So, I must reject both readings of the pivotal term *determination,* but this raises the important question of how it must be understood.

Fourth, Quine's way into the plurality of worlds is through the premise that incompatible total theories can account for all the possible evidence, and the premise that such theories must, on empiricist grounds, be true, and the premise that what there is is what there must be in order for a true total theory to be true. The aggregate of possible evidence is not ontologically neutral, since part of what there is is what there must be for all the possible evidence, which Quine assumes to take a sentential form, to be true. In other words, the incompatible total theories must share an empirical ontology. So Quine's views only support the thesis that there are many actual worlds in a limited sense, namely, there can be different ontologies, but only theoretical ontologies can differ, and empirical ontologies must be had in common. Thus, Quine's views do not show us the way to an account of the multiplicity of nonoverlapping actual worlds.

Fifth, Quine's ontological insight presupposes an inversion, namely, that a world is everything that there must be in order for all the true representations to be true. As far as I can determine, he does not make this inversion explicit, and so he leaves open the question of why one should accept it. In other words, why invert? Sixth, Quine does not answer the question about how there can be many disparate manifolds of true representations. I have argued that there is a hint of an answer in his work, but that it must be extrapolation from a single remark that may only have the status of an aside. In short, there are many disparate manifolds of true representations because there are many purposes. Seventh, consequently, Quine does not take purposiveness seriously enough, and as I have noted, the premise that representation producing beings are purposive beings will be essential to my argument that there are many actual worlds.

III
Motivating the Fundamental Ontological Idea
Goodman and Putnam

Whorf's work only contains an implicit account of the multiplicity of worlds and truths. One can cull from Quine's work a more or less explicit account of these multiplicities, but he would assert that there is just the one world and the one truth of natural science. Neither Whorf, nor Quine explains (1) why there are many actual worlds, (2) why there are many truths, and (3) why the aforementioned ontological inversion ought to be embraced, which is, I think, among the most puzzling things to be explained. So they have not done what I want to do, but I have only sought to elucidate these themes by showing how I see them developed, or able to be developed, in their work. In pursuit of their further elucidation, I will now draw on the work of Nelson Goodman. More specifically, I will attempt to elucidate these three themes by exploring three aspects of Goodman's metaphysical vision. I will begin with an examination of what I take to be Goodman's answer to the question: Why embrace the aforementioned ontological shift?

According to Quine, to be is to be the value of a bound variable. This thesis requires a reconception that amounts to a fundamental ontological shift, a Copernican revolution. Quine's thesis presupposes, however, that the idea that there is just one representation-independent world must be supplanted by the idea that a world is everything that there must be in order for all the true representations to be true. In other words, his thesis presupposes the renunciation of metaphysical realism, and the appropriation of something like the thesis that a world is an ideal sum of what can be represented by a manifold of true, or right, representations. As far as I can ascertain, he neither makes this ontological shift explicit, nor does he say why it should be embraced. Moreover, the same can be said about Whorf. Since this is a pivotal premise in my argument for a plurality of actual worlds, not to mention an essential element of my response to Davidson's critique of conceptual relativism, it behooves the present writer to answer questions such as the following. Why should the former idea be rejected? Moreover, what could possibly compel the latter? In short, why shift?

Part of Goodman's importance is that he provides us with both a proof that a shift is necessary, and a fuller articulation of the *terminus ad quem* of such a shift. The *terminus a quo* is, of course, the thesis that there is a unique world, and neither its existence, nor the way it is depends on the way it is represented. Given this, a world cannot be an ideal sum of what is representable by a manifold of right or true representations. If the world were such a sum, both the existence of the world, and the way of the world would then depend on the way it is represented, which on the hypothesis of metaphysical realism, it does not. It is, I think, instructive to interpret Goodman's proof in terms of a strategy that may have been first advanced by Kant. In a 1798 letter to Christian Garve, Kant wrote that "the antinomy of pure reason [for example, pure reason shows both that there must be a first moment, and that there cannot be a first moment] . . . is what first aroused me from my dogmatic slumber [which includes transcendental or metaphysical realism]." [1] There is a discernible and definite strategy here: since realism, metaphysical or transcendental, is an essential premise in an antinomy, and since antinomies are intolerable, the only alternative is to give up the relevant version of realism, and to adopt a version of the ontological shift that is now at issue. *Mutatis mutandis,* Goodman argues that since the realist thesis is an essential element of an enigma, which is as intolerable as any antinomy, the above described ontological shift must be embraced. The pivotal question is: What is this enigma?

There are statements that can both be false, but cannot both be true, for example, (1) *Socrates always flies,* and (2) *Socrates never flies.* Such statements are entitled contraries. Now, true statements can sometimes appear to be contraries. For example, (3) *the sun always moves,* and (4) *the sun never moves* are both true, and yet they appear to be contraries. It is important to note that Goodman's enigma is not that there are true contraries; it is not that there are contraries that are both true. It is also important to note that our reason for saying that (3) and (4) are both true is closely connected to, if not the same as, our reason for saying that they are not contraries. Our reason for saying that (3) and (4) are true is that they are elliptical for two much more complex statements, namely, (5) *there is a frame of reference under which the sun always moves,* and (6) *there is another frame of reference under which the sun never moves,* which are, given sufficient qualification, both true. Furthermore, our reason for saying that (3) and (4) are not contraries is that (5) and (6) are not contraries. In this case, our sophistication about frames of reference keeps us safe from the enigma of true contraries. According to Goodman, however, we are hoist by this very sophistication.

A frame of reference is a set of axes in terms of which the position or the motion of an object can be described; as Goodman writes, "frames of reference are just coordinate systems within which spatial relations are mathematically represented."[2] Goodman's enigma rests on what he takes to be two fundamental truths about frames of reference. The first truth is, as Goodman writes, that "nothing is at rest or is in motion apart from a frame of reference."[3] I will take it as obvious that apart from all frames of reference, there is no position, motion or rest. The second truth is, as Goodman writes, that: "Frames of reference . . . seem to belong less to what is described than to systems of description."[4] This is not obvious. The idea is that although a frame of reference is an essential element of some systems for describing objects, it is neither an object among the objects that may be described with the assistance of such a system, nor does it characterize any such objects. In less perspicuous words, although words that may have at least once seemed clearer to my readers, a frame of reference is empirically real and transcendentally ideal. Be this as it may: not only *can* a frame of reference be used to describe the spatial and temporal features of objects; a frame of reference *must* be used to so describe objects.

Moreover, although a frame of reference must be used to describe the spatial and temporal features of objects, a frame of reference does not itself describe any object. In other words, a frame of reference is a necessary condition for the representation of rest or motion, and perhaps the representation of any possible object, but a frame of reference is not itself a representation of any object, or any relation among objects. The latter part of this is not obvious. Why doesn't a frame of reference represent some object or objects? or some relation among objects? These are quite complex questions, and they are questions over which I shall not here worry, but the answer is, I think, that if some frame of reference were somehow a part of the world as it is in itself, then there would be, for example, an up and down to this world, which, as a matter of empirical fact, there is not. In any case, Goodman articulates his enigma by bringing these two truths together with the reflection that the realist, as he construes her, thinks that there must be a world as it is in itself, that is, apart from all systems of descriptions, and so there must be a world apart from all frames of reference. Moreover, this sort of realist thinks not only that there must be a world apart from all frames of reference, but that there must also be a framework-independent way that such a world is.

Kant has an apt image for all of this.[5] It is easy to imagine that the objects reflected in a mirror have a reality behind its surface, a farside reality. This illicitly presumed subsurface reality is the *focus imaginarius,* which is exploited by the story of Alice. The story of metaphysical realism exploits a similar imaginary focus, and herein lies the enigma. The metaphysical realist begins with a number of descriptions of objects that depend on an equal number of frames of reference. Then she imagines or supposes that these objects have a reality that is independent of these frames. The point of the image is that this supposedly framework independent reality is no more legitimate than the *focus imaginarius.* To see how this image or supposition breaks down, let us submit to it, and let us acquiesce in the thesis that there is a world apart from all frames of reference. If there is such a world, then there must be, according to the realist as construed by Goodman, a framework-independent way that it is, but this invites an obvious question: What is this way?

Goodman asks a remarkably simple question:

If I ask about the world, you can offer to tell me how it is under one or more frames of reference; but if I insist that you tell me how it is apart from all frames, what can you say?[6]

The answer to this clearly rhetorical question is that one can say nothing. Now, it is exactly here that Goodman's truths about frames of reference become relevant. There is, apart from all frames of reference, neither motion nor rest. Apart from all frames of reference, events are neither simultaneous nor successive, and so apart from all such frames, there is neither simultaneity nor succession. Moreover, although a frame of reference is an essential part of a system of description, it is not a part of what is thereby described. With respect to these kinds of spatial and temporal relations, therefore, apart from all frames of reference, there is no way that the world is. Goodman's enigma can be made clearer in the light of a certain contrast with the Parmenidean dictum that "you could not know what is not—that cannot be done— nor indicate it."[7] The relevant point is not that one cannot indicate what is not, instead it is that what one cannot indicate is not. The intuition that underlies Goodman's enigma, which constitutes its suppressed premise, is that where nothing can be said, there is nothing. In other words, where one can say nothing, there is nothing to say, and so there is nothing. Or, equivalently, where there is something, something can be said, which should not be confused with the thesis that wherever there is something to say, there is something. According to Goodman, the intolerable enigma is that if there are objects apart from all frames of reference, then there is nothing to say about them—that is, there is, in abstraction from all frames of reference (and note again that the realist's supposition is exactly that there is a world apart from all such frames) nothing to say about objects with respect to rest and motion—and so there are no such objects. Therefore, given Goodman's suppressed premise, there are no objects apart from all frames of reference. In short, if there are objects apart from all frames of reference, there are no objects apart from all frames of reference. This is an enigma, if anything is.

Goodman's enigma can also be expressed in the following manner. Reflection on what it is to be a frame of reference should make it clear that (1) there is, apart from all frames of reference, neither motion or rest, and (2) although a frame of reference may be an essential element of any system that can represent the spatial and temporal relations of things, no frame of reference is a thing—that is, object, property of an object, or relation among objects, et cetera—in the world as it is in itself. Now, the realist, as construed by Goodman, maintains that apart from all systems of representation, and so apart from all frames of reference, there is not only a world, but there is a way that this world is. Goodman asks: if there is, apart from all systems of description, and so all frames of reference, both a world, and a way that this world is, then what is this way with respect to rest and motion? If there are no frames of reference in the world as it is in itself, and there is neither rest nor motion where there are no frames of reference, then there is, with respect to rest and motion, no way that the world in itself is. Thus, the realist thesis that there is, apart from all frames of reference, both a world and a way that it is, and a pair of general truths about frames of reference, together lead to the enigma that there is such a way, but there cannot be such a way. Now, just as Kant didn't think that he had established an antinomy, Goodman does not think that he has established this enigma. It needs resolution. Moreover, just as Kant thought that the only way to resolve his antinomies, not to mention escape skepticism, is to reject realism, Goodman thinks that the only way to resolve his enigma is to reject the realist thesis upon which it is based.

Goodman's point has been well illustrated in a sphere outside that of physics, namely, that of economics. Richard D. Wolff and Stephen A. Resnick tell us, in their *Economics: Marxian versus Neoclassical*, that under the framework of neoclassical economic theory, there is a panoply of entities: individuals, markets, commodities, technologies, prices, money, income, savings, investments, individual preferences, utility, supply, demand, production, distribution, labor, capital, growth, GNP, interest rates, uncertainty, and so on.[8] They write that

> [f]or neoclassical economists, *society* is the collection of *individuals* in it. Individual *wants, thoughts,* and *deeds* combine to make society what it is. To understand an economy is then to make sense of the *aggregate effects* of *individual wants* and *acts.* Neoclassical theory does this by demonstrating how individuals maximize their material *self-interests* by utilizing their *owned resources* and the available *technology* in *market transactions.*[9]

They also tell us that under the framework of Marxian economic theory, there is an equally impressive array of different entities: class, surplus, capital, labor, labor power, commodities, values, production and distribution, accumulation of capital, crises, imperialism, *et cetera.* They write that "Marxian theory . . . will presume that any event occurs as the result . . . of *everything else* going on around that event and preceding that event."[10] Be this as it may, Wolff and Resnick note that

> [t]his partial and preliminary listing underscores a remarkable difference in the neoclassical and Marxian theories. Notwithstanding the considerable overlap in the words and phrases that appear in both theories, basic objects on one theory exist as secondary objects or are altogether absent in the other. Self-interest-maximizing individuals are as scarce in Marxian theory as surplus labor is in neoclassical theory. . . . Class exploitation is a key object for Marxian theory, while most neoclassicals would deny its existence; likewise, the self-interest-maximizing individual as specified in neoclassical theory would be rejected as an imaginary creation by most Marxists.[11]

At this point, Goodman can be paraphrased: If I ask about the economic world, you can offer to tell me how it is under the neoclassical and Marxian frames of reference; but if I insist that you tell me how the economic world is apart from all such frames, what can you say? Goodman's answer can be repeated: *one can say nothing.* The same intuitions are relevant: where one can say nothing, there is nothing to say, and so there is nothing. Thus, the economic world in itself is nothing. This is exactly the conclusion that Wolff and Resnick reach: "objects in and for one theory may literally not exist in another. . . . Objects of theories do not exist out there in the world just waiting for theories to observe [sic] and explain them."[12]

Once again, note that Goodman does not believe that he has established an enigma. Its point is similar to the point of Kant's antinomies, to wit, realism must be rejected, that is, it is necessary to reject the assumption that there is, apart from all frames of reference, both a world and a way that it is.[13] Goodman concludes:

> We are confined to ways of describing whatever is described. Our universe, so to speak, consists of these ways rather than of a world or of worlds.[14]

The world posited by metaphysical realism is, therefore, nothing, and so it is necessary to shift to another conception of what it is to be a world. Goodman's argument moves quickly, perhaps too quickly. It assumes many things, for example, it assumes that one may generalize from a thesis about frames of reference, that is, just one of many systems of description, to a thesis about all systems of description— including conceptual schemes—but it is not clear what justifies this. Moreover, it is not clear what justifies Goodman's implicit assumption that if there is, apart from all frames of reference, nothing to say about the motion or rest of objects, then there is nothing at all to say about these objects. There are many problems here, but before I attend to them, I will discuss the second of the three facets of Goodman's vision, which corresponds to the second of my three questions. Even if Goodman has given us a good reason to embrace the already discussed ontological inversion, why should it be thought that there is more than one actual world?

Even if the idea of a unique world in itself is intolerably enigmatic, it may be that the plurality of true or correct frame of reference dependent descriptions may all be transformable, or translatable, into one another. If so, there may be just one world, namely, whatever it is that is described by all intertransformable or intertranslatable true descriptions. If all the true framework relative descriptions were translatable into one another, the unique world might be defined as everything that is described by them, that is, if there is anything that is described by them. As Goodman himself puts this possibility:

> We might . . . take the real world to be that of . . . groups of them [that is, alternative right versions] bound together by some principle of reducibility or translatability.[15]

Or, in other words:

> [W]e may say . . . two versions deal with the same facts if we mean by this that they not only speak of the same objects but are also routinely translatable each into the other. As meanings vanish in favor of certain relationships among terms, so facts vanish in favor of certain relationships among versions.[16]

More generally, if all the correct representations were transformable into one another, the world might be defined as everything that is represented by such representations. Why, then, think that there are many actual worlds?

Goodman considers the example of the apparently conflicting descriptions of the sun's motion to be uninteresting, because they are easily transformable or translatable into one another, and this makes it seem that they are all somehow representations of the same thing, that is, the same world. He writes:

> The alternative descriptions of motion, all of them in much the same terms and routinely transformable into one another, provide only a minor and rather pallid example of diversity in accounts of the world.[17]

Moreover, Goodman provides this warning:

> If we are tempted to say that "both are versions of the same facts," this must no more be taken to imply that there are independent facts of which both are versions than likeness of meaning between two terms implies that there are some entities called meanings.[18]

Is it even possible for there to be a method that can transform any correct representation into any other apparently opposing yet also correct representation? Of any method that appeared to be so capable, it would be necessary to ask: how much opposition could such a method transform, if such a method could transform opposition?[19] It is instructive to recall Quine's alleged method for putting together incompatible yet empirically equivalent and complete theories. Goodman must answer the following sorts of questions. Does the set of right representations represent one and only one world? Can the set of right representations be put together in such a way that they represent just one world? According to Goodman, they do not, and they cannot.

Here, Goodman offers two arguments. The first assumes the form of an invitation to make a number of comparisons. In essence, he asks us to compare the scientific pictures of the world, the moral or political pictures of the world, and the many aesthetic pictures of the world. According to Goodman, if one looks, one should see that although all of these pictures are true or right, they cannot be put together in a way that results in a composite picture of one world. Moreover, there is no picture to which all the others can be reduced; Goodman asks, perhaps rhetorically, "How do you go about reducing Constable's or James

Joyce's world-view to physics?"[20] I think that Goodman would say that a similar point applies to neoclassical economic theory and Marxian economic theory as described by Wolff and Resnick; not only is it impossible to put these economic pictures together in a way that results in a composite picture of one economic world, but neither can be reduced to the other.

> Much more striking [than the alternative descriptions of motion considered above] is the vast variety of versions and visions in the several sciences, in the works of different painters and writers, and in our perceptions as informed by these, by circumstances, and by our own insights, interests, and past experiences. Even with all illusory or wrong or dubious versions dropped, the rest exhibit new dimensions of disparity. Here we have no neat set of frames of reference, no ready rules for transforming physics, biology, and psychology into one another, and no way of transforming any of these into Van Gogh's vision, or Van Gogh's into Canaletto's.[21]

The obvious question is why not simply link the manifold of versions, visions, works, and perceptions? and say that what they represent is the one and only world? Goodman answers:

> Such of these versions as are depictions rather than descriptions have no truth-value in the literal sense, and cannot be combined by conjunction. The difference between juxtaposing and conjoining two statements has no evident analogue for two pictures or for a picture and a statement.[22]

Nothing can serve as the linking mechanism whereby every element of the manifold of right or true representations can be put together. Juxtaposition would leave out statements, and conjunction would omit pictures. So the manifold of representations cannot be put together in a way that results in one composite representation of one world.

Goodman's second argument is based on a well known strategy for resolving apparent inconsistencies. *Bill is the cat* and *Bill is not the cat* are, for example, consistent, if the former *Bill* and the latter *Bill* do not refer to the same entity. More generally, what appear to be inconsistent statements *can* be shown to be consistent by establishing that certain terms refer to different objects. As Goodman writes, "contradiction [or: inconsistency] is avoided by segregation."[23] He thinks, moreover, that such a strategy supports the conclusion that "conflicting statements, if true, are true in different worlds."[24] Goodman's task is to show how this strategy supports this conclusion. The first step involves the example discussed above: *the sun always moves* and *the sun never moves*. Although these statements appear to be contraries, both are true. There can't be true contraries, however. So, the appearance of true contraries must be dispelled.[25] Such dispelling reveals the connection between the strategy and the conclusion.

One solution is that apparently contrary statements belong to different accounts. The idea is that according to one account, the sun always moves, and according to another account, the sun never moves. This solution does not work, however. There is little, if any, difference between these statements and the statements that generated the puzzle in the first place. Another solution is to relativize the relevant statements to different frames of reference. The idea here is that relative to one frame of reference, the sun always moves, and relative to another frame of reference, the sun never moves. However, this solution also does not work. Frames of reference are, as Goodman thinks of them, coordinate systems with which spatial and temporal relations can be mathematically represented. True yet contrary mathematical representations are as much of a problem as the apparently true yet contrary statements with which the present puzzle began. Goodman's solution is that such conflicting statements, if true, are true in different worlds. If Goodman's solution works, so to speak, there are many worlds, but what motivates his solution? Behind this solution stands the intuitive force of the well-known strategy for resolving apparent inconsistencies described above. If *the sun always moves* and *the sun never moves* are contrary yet true descriptions of the same world, the conflict is neither mitigated nor dispelled. As Goodman notes: "The apparent conflict between true descriptions shows that they are not descriptions of the same thing."[26] Therefore: "The earth that is truly described as in motion is not the earth that is truly described as at rest."[27] Thus, there are many actual worlds.

Goodman concludes that since a world is what is represented by a manifold of true representations, and the different manifolds of true representations cannot be put together in a way that results in a composite representation of just one world, there are many worlds. He writes, "the multiple worlds of conflicting true versions are actual worlds. . . . [I]f there is any actual world, there are many."[28] Since a world is what answers to a true, or correct version, and there are many such versions, indeed the purpose of much of Goodman's work is to lay out the ways in which many true versions can be made, there are many actual worlds.

This would seem to bring us to the third facet of Goodman's metaphysical vision, and the third of my questions: How can there be many truths? Unlike Protagoras and Whorf, however, Goodman does not first argue that there are many worlds, and then turn to the task of showing that each world has a complete and true description, that is, there are many truths. For Goodman, as for Quine, or at least as I have construed their words, there are many worlds because there are many truths. So, in discussing Goodman's metaphysical vision, one cannot begin by focusing exclusively on the issues of the quiddity and plurality of worlds, and then to turn to the issue of the plurality of truths. What it is to be a world, the plurality of worlds, and the plurality of truths are, for Goodman, three closely related issues, but the plurality of truths is not a consequence of his account of the quiddity and plurality of worlds. It should be clear that Goodman maintains that the opposite is the case: there are many actual worlds because there are many truths.

None of this entails that Goodman rejects the correspondence theory of truth, or the image that I have called the string theory of truth. As I understand Goodman, he is an advocate of this formalism, but he rejects, with Quine, one assessment of the priority of its elements. Formalism aside, *Fido is a dog* is true if and only if the object tied to *Fido* is an element of the set tied to *is a dog*. Clearly, then, truth can be defined, if objects, sets, and string constituted relations are taken as primitive. However, Goodman's move is to take truth as primitive, and to define the collections of objects that make up the ontologies of the manifold of actual worlds. Crudely put, on the one hand, reality and correspondence can be taken as primitive, and a true sentence can be defined as a sentence that corresponds to reality; on the other hand, truth and correspondence can be taken as primitive, and reality can be defined as that to which all the true sentences correspond. Thus, in addition to his acceptance and defense of the thesis that there are many actual worlds, Goodman also seems willing to endorse a notion of truth that is quite similar to that outlined in the preceding. He affirms that the familiar dictum " 'Snow is white' is true if and only if snow is white" must be revised to something like " 'Snow is white' is true in a given world if and only if snow is white in that world."[29]

If there are many actual worlds, and there is one total truth for each world, then Goodman would *seem* to have provided an account of how there can be many total truths. However, for Goodman, since a world is what answers to a manifold of true or right representations, and there are many such manifolds, the plurality of truths is a premise, not a conclusion.

As with the work of Whorf and Quine, Goodman's work is neither irrelevant to mine, nor does it do mine. It provides moral support for those of us who think monstrous thoughts about pluralities of actual worlds, but there are a number of reasons why his work does not do mine. First, there seems to be an irresolvable ambiguity in the midst of Goodman's metaphysical vision. In his "The Wonderful Worlds of Goodman," Israel Scheffler points out that in Goodman's work, there are two conflicting interpretations of the word *world*. On the one hand, there is a versional interpretation. Here, a world is, in Scheffler's words, "a true (or right) world-version."[30] Goodman seems to have the versional interpretation in mind, when he asks "In what sense are . . . there many worlds?" and he answers that "many different world versions are of independent interest and importance."[31] Moreover, he also seems to have the versional interpretation in mind, when he writes that "the world [is] displaced by worlds that are but versions."[32] Here, the pivotal idea is that a world should be equated with an ideally completable and true description. This very formulation leaves open, however, the possibility that there is some sphere or domain of objects that such a description might fail to get right, and this brings one to the second possible interpretation of the word *world*. So, there is, on the other hand, an objectual interpretation. In Scheffler's words, a world is "a realm of things (versions or nonversions) referred to or described by . . . a right world-version."[33] Goodman seems to have the objectual interpretation in mind, when he writes that "the multiple worlds I countenance are just the actual worlds made by and answering to true or right versions."[34] Scheffler's distinction makes it seem that worlds are one thing, and versions are another. Perhaps it should be said that this makes it seem that worlds are concatenations of things, and versions are not, but I will prescind from this issue here.

With Scheffler's distinction in hand, a realist might object to Goodman's metaphysical vision on the grounds that it is ambiguous between (1) there are many true *versions,* and (2) there are, in the above-described objectual sense, many *worlds.* Such a realist might reluctantly accept the first thesis, and adamantly reject the second thesis on the grounds that it is simply confused. If so, the metaphysical realist is then obligated to say exactly what the confusion is. What could her explanation be except a reiteration of the claim that there is the world, there are our representations, the world is independent of our representations, and so the world and our representations are distinct? In other words, to what could such an explanation amount, if not a reiteration of the distinction between the objectual and the versional interpretations of the word *world?* This is, I think, insufficient.

Someone who has embraced the aforementioned ontological shift, that is, who thinks that the limit of the world and the limits of representation somehow coincide, that is, who thinks that to be is to be representable, would not, or should not, accept Scheffler's distinction. Goodman acknowledges that

> a right version and its world are different. A version saying that there is a star up there is not itself bright or far off, and the star is not made up of letters.[35]

However, he would add that

> saying that there is a star up there and saying that the statement "There is a star up there" is true amount, trivially, to much the same thing, even though the one seems to talk about the star and the other to talk about a statement. What is more important, we cannot find any world-feature independent of all versions. Whatever can be said truly of a world is dependent on the saying—not that whatever we say is true but that whatever we say truly (or otherwise present rightly) is nevertheless informed by and relative to the language or other symbol system we use.[36]

To what, then, does the distinction between the objectual and the versional interpretations of the word *world* amount? Goodman does not offer a clear answer to this question, but he suggests that this is entirely illegitimate: "No firm line can be drawn between world-features that are discourse dependent and those that are not." [37]

This last point is closely related to a second deficiency in Goodman's metaphysical vision, namely, there is the highly dubious character of Goodman's premise: where nothing can be said, there is nothing. It should be noted that Goodman is neither alone, nor should his premise seem so alien as to also seem plainly wrongheaded. In his *Tractatus Logico-Philosophicus*, Ludwig Wittgenstein similarly affirmed that "*the limits of my language* mean the limits of my world." [38] Although he opposed this premise, in his *The View from Nowhere*, and in a somewhat different idiom, Thomas Nagel has more recently written:

> what there is is what we can think about or conceive of . . . the idea
> of something that we could not think about or conceive of makes no
> sense. [39]

Within the framework of metaphysical realism, however, Goodman's premise is, irrespective of idiom, plainly wrong. If the world is a world of representation-independent objects, it is possible for there to be something that cannot be represented. As Nagel writes:

> What there is and what we, in virtue of our nature, can think about
> are different things, and the latter may be smaller than the former. [40]

In other words, if there is a world of representation-independent objects, it is possible for there to be something about which nothing can be said. This vitiates Goodman's argument for adopting the ontological shift discussed above.

If what there is is some sort of ideal sum of what can be represented by the manifold of true, or right, representations, then Goodman's premise is far more plausible, if not obviously right. If the sphere of what there is and the sphere of what can be represented by some manifold of right or true representations are coextensive, then it is trivially true that where no representation can be produced, there is nothing. Recall the point of Goodman's argument: he wants to motivate the above-described ontological inversion, which seems to be a pivotal premise in the argument that there are many actual worlds. Also remember that this ontological inversion amounts to the thesis that the sphere of being and the sphere of the rightly or truly representable are identical and, moreover, that Goodman's strategy is to argue that realism is intolerably enigmatic. His argument presupposes this premise: where there is nothing to say, there is nothing. This premise is totally unacceptable to the realist, and it presupposes that the sphere of being and the sphere of the representable are identical. So Goodman's argument is circular. In short, Goodman argues that since realism is an enigma, the ontological inversion must be accepted, but his argument for thinking that realism is an enigma rests on the premise that *where nothing can be said, there is nothing,* which only seems acceptable in the context of the very ontological inversion that Goodman seeks to motivate. This is important, since the circularity of Goodman's argument leaves unfulfilled the task of explaining why the aforementioned ontological inversion ought to be embraced, and without such an explanation, there is, I think, little hope of explaining why there are a plurality of actual worlds.

There is a third problem with Goodman's metaphysical vision, which also concerns his defense of this ontological shift. As I noted above, in his argument, Goodman assumes that one may generalize from a thesis about frames of reference, that is, just one of many systems of description, to a thesis about all systems of description, but it is not clear what justifies this. Conceptual schemes are systems of description, and if they are like frames of reference in that they are not part of the world, then Goodman may well be able to press the above-described argument. But, although it may be obvious that frames of reference are not part of the world, it is not at all obvious that conceptual schemes are in no way a part of the world. Moreover, recall that it is essential to metaphysical realism that independently of both our actual representations, and our capacity to represent, there is an unique order of objects that possess various properties, and that these properties are also independent of both our actual representations and our capacities to represent. In other words, there are objects that are distinct by virtue of the properties that they possess, or fail to possess, independently of whatever lexicon of predicates we may happen to possess. Indeed, as G. H. Merrill has pointed out:

> [T]he world must be represented *not* simply as a *set,* but as a set
> *together with* a class of relations among the members of that set. To
> describe *the world* is to describe the entities (or kinds of entities) in it

and their relations to one another. . . . [I]t is this stronger position that the realist traditionally [?] holds.[41]

David Lewis has made a similar point:

> [R]ealism needs realism. That is: the realism that recognizes a non-trivial enterprise of discovering the truth about the world [which is guaranteed by the uniqueness and independence of the world, which is a principal motivation for accepting realism] needs the traditional [?] realism that recognizes objective sameness and difference, joints in the world, discriminatory classifications not of our own making.[42]

So, since it is not clear whether the argument about frames of reference can be legitimately extended to include conceptual schemes, Goodman's argument may not only move too quickly, but it may beg some important questions.

In the foregoing, I considered Goodman's proof for adopting a certain ontological shift, and I noted that his proof followed one of two strategies that were advanced by Kant. Its basic idea was that since realism is intolerably enigmatic, that is, an essential premise in an antinomy, it is necessary to both reject it, and shift to some version of antirealism or idealism, or even *irrealism,* as Goodman entitles his position.[43] In short, his proof did not work, and so it is, within the context of this work, still necessary to motivate this sort of shift, not to mention the necessity of resolving the myriad of other problems that have arisen up to this point. In this section, I will investigate Hilary Putnam's proof for the necessity of embracing this type of shift, a proof which follows the second Kantian strategy.

In his *Prolegomena,* Kant wrote that "my remembering David Hume [to wit: his skepticism] was the very thing which many years ago first interrupted my dogmatic slumber [to wit: his realism]."[44] There is a discernible and definite strategy here: the basic idea is that since realism entails skepticism, and skepticism is intolerable—as intolerable as any antinomy—we should shift to some other metaphysical view. Be this as it may, it must be acknowledged that realist intuitions have great power. So, if one's objection to realism is that it entails skepticism, one is obligated to establish this entailment, and one is *prima facie* obligated to provide an equally powerful case against skepticism. For Kant, it seems that skepticism is merely intolerable, and if his ontological or transcendental turn dispels it, he takes his turn to be *ipso facto* justified. The justification of transcendental idealism, and so the repudiation of transcendental realism, comes, in part, with the latter's mere association with skepticism. In his *Reason, Truth and History*, Hilary Putnam objects to realism for a similar reason.[45] Following, in its broadest outlines, what I have described as the second Kantian strategy, he also argues that realism is refuted by virtue of its association with skepticism, but he, unlike Kant, offers us an ostensible refutation of skepticism. Now, I wish that Putnam's argument were sound, but I think that it is not. In this section, I will say what his argument is, where he thinks it takes us, and I will explain why I think it fails. In conclusion, I will explore the prospects of reconstructing his argument in a way that might lend support to the thesis that there are many actual worlds and truths.

Let us be clear about the theses involved. Once again, metaphysical realism, to use Putnam's idiom, includes the thesis that there is just one actual world, which consists of a multiplicity of representation independent objects, and the way that the world is, or the way that these objects are, is also representation independent.[46] This is essential. Additionally, metaphysical realism includes the theses that there is just one true and complete representation of this world, and that truth is, more or less, a correspondence between some representation and some segment of the world. As Putnam understands it, metaphysical realism is, in short, the view that

> [1] the world consists of a fixed totality of mind-independent objects
> ... [2] there is exactly one true and complete description of the way
> the world is ... [3] truth involves some sort of correspondence.[47]

To what alternative metaphysical picture does Putnam think his argument takes us? Contrary to the realist thesis that there is just one actual world that consists of a multiplicity of representation independent objects, after the shift, which Putnam's proof aims to motivate, *"what objects does the world consist of?* is a question that only makes sense to ask *within* a theory or description."[48] Putnam illustrates this with an example drawn from mereology—the axiomatic analysis of the whole-part relation.[49] Suppose that there are three objects: x_1, x_2, and x_3. He asks: how many objects are there? The answer appears obvious: there are three. However, suppose that for any two objects, there is a third object that is their mereological sum. Given this mereological principle, if there is no null object, there are then seven objects, to wit: (1) x_1, (2) x_2, (3) x_3, (4) $x_1 + x_2$, (5) $x_1 + x_3$, (6) $x_2 + x_3$, and (7) $x_1 + x_2 + x_3$.[50] So, are there three objects or seven? Or, more generally, what is there? Putnam maintains that the answers to such questions are relative to either some method of counting, or some theory or system of description. According to metaphysical realism, there is an independent something that gets counted differently, but how many parts does this something have? This question can only be answered in a way that is dependent on some method of counting, and on either the answer of three or seven, "we have not a neutral description, but rather a *partisan* description."[51] Putnam maintains, therefore, that no theory or description independent answer can be given to the question, What is there? Moreover, he denies that there is just one true description of the world, rather: "there is more than one 'true' theory or description of the world."[52] Along with this, he denies that truth is correspondence, rather: " 'Truth' . . . is some sort of (idealized) rational acceptability."[53]

Be this as it may, as I have noted, realist intuitions are deeply entrenched, and so Putnam is obligated to motivate this alternative. Once again, his strategy is to argue that since metaphysical realism entails skepticism, and skepticism is intolerable, so is metaphysical realism. What is this skepticism? Why is it so bad? Skepticism is, in this context, the thesis that any nontautologous representation could be false, even an ideal representation. In other words, even a representation that is consistent, maximally simple, conservative, empirically adequate, and so on, could be false. Given the foregoing explications, Putnam's claim that metaphysical realism entails skepticism is equivalent to the claim that if there is just one representation independent actual world, and truth is, more or less, the correspondence between some representation and some segment of this unique world, then any nontautologous representation could be false, even an ideal representation. Why should one think, however, that metaphysical realism entails skepticism?

An essential part of metaphysical realism is that the one and only actual world is representation independent. As construed by the metaphysical realist, representations constitute neither the being, nor the quiddity of the world. Consequently, there is no necessary connection between our representations and the way the world is, even if the representation is ideal. So any representation could fail to correctly represent the way the world is, that is, any representation could be false. This is even true of an ideal representation. One way in which a representation, even if ideal, could be false is this: every sentient being could be a brain in a vat whose afferent and efferent nerve endings are connected to a supercomputer that generates impulses that make it seem to the bevatted brains that the world is the way it seems to be to us who have presumed ourselves to be unbevatted. This is a pantemporal claim: every sentient being has been, is and will be such a brain. This is, of course, a cybernetic version of Cartesian skepticism. Another way in which an ideal representation could be false is that there could be "an evil genius, as clever and deceitful as he is powerful, who has directed his entire effort to misleading me."[54] As Putnam only focuses on the former possibility, so will I. In this case, our world picture, even if it were refined to the point of being ideal, would be mostly wrong. What if the result of refining our present world picture were to include the proposition that every sentient being is a bevatted brain? It might not seem to us that this could be the result of refining our world picture to the point at which it is ideal, but we are entrenched. I will here ignore this sort of problem. In any case, according to Putnam's scenario, although we would think of ourselves as being justified in believing that we possess pairs of hands, and that we walk, we would have no hands, and we would not walk. It would seem to us that we have hands, but these hands would only be computer-generated images, or something of this sort.

The above point merits reiteration. The realist maintains that both the existence of the world, and the way of the world are representation independent. It follows that there is, at most, a contingent connection between our representations and the existence or the essence of the world. Although I may believe that I am not a bevatted brain, given the contingency of the relation between my representations and the being and way of the world, I could be a bevatted brain. If our representations constituted the way the world is, this relation would be necessary, but realists adamantly reject the thesis that our ideas either bring about the being, or constitute the way of the world. In short, metaphysical realism entails that we could all be brains in vats. Or, metaphysical realism entails skepticism. Putnam argues, however, that it is impossible for us all to be brains in vats, and so metaphysical realism must be rejected. How could Putnam possibly show that it can't be that every sentient being is a bevatted brain? Does it not seem obvious that there is a possible world where every sentient being is a brain in a vat?

Putnam summarizes his argument in the following manner:

> [I]f we are brains in a vat, then "We are brains in a vat" is false. So it is (necessarily) false.[55]

As Gary Iseminger has pointed out, this argument resembles the *consequentia mirabilis* of the mediaevals.[56] In other words, it seems to have this valid structure: (i) *if p, then not-p*; (ii) *therefore: not-p*. On this reading of its structure, Putnam's argument seems to be the following:

1. If all sentient beings are brains in a vat, some sentient being is not a brain in a vat.

2. Therefore: some sentient being is not a brain in a vat.

However, it is obvious from Putnam's summary that his argument does not have the form of the *consequentia mirabilis*. His argument is this:

3. If all sentient beings are brains in a vat, then *All sentient beings are brains in a vat* is false.

4. Therefore: *All sentient beings are brains in a vat* is necessarily false.

However, the problem with this argument is that it is fallacious. From the premise that (i) *if p, x is false,* it does not follow that (ii) *x is necessarily false.* Or, more precisely, this version of Putnam's argument has the following invalid structure: (i) *if p, x is false;* (ii) *therefore: x is necessarily false.* What, then, is to be made of Putnam's argument?

It should be clear that Putnam desires to show that it can't be that all sentient beings are bevatted brains. As he sees things, if this were forthcoming, then so would the refutation of one seemingly important version of skepticism, and therewith would come the refutation of metaphysical realism. It might seem evident that only two things are needed for a valid argument that yields the conclusion that Putnam desires: one, the premise of the last argument considered above, namely (3), and two, the additional and trivial premise that: it must be that if *All sentient beings are bevatted brains* is false, some sentient being is not a bevatted brain. It might also seem evident that this trivial premise is justified by Tarski's semantic conception of truth, which is itself trivial. If we add this seemingly trivial premise to the premise of the last version of Putnam's argument above, we get the following:

A. It must be that if all sentient beings are bevatted brains, *All sentient beings are bevatted brains* is false. [?]

B. It must be that if *All sentient beings are bevatted brains* is false, some sentient being is not a bevatted brain. [Tarski?]

C. It must be that if all sentient beings are bevatted brains, some sentient being is not a bevatted brain. [A, B]

D. Some sentient being must not be a bevatted brain. [C, *consequentia mirabilis*][57]

Obviously, two questions may be asked about this argument. First: why premise (A)? Second: why premise (B)? In answering these questions, I shall argue for two theses: (1) The basic reason for (A) is ironically also a reason why Putnam's bevatted brains scenario does not depict a case in which most of our beliefs are false. In fact, Putnam has unwittingly shown us that if we were bevatted brains, most of our beliefs would be true. (2) Given the basic reason for (A), (B) is not a consequence of Tarski's account of truth, and so the reason for (B) rests on a mistake.

A key premise of Putnam's argument for (A) may be entitled *the causal theory of reference*. This is the thesis that anyone who refers to an object must stand in an appropriate causal relation with it. How are we to render precise this notion of an appropriate causal relation? As far as I can tell, no one has yet answered this question. It's not that there is a fully developed theory that shows that reference is a kind of causal relation, and that specifies the nature of this relation. It seems that the causal theory of reference is, at this time, nothing more than a number of intuitions about the general manner in which a congeries of philosophical issues might be resolved. Michael Devitt is as ardent a proponent of the causal theory of reference as anyone, but he writes of it in terms of *hope* and *optimism*.[58] Within the context of Putnam's argument, however, the causal theory of reference does not need to be any more than this, and so this question does not need to be answered. Our intuitive grasp of what such a theory would have to be like is, I suppose, all that is required. All that is needed is the intuition that reference is, or rests on, a causal relation, and the intuition that certain causal relations are, and others are not sufficient for reference.

Premise (A) (it must be that if all sentient beings are brains in vats, then *All sentient beings are brains in vats* is false) is a consequence of these intuitions. A bevatted brain would not stand in the sorts of causal relations with vats, brains, and so on, that are required for it to successfully refer to them. A bevatted brain would be causally related to the computer, the vat, the nutrients, and so forth, but not in a way that is sufficient for it to be able to refer to them. Similarly, if the bevatted brains hypothesis is momentarily put aside, it can be seen that although Karl may be causally related to the oxygen that he breathes when he says *Fido is a dog*, his words do not thereby refer to that oxygen. The intuition is that the causal relations that a bevatted brain would bear to the computer, vat, and so on, would not be sufficient for its representations, or sentences, to refer to the computer, vat, et cetera.

Suppose, however, that the bevatted brains prevailed in referring. To what then would they refer? There are a number of options here. Putnam writes:

> [W]hen the brain in a vat (in the world where every sentient being is and always was a brain in a vat) thinks [or: says?] "There is a tree in front of me," his thought [or: sentence?] does not refer to [1] actual trees. . . . [I]t might refer to [2] trees in the [computer-generated] image, or to the [3] electronic impulses that cause tree experiences, or to [4] features of the program that are responsible for those electronic impulses.[59]

Thus, Putnam presents four possibilities. Assuming that a bevatted brain would be capable of referring, it might refer to: (1) actual trees, (2) computer-generated images, (3) the impulses that cause these images, or (4) features of the computer's program that produce these impulses. Since the bevatted brains would not, given our supposed intuitions, stand in the sorts of causal relations that are necessary for their successful reference to actual trees, they obviously would not be referring to actual trees. Putnam and others have assumed that bevatted brains would refer, if they prevailed in referring at all, to computer generated images. Jane McIntyre writes, "a brain in a vat could only refer to *images* of brains and *images* of vats."[60] Carol A. Van Kirk writes, "if the [bevatted] hypothesis were true, 'vat' would refer not to actual vats but to 'vats in the image.' "[61] Thomas Tymoczko writes, "we should interpret the brains' word [phrase?] 'elm trees' as referring to trees-in-the-image [elm-trees-in-the-image?]."[62] To borrow a phrase that is currently in the air, if a bevatted brain refers, it refers to the virtual reality, or virtual objects, generated by the supercomputer. In more philosophical words, were a bevatted brain to be capable of reference, it would refer to some phenomenal reality, or phenomenal objects—perhaps: phenomenological reality or phenomenological objects—generated by the computer. It has also been assumed that nothing depends on this, and I will here work within the confines of this assumption.

If a bevatted brain prevailed in referring, it would, I here assume, refer to computer generated images, or, in other words, it would refer to computer generated virtual objects. Now, suppose that a bevatted brain asks, "Could I be bevatted?" or "Am I bevatted?" To what would its words then refer? Putnam has put the answer quite simply:

> [I]f . . . we are really brains in a vat, then what we now mean by "we are brains in a vat" is that *we are brains in a vat in the image.*[63]

This is the key to (A)—if all sentient beings are brains in vats, then *All sentient beings are brains in vats* is false. *Ex hypothesi,* in the computer-generated image, we would not be bevatted brains. In other words, our virtual or phenomenal reality would not be one in which we are brains in a vat. It is, however, exactly the way of the elements of this virtual reality that figure in the evaluation of the truth and falsity of the beliefs or representations of the bevatted brains. For example, *The cat is on the mat* is true in the language of the bevatted brains just when *the computer-generated cat image* bears *the computer-generated on relation* to *the computer-generated mat image.* Therefore, if we are all brains in a vat, then *All sentient beings are brains in a vat* is false. As Putnam writes, this is false because

> part of the hypothesis that we are brains in a vat is that we aren't brains in the image (that is, what we are "hallucinating" isn't that we are brains in a vat). So, if we are brains in a vat, then the sentence "We are brains in a vat" says something false (if it says anything). In short, if we are brains in a vat, then "We are brains in a vat" is (necessarily) false.[64]

If we are bevatted, then *We are bevatted* is true if and only if our virtual reality is one in which we are bevatted. Our virtual reality would, if we were bevatted brains, be identical to our de facto phenomenological reality, that is, everything would seem the same. Our de facto phenomenological reality is not one in which we are bevatted brains, however. So, if we are bevatted brains, then since our virtual reality is not one in which we are bevatted brains, *We are bevatted brains* is false. Thus, if we are bevatted brains, *We are bevatted brains* is false. This, in short, is Putnam's justification for (A).

Before I proceed to my discussion of Putnam's argument for (B) (it must be that if *All sentient beings are brains in vats* is false, then some sentient being is not a brain in a vat), I should note that there is reason to doubt that Putnam's justification for premise (A) is consistent with his implicit assumption that the bevatted brain scenario is one that illustrates the skeptical thesis that any representation could be false. How could this be? How could it be, for example, that my present perceptual representation that I possess two hands is false? Putnam answers that it would be false, and so it could be false, if every sentient being were a brain in a vat. He argues that this scenario just could not obtain, but for the moment, let us bracket the question of whether or not his argument succeeds. Instead, let us consider whether or not the bevatted brains scenario is one according to which my present perceptual representation that I am possessed of two hands is false.

Putnam argues that if we are bevatted, and the causal theory of reference holds, then *We are bevatted* is true just when our virtual reality is one in which we are bevatted. Since this computer generated virtual reality is qualitatively identical with what we would experience were we to be unbevatted or embodied brains, and since we do not experience ourselves as bevatted, our virtual reality is not one in which we are bevatted. Therefore, *We are bevatted* is false. This way of thinking about the content, or reference, of a bevatted brain's beliefs provides a powerful reason for saying that were I bevatted, my representation of myself as possessed of two hands would not be false, and that it would be true. An essential part of Putnam's story is that if we were bevatted, the vast majority of such perceptual and doxastic representations would be false. It would seem that I possess a pair of hands, but since there are, *ex hypothesi,* no hands, I would be deceived. But, Putnam himself tells us why this analysis is wrong: if we are bevatted, *I possess two hands* is true just when our virtual reality is one in which the virtual me virtually possesses a virtual pair of hands. *Ex hypothesi,* our virtual reality, were we to be bevatted brains, would be qualitatively identical with the phenomenological reality of embodied brains. Since we would experience me as possessing a pair of hands, our virtual reality would be one in which I would possess two hands, and so *I possess two hands* would be true. Putnam himself makes a similar point:

> [T]he brain is *right,* not *wrong* in thinking "There is a tree in front of me." Given what "tree" refers to . . . and what "in front of" refers to . . . then the truth conditions for "There is a tree in front of me" when it occurs . . . are simply that a tree in the image be "in front of" the "me" in question. . . . And these truth-conditions are certainly fulfilled.[65]

Is my perceptual representation of myself as possessed of two hands false according to the bevatted brain scenario? No, since its truth conditions would concern the elements of a virtual reality that would, *ex hypothesi,* obtain. So, Putnam's scenario does not do the work he wants. Now, I will not rest my criticism of Putnam's argument on this, and so I will now turn to the question of premise (B).[66]

As I noted above, it might appear that the only additional thing that is needed for a valid argument that yields, or at least appears to yield, the conclusion that Putnam desires is the trivial premise that it must be that if *All sentient beings are brains in a vat* is false, some sentient being is not a brain in a vat. I also noted that it might appear that this premise is provided by Tarski's account of truth. The idea turns on a consequence of Tarski's account of truth, namely, that it will entail biconditionals such as: it must be that *Snow is white* is true in some language just when snow is white, and it must be that *Snow is white* is not true, or false, in some language just when some snow is not white—leaving the quantification implicit. It would seem that Tarski's account would also entail that if *All sentient beings are bevatted* is false in some language, some sentient being must not be bevatted. This is wrong. Reflection on this additional premise will show that and how this supplemented version of Putnam's argument fails.

Here, it is, I think, necessary to enter into the details of Tarski's account of truth, since it constitutes an important part of the background of the preceding reconstruction of Putnam's argument, and these details, although often mentioned, are rarely articulated. Tarski's account of truth is an account of truth for a very special kind of language, namely, a formalized language. Let me first give an example of such a language, and then show how Tarski defines truth for it. I will call this language Q.[67]

Like all languages, Q has what might be thought of as an alphabet. Here, this is a list of the primitive symbols from which all the other symbols of Q are constructed. In addition to *the positive integers*, the primitive symbols of Q include: a, F, x, $\sim$, $\supset$, , (, and). Among these, we have the five following symbols:

1. *Logical connectives:* $\sim$ and $\supset$
2. *Universal quantifier:*
3. *Brackets:* (and).

Other symbols of Q, which are constructed from the elements of this list of primitive symbols, where i is a positive integer, include the following:

4. *Constants:* a_i
5. *Variables:* x_i
6. *Predicates:* F_i

What do these symbols mean? Although this question will receive a more detailed answer, the following should serve as a rough guide. The *logical connectives* work almost exactly like the words *not* and *if . . . then*. The *universal quantifier* is similar to *all* in ordinary language. Moreover, the *brackets* function as punctuation. Now, the *individual constants* function like names, for instance, *Fido*. The *individual variables* are like the pronoun *it,* except that there are infinitely many of them. (Note that together the constants and the variables are the *terms*.) The *predicate symbols* work like ordinary n-place predicates, for example, the one-place predicate *is a dog*.

Among the nonprimitive symbols of Q, there are the well-formed formulas, or wffs. These are, simply put, the declarative sentences.

1. If F_i is a n-place predicate symbol, and $t_1, \ldots , t_n$ are n terms, then $F_i t_1, \ldots , t_n$ is a wff, and it is an atomic wff.

2. If A is a wff, and x_i is the i-th variable, then $x_i A$ is a wff.

3. If A is a wff, then $\sim A$ is a wff.

4. If A and B are wffs, then (A $\supset$ B) is a wff.

5. Nothing else is a wff.

This only concerns syntax, and so this leaves open the question of what these symbols mean, that is, it leaves open the question of their interpretation. Although these symbols are subject to the rough sort of characterization given above, in the context of a formalized language, an interpretation is a quite specific kind of thing. There are two parts to an interpretation of a language such as Q. The first part consists of a nonempty set, D. This is the domain of the interpretation. For example, D might be the set of positive integers, and if it is, talk in Q will be interpreted, so to speak, as talk about the positive integers. The second part is a function, I. Very roughly, this function determines the elements of D about which the various symbols of Q talk. On the one hand, I assigns to each individual constant some member of D. For example, it might be that $I(a_1) = 1$. In this case, a_1 is, very roughly, taken to talk about the number one. On the other hand, I assigns to each n-place predicate symbol a subset of D^n, that is, a subset of the n-th Cartesian product of D, where D^1 is, for example, the set of 1-tuples of the elements of D. For example, it could be that $I(F_1) = \{<y>$:y is an even number$\}$. In this case, F_1 is, once again very roughly, taken to talk about the even numbers. I will merely note that the connectives are given their usual truth-functional meanings.

   The notion that I am out to render more precise is the notion of truth in Q relative to an interpretation. But, there are three preliminaries, to wit, (1) the notion of satisfaction, (2) the notion of a denumerable sequence of elements of D, and (3) the notion of a star function relative to a given denumerable sequence of elements of D.

   A *sequence* is a function from some subset of the positive integers to some set of objects. For any two sequences, s and t, s = t just when $s_i = t_i$, for all i. In other words, s = t just when the i-th term of s is the i-th term of t, for all i. The sequences that are relevant here are infinite sequences of elements of the domain of some interpretation, that is, functions from the entire set of positive integers, which is, after all, a subset of itself, to the domain of the relevant interpretation. Were the domain of interpretation to be the set of positive integers, such a sequence could be $(1, 2, 3, 4, \ldots)$, and another could be $(1, 1, 1, 1, \ldots)$, and yet another could be $(1, 1, 1, 2, \ldots)$. We are now in a position to define the notion of a star function relative to a given denumerable sequence of elements of D.

Let s be an arbitrary denumerable sequence of elements of D. Now, for each interpretation, I, there is a star function, s^*, whose domain is the set of terms of Q—the union of the constants and the variables of Q—and whose range is D. Now, s^* is defined as follows. There are two cases:

1. In the case of an *individual constant*, a_i, $s^*(a_i) = I(a_i)$, that is, $s^*(a_i)$ is the element of D that I assigns to a_i

2. In the case of a *variable*, x_i, $s^*(x_i) = s_i$, that is, $s^*(x_i)$ is the i-th term of s, which is an element of D.

For example, suppose three things: (1) the term in question is a_1, (2) $I(a_1) = 2$, and (3) s is $(1, 3, 5, 7, \ldots)$. Then, $s^*(a_1) = I(a_1) = 2$. Or, suppose, for example, that (1) the term in question is x_3, and (2) s is as before, then $s^*(x_3) = s_3 = 5$. Now, *satisfaction* can be recursively defined.

It is well-formed formulas that are, or are not, satisfied by the infinite sequences of elements of the domain of some interpretation, and there are four cases to be defined:

1. the case where the formula in question has the form $F_i t_1$, $\ldots, t_n$, where F_i is a n-place predicate symbol, and where t_1, $\ldots, t_n$ are evidently n terms,

2. the case in which the formula has the form $\forall x_i A$, where A is itself a well-formed formula, and where x_i is obviously the i-th variable,

3. the case where the formula has the form $\sim A$, where A is itself a well-formed formula, and finally

4. the case in which the formula has the form $(A \supset B)$, where A and B are themselves well-formed formulas.

In the first case, s satisfies the relevant formula just when the n-tuple $<s^*(t_1), \ldots, s^*(t_n)>$ is an element of $I(F_i)$, that is, this n-tuple is an element of the set of n-tuples of D of I that I assigns to F_i.[68] In the second case, s satisfies the formula in question just when every denumerable sequence of elements of D that differs from s in at most the i-th term satisfies A. In the third case, s satisfies this formula just when s does not satisfy A. In the last case, s satisfies this formula just when s does not satisfy A or s satisfies B.

It is helpful to have examples. Let $I(a_1) = 5$, and let $I(F_1) = \{<y>$:y is an even number$\}$. Moreover, let s be $(1, 3, 5, 7, \ldots)$; one can suppose that s_i is the i-th odd integer. Then: s satisfies F_1a_1 just when $<s^*(a_1)>$ is an element of $I(F_1)$, and so s satisfies F_1a_1 just when 5 is an even number. Since 5 is not an even number, s does not satisfy F_1a_1. Does s satisfy F_1x_3? Once again, s satisfies F_1x_3 just when $<s^*(x_3)>$ is an element of $I(F_1)$. Since $s^*(x_3) = s_3 = 5$, and $I(F_1) = \{<y>:y$ is an even number$\}$, and 5 is not an even number, s does not satisfy F_1x_3.

Does s satisfy $\forall x_2(F_1x_2)$? Recall that s satisfies $\forall x_2(F_1x_2)$ just when every denumerable sequence of elements of D that differs from s in at most the second term satisfies F_1x_2. Now, let t be $(1, 7, 5, 7, \ldots)$, that is, let t be a denumerable sequence of elements of D that differs from s in at most the second term. Given the above account of satisfaction, t satisfies F_1x_2 just when $<t^*(x_2)>$ is an element of $I(F_1)$, and so t satisfies F_1x_2 just when 7 is an even number. Since $t^*(x_2) = t_2 = 7$, and 7 is not an even number, t does not satisfy F_1x_2, and so s does not satisfy $\forall x_2(F_1x_2)$. Since the remaining two cases are more or less self-evident, I will now pass on to the notion of truth in Q relative to an interpretation I.

What Tarski said, and what the reconstruction of Putnam's argument, which is being considered here, appropriates, is essentially this: a formula of Q is true for a given interpretation I of Q just when *every* denumerable sequence of members of the domain of I satisfies it.[69] In other words, a sentence is true relative to a given language and its interpretation just when every denumerable sequence of members of the domain of the interpretation satisfies it. Similarly, a formula of Q is false for a given interpretation I of Q just when *no* denumerable sequence of members of the domain of I satisfies it. The pivotal point here is that this is the notion of truth that is operative in the reconstruction of Putnam's argument that is being considered here.

As a first step toward making clearer the role that Tarski's account of truth plays in this reconstruction of Putnam's argument, I will establish an instance of what Tarski demanded from a theory truth, namely, Convention T, or what Tarski referred to as the test of the material adequacy for an account of truth.[70] According to Tarski, a materially adequate account of truth must entail all the biconditionals of the form: Φ is true in Q (for an interpretation I) if and only if p, where Φ is a structural descriptive name of a sentence in the object language, and p is a translation of Φ into a sentence of the metalanguage, that is, the language in which the definition of *true in Q* is given. Convention T is, it is instructive to note, analogous to the requirement that any definition of an ordered pair be such that if $<a,b> = <x,y>$, then $a = x$ and $b = y$. Tarski's famous example is: *snow is white* is true if and only if snow is white.

Be this as it may, a much simpler example of Convention T is: *Fido is a dog* is true in some language, which is presumably English, just when Fido is a dog. *Fido is a dog* is not a well-formed formula of Q, but I will pretend, for the sake of illustration, that this can be ignored. Moreover, since I'm only explaining this for the sake of illustration, it too can be ignored. In any case, if *Fido is a dog* could be represented in Q, it would be represented as F_1a_1, where $I(F_1) = I(is\ a\ dog)$, and $I(a_1) = I(Fido)$. For the same reason, also suppose that $I(F_1) = \{<y>: y$ is a dog$\}$, and $I(a_1) = $ Fido. Let me show how Tarski's account of truth for Q relative to this interpretation function entails my example.

1. Suppose that it is not that *Fido is a dog* is true just when Fido is a dog, that is, suppose that it is not that F_1a_1 is true just when Fido is a dog.

2. From (1) it follows that either (a) F_1a_1 is true and Fido is not a dog, or (b) F_1a_1 is not true and Fido is a dog.

3. Suppose that F_1a_1 is true and Fido is not a dog.

4. From (3) and Tarski's account of truth, it follows, in short, that every sequence of elements satisfies F_1a_1. Specifically, s satisfies F_1a_1.

5. Given (4) and the definition of satisfaction, $<s^*(a_1)>$ is an element of $I(F_1)$.

6. Given (5), since $I(F_1) = \{<y>: y$ is a dog$\}$, $<s^*(a_1)>$ is an element of $\{<y>: y$ is a dog$\}$, and so $s^*(a_1)$ is a dog.

7. Given (6) and the above account of a star function relative to a sequence, $s^*(a_1) = I(a_1)$, and since $I(a_1)$ = Fido, Fido is a dog, which contradicts (3). So, the supposition at (3) must be rejected.

8. From (7) and (2) (b), that is, F_1a_1 is not true and Fido is a dog.

9. Given Tarski's account of truth, and (8), it follows, in short, that no sequence satisfies F_1a_1. Specifically, s does not satisfy F_1a_1.

10. From the above account of satisfaction, and (9), it follows that $<s^*(a_1)>$ is not an element of $I(F_1)$.

11. Since (10), and since $I(F_1) = \{<y>: y$ is a dog$\}$, $<s^*(a_1)>$ is not an element of $\{<y>: y$ is a dog$\}$, and so $s^*(a_1)$ is not a dog.

12. Given (11) and the above account of a star function relative to a sequence, $s^*(a_1) = I(a_1)$, and since $I(a_1)$ = Fido, Fido is not a dog, which contradicts (8). So, the assumption at (1) must be wrong, and so: *Fido is a dog* is true just when Fido is a dog. (Q.E.D.)

Tarski's idea is that a materially adequate account of truth for a formal language must entail this sort of biconditional for every sentence of the language in question. The point of going through this example is to get my reader to clearly understand how the mechanism of Tarski's account of truth works. The pivotal question is: What role does Tarski's account of truth play in the present reconstruction of Putnam's argument? Roughly put, it is supposed to provide the link between *All sentient beings are bevatted,* and *Some sentient being must not be bevatted.* More specifically, it is supposed to provide the premise that: if *All sentient beings are bevatted* is false, it must be that some sentient being is not bevatted. My claim is that Tarski's account of truth provides neither this link, nor this premise.

With Putnam, let us suppose four things. First, we are brains in a vat. Second, the causal theory of reference. Third, our language is sufficiently like Q to give an interpretation of it. So, there will be a set of individual constants, which will be mapped onto the elements of some set, D. There will be a set of n-place predicates, which get mapped onto subsets of D^n. Et cetera. Putnam's fourth and pivotal supposition is that our intuitions about the intimate relation between causality and reference imply that every element of D is something like a computer-generated image. In short, every element of D is a computer-generated virtual entity. Putnam suggests that the contents of D might be computer-generated images, or electronic impulses that cause these images, or features of the computer program that generate such electronic impulses. As I have noted, it does not matter whether the domain of the interpretation is a set of images, electronic impulses, or facets of the machine's program; I believe that the present reconstruction of Putnam's argument fails on all three construals of the contents of D, but I will focus, as does Putnam, on the construal according to which the elements of D are computer-generated images.

I have developed the foregoing account of Q and its interpretation for the sake of being able to show that and how the current revision of Putnam's argument fails. What I propose to do is to go through the mechanics required to show that Tarski's account of truth does not give Putnam the premise that it must be that if *All sentient beings are brains in a vat* is false, some sentient being is not a brain in a vat. I claim that all it gives him is the premise that it must be that if *All sentient beings are brains in a vat* is false, some computer-generated image of a sentient being is not a computer-generated image of a bevatted brain. If my claim is not obvious, it can be established in the following manner. If the elements of D are computer-generated images, then: $I(is\ a\ sentient\ being) = I(F_1) = \{<y>: y$ is a computer-generated image of a sentient being$\}$, and $I(is\ a\ brain\ in\ a\ vat) = I(F_2) = \{<y>: y$ is a computer-generated image of a brain in a vat$\}$. Given this, let us see what Tarski's account of truth entails. Once again, Putnam needs it to entail that: it must be that if *All sentient beings are brains in a vat* is false, some sentient being is not a brain in a vat. But this is quite different from what it does entail. Once again, although *All sentient beings are brains in a vat* is not a sentence of Q, I will pretend, for the purpose of explication, that this can be ignored. Here are the required mechanics:

1. Suppose that *All sentient beings are brains in a vat* is false, that is, suppose that $\forall x_1(F_1x_1 \supset F_2x_1)$ is false. Moreover, given the causal theory of reference, every element of D of I is a computer-generated image, and so it must be that $I(F_1) = \{<z>: z$ is a computer-generated image of a sentient being$\}$ and

$I(F_2) = \{<z>: z$ is a computer-generated image of a brain in a vat$\}$.

2. By Tarski's account of truth and (1), no sequence satisfies $\forall x_1(F_1x_1 \supset F_2x_1)$, and so s does not satisfy it.

3. By the definition of satisfaction, s satisfies $\forall x_1(F_1x_1 \supset F_2x_1)$ just when every sequence that differs from s in at most the first place satisfies $F_1x_1 \supset F_2x_1$.

4. By (2) and (3), some sequence that differs from s in at most the first place fails to satisfy $F_1x_1 \supset F_2x_1$. Let it be t.

5. By the definition of satisfaction, t satisfies $F_1x_1 \supset F_2x_1$ just when t does not satisfy F_1x_1, or t satisfies F_2x_1.

6. By (4) and (5), t satisfies F_1x_1, and t does not satisfy F_2x_1.

7. By the definition of satisfaction, and (6), $<t^*(x_1)>$ is an element of $I(F_1)$, and $<t^*(x_1)>$ is not an element of $I(F_2)$.

8. By (1) and (7), $t^*(x_1)$ is a computer-generated image of a sentient being, and $t^*(x_1)$ is not a computer-generated image of a brain in a vat.

9. By (8), some computer-generated image of a sentient being is not a computer-generated image of a brain in a vat.

10. By (1) through (9), if *All sentient beings are brains in a vat* is false, then some computer-generated image of a sentient being is not a computer-generated image of a brain in a vat. (Q.E.D.)

Nota bene: This conclusion is not the premise that the reconstruction of Putnam's argument needs. In other words, this conclusion is not premise (B) of the above version of his argument.

If we add what was supposed to be a trivial premise to the premise of my initial version of Putnam's argument, namely (3), that is, add the above result of Tarski's account of truth, we get an argument that runs as follows:

A. If all sentient beings are brains in a vat, *All sentient beings are brains in a vat* must be false. [The Causal Theory of Reference.]

B'. If *All sentient beings are brains in a vat* is false, then it must be that some computer-generated image of a sentient being is not a computer-generated image of a brain in a vat. [Tarski: the conclusion of the mechanics articulated above.]

C′. It must be that if all sentient beings are brains in a vat, then some computer-generated image of a sentient being is not a computer-generated image of a brain in a vat. [A,B′]

D. Not all sentient beings must be brains in a vat. [???][71]

To work, this reconstruction of Putnam's argument needs a premise with an antecedent that is the same as the consequent of (A), and with a consequent that contradicts the antecedent of (A). If he could get this, (C) could be: if all sentient beings are brains in a vat, some sentient being must not be a brain in a vat. Then, Putnam could get (D). But, Tarski's account of truth cannot provide such a premise. It can only provide (B′), and this is not sufficient. So, even when Putnam's argument assumes the form of what seems to be its best reconstruction, it is not a version of the *consequentia mirabilis*. Instead, it is a *non sequitur.*

This technical point can be expressed in terms of what I have above entitled *the string theory of truth*, which is an image of what it is for a sentence to be true that preserves, I think, the intuitions of the correspondence theory of truth. The basic idea can be explained in terms of the example of what it is for *Fido is a dog* to be true. First, let there be an object and a name, let the latter be: *Fido*. Now, take some string, tie one end of the string to the name, and tie the other end to the object. Second, let there be a property and a predicate, let the latter be: *is a dog*. Now, take some more string, tie one end of the string to the predicate, and tie the other end to the set of all the objects that have the property. (I'll leave aside the incisive question of how a string can be tied to a set.) The idea is that *Fido is a dog* is true just when the object tied to *Fido* is an element of the set tied to *is a dog*.[72] This idea can be used to show that the above reconstruction of Putnam's argument does not work.

The first premise of the above reconstruction of Putnam's argument is that: (A) if we are bevatted, *We are bevatted brains* must be false. Given the causal theory of reference, if we were bevatted, our strings could only be tied, so to speak, to either computer-generated phenomenal objects, or sets of computer-generated phenomenal objects. So, roughly put, the objects tied to *we* would be computer-generated images of us, and the set tied to *are bevatted brains* would be the set of computer-generated images of bevatted brains. Moreover, *We are bevatted brains* would be true just when the objects tied to *we* were elements of the set tied to *are bevatted brains*. Now, the assumption of Putnam's thought experiment is that the computer-generated phenomenal world of the bevatted brains is qualitatively identical with the phenomenal world of those of us who have presumed ourselves to be unbevatted, and that in our phenomenal world, it does not seem to us that we are brains in vats. So, even if we were bevatted, it wouldn't seem to us that we were. In other words, the computer-generated images of us would not be members of the set of computer-generated images of bevatted brains. It follows, and this is the important point, that *We are bevatted brains* would not be true, that is, it would be false, which gives us Putnam's first premise.

All would be well with the above reconstruction of Putnam's argument, if its second premise were: (B) if *We are bevatted brains* is false, it must be that one of us is not a bevatted brain. But, this premise is not available to Putnam. Given the reasons for his first premise, the only available premise is this: (B') if *We are bevatted brains* is false, it must be that some computer-generated image of one of us is not a computer-generated image of a bevatted brain. Since, according to the causal theory of reference, our strings can only be tied to computer-generated phenomenal objects, or sets of computer-generated phenomenal objects, *We are bevatted brains* is true just when the objects tied to *we* are elements of the set tied to *are bevatted brains*. So, if *We are bevatted brains* is false, or not true, it must be that some computer-generated image of one of us is not a computer-generated image of a bevatted brain. Of the two premises discussed here, namely, (B) and (B'), this is, once again, the only one available to Putnam, and even if it is conjoined with his first premise, namely, (A), it does not deliver the conclusion that he desires: some of us must be unbevatted. So Putnam has refuted neither skepticism, nor metaphysical realism.

At this juncture, there are two pivotal questions. (1) Can Putnam's argument for internal realism be successfully reconstructed? In short, I think not. (2) What can be appropriated from my reconstruction of Putnam's argument that will further the task of making sense of the thesis that there are many actual worlds and truths? Suspend this question for now; the answer will emerge from an investigation into the first question. Recall the basic structure of Putnam's argument for his internal realism. There are three basic premises. First, metaphysical realism and internal realism are mutually exclusive and jointly exhaustive. Putnam neither states this, nor does he argue for it, but it is implicit, and although this is dubious, I will not question it here. Second, metaphysical realism entails skepticism. This seems clear enough. Third, skepticism is incoherent. Putnam's argument for this premise is, as I have argued, flawed, but what if it is not necessary to provide an argument for it? Recall that for Kant, skepticism is merely intolerable, and if his ontological or transcendental turn dispels it, his turn is *ipso facto* justified. The justification of transcendental idealism, and the repudiation of transcendental realism, comes, in part, with the former's seeming capacity to dispel skepticism, and the latter's association with it. In any case, from these premises, it follows that metaphysical realism is false, and so Putnam's internal realism is vindicated.

Again, the problem with Putnam's argument is located in his ostensible refutation of skepticism. In addition to its being formally flawed, it is, as it seems to me, confused in that it presupposes both that a substantive philosophical thesis, to wit, skepticism, can be refuted by means of trivial, and perhaps merely formal, premises about truth and reference, and that a substantive and deeply rooted philosophical thesis, to wit, metaphysical realism, can be likewise refuted. This cannot be. No substantive thesis follows from a formal thesis, and no formal thesis contradicts any substantive thesis. So, if there is a successful reconstruction of Putnam's argument, it must contain at least one substantive premise. It is difficult to see what this premise could be. It cannot be Putnam's internal realism, that is, his thesis that "*what objects does the world consist of?* is a question that only makes sense to ask *within* a theory or description."[73] Because internal realism would then be a premise in an argument to establish internal realism, and this would be evidently circular. Or, because, internal realism would then be a premise in an argument to establish the incoherence of skepticism, the supposition of this incoherence would be a premise in an argument to establish internal realism, and so such a reconstruction of Putnam's argument would again be irremediably circular. Allegations of circularity aside, it should not be this, because the metaphysical realist's intuition that the world consists of representation independent objects is deeply rooted, and its legitimate displacement requires a philosophical argument based on a substantive and equally intuitive premise, and internal realism does not fill the bill. A clue to the identity of the needed premise lies in this: the intuition that skepticism is wrongheaded is at least as deeply rooted as the metaphysical realist's intuition that the world consists of representation independent objects. Is not internal realism *prima facie* justified, if metaphysical realism entails skepticism, and internal realism entails that it is a deep mistake? More to the point of the thesis that there are many actual worlds and many truths, is not an ontological shift that supports this thesis *prima facie* justified, if without it, we face skepticism, and with it, we escape it? But I get ahead of myself.

Putnam's argument could begin with the thesis that skepticism is, so to speak, false. On the one hand, since metaphysical realism entails skepticism, it is ruled out. Moreover, given that it and internal realism are mutually exclusive and jointly exhaustive, internal realism follows. On the other hand, if it should turn out that internal realism rules out skepticism, it is all the more vindicated, since it gets that issue right, that is, since it is, so to speak, epistemologically correct. In short, let the substantive premise be that skepticism is wrongheaded, or something of this sort, and internal realism, or my hitherto elusive ontological shift, may be vindicated. This obviously depends, however, on whether internal realism, or some version of an ontological shift, can be shown to be epistemologically correct, and this in turn depends on what Putnam's doctrine, or this shift, and skepticism are.

I will now focus on internal realism, and I will begin by contrasting it with metaphysical realism. It would make sense to ask for a theory or description independent answer to the question *What objects does the world consist of?* were there to be just one actual world that consisted of a multiplicity of representation-independent objects. Representation-independent objects would be distinct from one another by virtue of the properties that they possess, or fail to possess, independently of whatever concepts or predicates we would happen to possess. Roughly put, a complete enumeration of these representation-independent objects, not to mention all their representation-independent properties, would constitute an answer to Putnam's question *What objects does the world consist of?*, or, more simply: *What is there?*, that made sense independently of theory and mode of description. It is irrelevant to object that since we could use different names or different predicates, our description would thereby be theory- or description-dependent. Any answer to Putnam's question that employs names or predicates that do not match up with the world's representation-independent objects and properties must simply be wrong. Names and predicates that do not reflect the world's objects and properties cannot be part of a correct answer to Putnam's question. Thus professes the metaphysical realist. How does internal realism differ from this?

Putnam tells us that there can be no theory or description independent answer to the question *What is there?* Recall the illustration that Putnam draws from mereology, which was discussed above: If there are three objects, how many objects are there? If we do not count mereological sums as objects, it is clear that the answer to this question is: there are three objects; if, however, for any two objects, there is a third object that is their mereological sum, and there is no null object, then the answer is: there are seven objects. So, are there three objects or seven? Obviously, it depends on how one counts, and so Putnam concludes that the answers to such questions are relative to either some method of counting, or some theory or system of description. According to metaphysical realism, there is a representation-independent something that gets counted differently, but Putnam inquires: How may parts does this something have? This question can only be answered in a way that depends on some method of counting, and on either the answer of three or seven, "we have not a neutral description, but rather a *partisan* description."[74] Putnam concludes, and this is essential to his internal realism, that no theory or description independent answer can be given to the question *What is there?*

This would seem to entail that independently of theory or mode of description, there are no objects of which the world consists. In short, if there were such objects, there could be a theory or description independent answer to Putnam's question, but since there can be no such answer, there can be no such objects. Moreover, since there is then little left to the world as construed by the metaphysical realist, there is no theory- or description-independent world either. But then skepticism is thereby refuted, since it supposes that there is such a world. This must be explained.

Putnam addresses himself to a form of skepticism that was suggested by Descartes when he wrote that there could be "an evil genius, as clever and deceitful as he is powerful, who has directed his entire effort to misleading me."[75] The basic skeptical idea here is: Even if objects were to cohere in a manner that is required for them to be evidence for some picture of the world, it would still be possible for these objects to be illusions, and for this picture to be false.[76] Putnam's bevatted brains scenario is a cybernetic version of the Cartesian scenario of an omnipotent and deceptive evil genius, since it also shows how it is possible for objects to cohere in a manner that is required for them to be evidence for some picture of the world, and yet be such that they are illusory, while the picture for which they presumably provide evidence is false. Putnam rightly sees, I think, that both scenarios presuppose some version of metaphysical realism. It is because what is the case is independent of us and our representations that it is possible for objects or our representations to lack verisimilitude, that is, to be illusory or false, no matter what evidential virtues our representations may happen to possess. Now, one way to escape the skepticism suggested by these scenarios is to reject this very presupposition. In other words, one alternative is to maintain that what is the case somehow depends on our representations, but in a way that closes, so to speak, the gap that makes it possible for coherent objects to be evidence for some world picture, and yet be such that together, they are illusory or false. Putnam thinks that his internal realism achieves this by establishing that one ostensible side of this gap is a fiction. In other words, it does this by showing that independently of theory or mode of description, there are no objects of which the world might consist, and so there is no world as construed by the metaphysical realist. Consequently, there is no world that we might fail to correctly represent, and so Cartesian skepticism, in both its demonic and cybernetic forms, is false.

As I noted above, the justification of internal realism, and perhaps the justification of an ontological shift that would support the thesis that there are many actual worlds, could begin with the premise that skepticism is simply wrongheaded. This would rule out metaphysical realism, since it entails skepticism. Thus, were internal realism and it mutually exclusive and jointly exhaustive, internal realism would be justified. Since internal realism seems to rule out skepticism, it is all the more vindicated, since it gets this issue right. In short, by letting the substantive premise be that skepticism is wrongheaded, internal realism is vindicated. Or, is it? There is, I think, an error in this reconstruction of Putnam's justification of internal realism. To locate this error, recall that the success of this reconstruction depends on whether internal realism is epistemologically correct, and this, in turn, depends on what skepticism is. There is a form of skepticism that Putnam has not considered, however, and its consideration not only undermines the thesis that internal realism gets skepticism right, but it undermines it by bringing us to see that internal realism and metaphysical realism share essentially the same conception of what it is to be an object.

Query: does internal realism entail that skepticism *simpliciter* is false? No, and so, I think, internal realism doesn't amount to a fundamental ontological shift that supplants the metaphysical realist's intuitions about what it is to be an object. For the time being, I will place aside the question of this consequence, and I will focus on this negative answer. To justify this answer, it is necessary to distinguish Cartesian skepticism from another form of skepticism that was suggested by Hume when he wrote that "it implies no contradiction that the course of nature may change, and that an object, seemingly like those which we have experienced, may be attended with different or contrary effects."[77] For example, it is, as Hume noted, possible for "a body, falling from the clouds, and which, in all other respects, resembles snow . . . [to have] . . . the taste of salt or feeling of fire."[78] Or, it is, again as Hume noted, possible for "all the trees . . . [to] . . . flourish in December and January, and decay in May and June."[79] Or, as Kant worried, it is possible for "the country on the longest day . . . [to be] . . . sometimes covered with fruit, sometimes with ice and snow."[80] The Humean skeptic maintains that the behavior of objects could go awry in any of these ways. More generally, the basic skeptical idea here is that the behavior of objects might fail to cohere in a manner that is necessary for them to be evidence for any world picture. Even if internal realism and Cartesian skepticism are incompatible, because internal realism rules out the gap that makes this skepticism possible, there is still Humean skepticism, and so to answer the above query, it is necessary to ask whether internal realism rules out Humean skepticism.

Cartesian skepticism presupposes that what there is in no way depends on our representations. So, there is, in a manner of speaking, a gap between our representations and what there is, and so any representation might be false, even if it is ideal. According to Putnam, since there is no theory- or description-independent answer to the question *What is there?*, there are no representation independent objects of which the world might consist, and so there is no world as construed by the metaphysical realist. But, then, Cartesian skepticism is wrong-headed, since there is no world that we are constantly in danger of having misrepresented. Now, there is, in Humean skepticism, some-thing analogous to the gap of Cartesian skepticism, and the question for internal realism is whether it is capable of closing it. This gap consists of the fact that the past course of nature does not necessitate its future course, or the past behavior of objects does not necessitate their future behavior, or the content of our past experience does not necessitate that of our future experience. So, our experiences, or their objects, might fail to cohere in a manner that is necessary for either of them to evidentially support, or for there to be, any world picture. Now, to justify a negative answer to the query of the last paragraph, it is necessary to show that internal realism does not rule out Humean skepticism.

I will proceed by contrast once more. According to metaphysical realism, objects do not depend on our representations, but this does not entail that the past behavior of objects must cohere with their future behavior, and so it does not entail that the behavior of objects must cohere in a way that is necessary for them or the things they do to be evidence for some picture of the world. This may be put in another way. Like Cartesian skepticism, Humean skepticism presup-poses a kind of gap, to wit, a gap between the past and future behavior of objects. Because of this gap, it is possible for objects to fail to cohere, and so they may not be able to evidentially support any vision of the world. This gap is not closed, even if, as the metaphysical realist maintains, the world is as objective as it can be. Put shortly, the objec-tivity of the world does not ensure the coherence of objects. So, even if metaphysical realism is granted, Humean skepticism is not thereby refuted.

The situation is similar for internal realism. Even if no theory independent answer can be given to the question *What is there?*, it does not follow that the past behavior of objects necessitates their future behavior, and so they may fail to cohere. This too may be put in another way. The gap of Humean skepticism is not closed, even if, as the internal realist maintains, the question *What is there?* has no theory-independent answer. The dependency of all possible answers to some question on some theory or other does not ensure, by itself at least, that objects will behave coherently. So, and this is a pivotal point, *internal realism is compatible with Humean skepticism.* Even if, as Putnam maintains, truth were some sort of idealized rational acceptability, this rationality would only be ideal, and so this would not rule out the possibility that objects might be so incoherent that no world picture would be acceptable. If Putnam built coherence into truth in a way that guaranteed that objects would be able to provide evidence for some world picture, he would have then ruled out Humean skepticism by fiat. Internal realism would rule out Humean skepticism because it would be so defined that the ideal of coherent objects evidentially supporting some world picture would necessarily be realized, and a substantial result would then rest on a gratuitous definition. So, since internal realism does not rule out Humean skepticism, it does not rule out skepticism *simpliciter,* and this shows, I think, that Putnam's view does not amount to a fundamental ontological shift that supplants the metaphysical realist's intuitions about what it is to be an object. Why?

Do internal realism and metaphysical realism embrace essentially different conceptions of what it is to be an object? As far as I can ascertain, there is, in Putnam's exposition of internal realism, no explicit explanation of what it is to be an object, but such an explanation is implicit. Internal realism might fail to get Humean skepticism right, because its conception of what it is to be an object is not essentially different from that of metaphysical realism. In which case, one is entitled to suspect that internal realism and metaphysical realism are essentially the same. In this regard, recall, once again, Putnam's mereological example, and note that any answer to the question *How many objects?* is always relative to some method of counting, but given a specific method of counting, the answer to this question is completely determinate. This is an ambiguous fact, if it is indeed a fact. On the one hand, this might be because a method of counting somehow constitutes the objects counted. In this case, since objects would then depend on such a method, they would be theory- or mode-of-description-dependent, and so internal realism and metaphysical realism would embrace essentially different conceptions of what it is to be an object. On the other hand, however, this might be because there are objects that are independent of all methods of counting, and that somehow necessitate a specific and determinate answer. Note well, however, that in this case, objects are independent of us and our representations. The important point is that there is, then, reason to suspect that on the issue of what it is to be an object, Putnam's internal realism does not essentially differ from metaphysical realism.

Does it follow from the supposition that neither internal realism nor metaphysical realism is, with respect to Humean skepticism, epistemologically correct, that they contain essentially the same conception of what it is to be an object? Yes, because, in essence, they both get Humean skepticism wrong for the same reason, namely, it is because objects are independent of our representations that they need not cohere. In other words, internal realism does not get Humean skepticism right, because although it differs from metaphysical realism on the issue of whether there can be a theory or description independent answer to the question *What is there?*, it does not essentially differ from metaphysical realism on the question of what it is to be an object. This must be explained. Internal realism and metaphysical realism are both compatible with Humean skepticism. For internal realism, this means that although there can be no representation independent answer to the question *What is there?*, there is still a gap between the past and the future. Even though there is, according to internal realism, a way in which objects are representation-dependent, objects are independent in that they may still behave in ways that make them unrepresentable, that is, they may still behave in ways that make it impossible to coherently represent them. So, even given internal realism, there is a way in which objects are independent of our representations. For metaphysical realism, objects are representation-independent; this is essential to it. Therefore, for both metaphysical realism and internal realism, objects are representation-independent, and so they do not embody essentially different conceptions of what it is to be an object.

What if Putnam offered the following? Suppose that if internal realism and Humean skepticism are compatible, objects are representation-independent. Objects are not representation-independent. Why? Because there are no theory- or description-independent answers to Putnam's question *What is there?* If there were representation-independent objects, there could be a theory- or description-independent answer to Putnam's question, but since there can be no such answer, there can be no such objects. Therefore, internal realism and Humean skepticism are incompatible. Since internal realism is, so to speak, true, that is, since there are no theory- or description-independent answers to the question *What is there?*, Humean skepticism is wrongheaded. If Putnam did offer this, he would then seem to have undermined the claim that internal realism and metaphysical realism embrace essentially the same conception of what it is to be an object, since this claim itself rests on the premise that internal realism is, with respect to Humean skepticism, epistemologically incorrect. Putnam's dormant offering rests, however, on his dubious inference from the premise that no theory- or description-independent answer can be given to the question *What is there?*, to the conclusion that objects are somehow theory-, description-, or representation-dependent. How could a fact about a question be relevant to the representation-dependency or otherwise of objects? Isn't it evident that even if all the possible answers to some question about some set of objects depends on some theory or other, it doesn't follow that these objects depend on some theory? To suppose that it does follow is to have already embraced the sort of ontological turn that I am out to clarify.

This brings me back to a pivotal question raised above: Can Putnam's argument for internal realism be successfully reconstructed? I think not, because given that internal realism is compatible with Humean skepticism, it is also compatible with at least a modicum of representation-independence on the part of objects, and this is compatible with Cartesian skepticism, and so Putnam's argument, or all of its reconstructions, must fail. Why? Because the essential point (premise?) is that internal realism is, relative to Cartesian skepticism, epistemologically correct, but given the above, this is just plain wrong. If internal realism and Humean skepticism are compatible, objects are representation-independent. But, if objects do not depend on our representations, there is a gap between what is the case and what we represent it to be, that is, our representations do not constitute the being or essence of objects. Given this gap, however, any nontautologous representation might fail to represent the way things are, and so any could be false, and so the scenarios described in both the demonic and the cybernetic forms of Cartesian skepticism could obtain. But, then, internal realism and Cartesian skepticism are compatible. Therefore, since a conceptual keystone of Putnam's argument is that internal realism is, with respect to Cartesian skepticism, epistemologically correct, if a reconstruction of Putnam's argument is an argument that rests on this keystone, there cannot be a successful reconstruction of Putnam's argument.

This brings me back to another pivotal question: What can be appropriated from my reconstruction of Putnam's argument that will further the task of making sense of the thesis that there are many actual worlds and truths? The lesson is this: The way to justify an ontological turn, which will explain the thesis that there are many actual worlds and truths, is to show that it gets both Cartesian and Humean skepticism right. This constitutes a test for any such turn. Is there an ontological turn that evades these forms of skepticism? If there is, it involves a much more radical turn than Putnam's internal realism, who himself seems to be in need of an awakening from his own dogmatic slumbers. If there is an escape from skepticism, it involves returning to Kant's primordial articulation of the very ontological turn that Protagoras, Whorf, Quine, Goodman, and Putnam have either failed to see, or have failed to get right. Or, this is what I will argue. So, with the above test in hand, I now turn to Kant to attempt to extract a viable version of an ontological shift that will support the thesis that there are many actual worlds and truths.

IV
Why There Are Many Actual Worlds
Kant's Copernican Revolution and Our Purposiveness

My project is, once again, to determine whether any sense can be made of the theses that there are many actual worlds, and that there are many truths. At this stage, the proposal under consideration is that the ontological shift of Kant's Copernican revolution can be appropriated to bring this project to completion. How? In his *"The World Well Lost,"* Richard Rorty suggests the following:

> Since Kant, we find it almost impossible not to think of [1] *the mind as divided into active and passive faculties, the former using concepts to "interpret" what "the world" imposes on the latter.* We also find it difficult not to [2] *distinguish between those concepts which the mind could hardly get along without and those which it can take or leave alone*—and we think of truths about the former concepts as "necessary" in the most proper and paradigmatic sense of the term. But as soon as we have this picture of the mind in focus, it occurs to us, as it did to Hegel, that [3] *those all important a priori concepts,* those which determine what our experience or our morals will be, *might have been different.* We cannot, of course, imagine what an experience or practice *that* different would be like, but we can abstractly suggest that [4] *the men of the Golden Age, or the inhabitants of the Fortunate Isles, or the mad, might shape the intuitions that are our*

common property in different molds, and [5] *might thus be conscious of a different "world."*[1]

The basic idea is, I surmise, this. Suppose that we both think and intuit, and that thinking is casting what is intuitively given into conceptual molds. Moreover, suppose that experience is a product of this casting, and that a world is an ideal sum of what can be experienced. *On the one hand,* if there can be only one repertoire of conceptual molds, there can be only one world. Or, this is what Kant seems to have thought. On the other hand, if there can be many essentially different sets of conceptual molds, and the intuitively given can be cast into them, so that different experiences result, then there can be many actual worlds. Furthermore, if each actual world were to have a complete description, there would be, in the sense that I have explained above, many truths.

Rorty's suggestion involves a number of dubious suppositions. Now, I do not find it difficult to suppose that we both think and intuit. I know that some thinkers think that no one thinks, but I will not pursue this issue here. There is, however, some difficulty in supposing that thinking is casting the intuitively given into conceptual molds. The basic problem is that since the casting metaphor is far less perspicuous than the intuitions of metaphysical realism, and an essential part of the aim of Rorty's suggestion, which is supported by the metaphor that thought is casting, is to supplant these intuitions, the unclear supplants the clear. The same can be said about the notion that experience is a product of the conceptual molding of the intuitively given. Additionally, if what it is to be a world is characterized in terms of ideal sums and experience, it is still an open question whether a world is the ideal sum of (i) what *is* experienced, (ii) what *is* and *can be* experienced, or (iii) what *is* and *can be* experienced *plus* whatever may be connected by rules to what *is* and *can* be experienced. Also note that the word *world* is ambiguous in another way, since it can mean (i) that which imposes on the passive faculty of sensuous intuition, and it can mean (ii) that of which we are supposed to be conscious after the active faculty of thought has interpreted what the world, in the just-mentioned sense, has imposed on the passive faculty of intuition. These issues aside, there is also the dubious supposition that not only can there be essentially different sets of conceptual molds, but the given can be cast into them. I have already noted Davidson's objections to the former, and the metaphysical realist might object to the latter on the grounds that since the given is a representation of what is itself representation-independent, that is, since the intuitively given is, or involves, the sensuous presence of what is itself representation-independent, it comes structured, and so it cannot be cast into alternative conceptual molds. To suppose that the given can be cast in many ways is to beg an important ontological question.

Rorty himself objects to this account of world and truth multiplicity because he thinks that the Kantian picture upon which it depends itself depends on a pair of distinctions that ought to be rejected. One is the distinction between the given and the conceptual, and the other is the distinction between the analytic and the synthetic. With respect to the former, Rorty focuses on the intuitively given, and he offers a dilemma:

> Insofar as a Kantian intuition is effable, it is just a perceptual judgment, and thus not *merely* 'intuitive'. Insofar as it is ineffable, it is incapable of having an explanatory function.[2]

This needs to be elucidated. The intuitively given is either characterless or not. On the assumption of the latter, the intuitively given possesses some character, and so it is already conceptually molded. (If possessing determinate features is essentially different from being conceptually molded, as the metaphysical realist might maintain, this is a *non sequitur*. I will disregard this issue here.) But, then, since it is exactly the given that is supposed to be conceptually molded, the given is not the given. But this cannot be, and so the former must be assumed, that is, it must be that the intuitively given is characterless.

If the given is characterless, it is more like Aristotelian matter, or primary matter, than like any determinate object, for example, this man or that horse. For Aristotle, matter is supposed to be the stuff that underlies change from one kind of thing into another kind of thing, for example, the change of an apple into a man by digestion. Aristotle asserts: " 'Matter' . . . is to be identified with the *substratum* which is receptive of coming-to-be and passing-away."[3] Consequently, matter can be neither apple nor man, but it is what can be anything. So, it cannot, in and by itself, be anything specific. If it were something specific, it would be limited in what it can become. That Aristotle maintained this is evidenced by his having written:

> When all else is stripped off [a thing or substance] evidently nothing
> but matter remains. . . . By matter I mean that which in itself is *nei-*
> *ther* a particular thing *nor* of a certain quantity *nor* assigned to any
> other of the categories by which being is determined. . . . [T]he ulti-
> mate substratum is of itself *neither* a particular thing *nor* of a particu-
> lar quantity *nor otherwise positively characterized.*[4]

Although explanation is a quite complicated thing, it seems clear that
in giving an explanation, one tells a story about something that makes
it clear why the thing to be explained is the way that it happens to be.
But telling a story about something involves asserting that something
has certain characteristics, which are somehow related to the thing to
be explained. This could be unraveled further, but the point is that if
the Aristotelian conception of matter is to have any explanatory power,
it must entail that this matter has at least some character. So, if matter
is, according to the Aristotelian conception, characterless, it cannot
explain anything, including coming-to-be and passing-away.

George Berkeley argued not only that the conception of a characterless something could do no explanatory work, but that a characterless stuff would be nothing. With respect to the former, he put the
point well, when he wrote:

> It is said extension is a mode or accident of matter, and that matter is
> the *substratum* that supports it. Now I desire that you would explain
> what is meant by matter's *supporting* extension: say you, I have no
> idea of matter, and therefore cannot explain it. I answer, though you
> have no positive, yet if you have any meaning at all, you must at least
> have a relative idea of matter; though you know not what it is, yet
> you must be supposed to know what relation it bears to accidents,
> and what is meant by its supporting them. It is evident *support* cannot
> be taken here as taken in its usual or literal sense, as when we say
> that pillars support a building: in what sense therefore must it be
> taken?[5]

On the one hand, matter is supposed to be characterless, but then no
sense can be given to the claims that it supports various characteristics,
and that it is the substratum that persists through coming-to-be and
passing-away. On the other hand, matter is supposed to support various characteristics, or to be the substratum that persists through coming-to-be and passing-away, but since supporting things have a certain

character, as do persisting things, whatever sense can be given to these suppositions must conflict with the view that matter is characterless. So, not only cannot such a conception of matter explain coming-to-be and passing away, or such characteristics with which we are acquainted, it can't explain anything.

Moreover, with respect the point that a characterless stuff would be nothing, Berkeley thought that he could show that all the features that matter is supposed to have in itself are subjective, and so they are not possessed by matter in itself. He concludes that since matter is then characterless, it is nothing. Suspend the point about all the supposed features of matter being demonstrably subjective; it is this last inference that is important here. Berkeley writes:

> [W]hat if we . . . assert . . . that matter is an unknown *somewhat,* neither substance nor accident . . . ? . . . [Y]ou may . . . use the word *matter* in the same sense, that other men [sic] use *nothing,* and so make those terms convertible. . . . [T]his is what appears to me to be the result of that definition, the parts of whereof when I consider with attention, either collectively, or separate from each other, I do not find that there is any kind of effect or impression made on my mind, different from what is excited by the term *nothing.*[6]

His point is somewhat obvious: the characterless is equivalent to nothing. Moreover, this excursus should make Rorty's point clearer: if the intuitively given were characterless, its conception could do no explanatory work, and it would be nothing. Now, Rorty's dilemma may be put as follows. The intuitively given is either characterless or not. If the given were to possess some character, it would already be conceptually molded. But, then, since the given is what gets conceptually molded, the given is not the given. This can't be. So, it must be that the intuitively given is characterless, but its conception would be, to repeat the point just made, incapable of doing any explanatory work, and it would be nothing. Rorty concludes that the very idea of the given must be rejected, and so must the distinction between the given and the conceptual. More importantly, he concludes that "the suggestion that our concepts shape neutral material no longer makes sense once there is nothing to serve as this material."[7] But, then, the suggestion that alternative concepts might shape some neutral material in alternative ways, and the whole Kantian-based suggestion about how there can be many actual worlds and truths, which were delineated above, also fail to make sense.

Rorty's dilemma would lack force, if he had somehow misallocated the Kantian picture. In other words, his dilemma wouldn't be so pointed, if there were no textual justification for thinking that Kant himself maintained that experience is a product of thought shaping or molding some conceptually neutral material delivered by sensuous intuition. However, on the very first page of the first edition of the *Critique of Pure Reason,* Kant wrote that: "Experience is, beyond all doubt, the first *product* to which our understanding gives rise, in *working up the raw material of sensible impressions.*"[8] Moreover, on the very first page of the second edition of that work, he wrote:

> [O]bjects affecting our senses partly of themselves *produce* representations, partly arouse the activity of our understanding to compare these representations, and, by combining or separating them, *work up the raw material of the sensible impressions* into that knowledge of objects which is entitled experience.[9]

So, there can be no doubt that Kant thought, at least sometimes, that the understanding, that is, the faculty of thought, produces experience by working up the conceptually raw material of sensible impressions. There is, therefore, some reason to think that Rorty's suggestion doesn't involve any misallocation of the Kantian picture. If there were some misallocation, there might then be a reconstruction of his suggestion that is based on an alternative reading of the Kantian picture, and that successfully avoids his dilemma. Theodore W. Schick, in his "Rorty and Davidson on Alternate Conceptual Schemes," has suggested another way to understand the Kantian picture, and so, it is an open question whether Rorty's suggestion can be successfully reconstructed.[10]

Schick proposes an account of the given that he claims avoids the dilemma associated with the apparently inevitable opposition between characterless or conceptualized. He writes:

> Consider . . . the perception of an ambiguous figure like the duck-rabbit. What we see that figure as will be determined by what concepts we use to organize *our visual experience*. But we cannot use any concepts whatsoever. We cannot, for example, see the duck-rabbit as an octopus. The best explanation of this fact is that *our visual experi-*

ence of the figure has certain qualities which serve to delimit the ways in which we can see it.[11]

The point is simple: the only explanation for the fact that the duck-rabbit can't be seen as an octopus is that the given is not characterless. But, as Schick writes, "to say that it [the given] has properties is not to say that it is [or] has been conceptualized."[12] Therefore, the given is neither characterless nor conceptualized. If the possession of determinate features is essentially different from being conceptually molded, as the metaphysical realist might maintain, then, as I noted above, one branch of Rorty's dilemma is a *non sequitur.* On the basis of this, Schick rejects the premise of Rorty's dilemma, to wit: the given is either characterless or not, and if not, then it is conceptualized.

It is unclear how Schick would make sense of the Kantian text where it is written that "the combination *(conjunctio)* of the manifold in general can never come to us through the senses."[13] I will not pursue this issue here. It is more important to explain why Schick's exit from Rorty's dilemma can't be appropriated here. Basically, it is because it is incompatible with Rorty's suggestion about how there can be many actual worlds and truths. Suppose that the given is neither characterless nor conceptualized, or that it is, in other words, conceptually neutral without being formless. According to Rorty's suggestion, thinking is casting what is intuitively given into conceptual molds. Moreover, experience is supposed to be a product of this casting, and a world is supposed to be an ideal sum of what can be experienced. If there were many essentially different sets of conceptual molds, and the intuitively given could be cast into them, so that different experiences result, then there would be many actual worlds. However, even if the given can be conceptualized in many ways, and the result is a plurality of experiences, and so a plurality of worlds, the given will, according to Schick's claim, possess features that will be common to all worlds, that is, worlds as understood in the context of Rorty's suggestion. So there will not be a plurality of distinct actual worlds, not to mention a plurality of truths.

It is still an open question, therefore, whether Rorty's suggestion can assume a form that is not subject to his dilemma. A clue to an adequate reconstruction of Rorty's suggestion lies in an ambiguity in Schick's phrase *visual experience.* It may mean (1) the reference of someone's visual experience, for example, the ambiguous figure, or it may mean (2) the visual experience itself *qua* episode in someone's stream of consciousness. Recall that Kant thought, at least sometimes, that the understanding produces experience by working up the conceptually raw material of sensible impressions. Or, is it that the understanding produces experience by working up the raw material of the sensible impressions themselves? There is a significant difference here, since there is a significant distinction between providing raw material and being raw material. In the first edition of the *Critique,* sensible impressions seem to provide the raw material upon which the understanding works. In other words, the idea seems to be that sensible impressions deliver some conceptually neutral, and perhaps featureless, stuff that the understanding works up into experience. In the second edition, however, sensible impressions themselves seem to be the raw material, the conceptually neutral stuff, upon which the understanding works. The idea seems to be that the understanding works up sensible impressions themselves, but in the sense that the understanding compares, combines and separates them, and where experience just is the concatenation of impressions that have thereby been ordered.

So, Rorty and Schick share, I think, an assumption. They both maintain that the given is something other than our sensible impressions themselves. They both believe, perhaps mistakenly, that the given is what is delivered by our sensible impressions. In another idiom, one might say that they both believe that the given is the reference of our sensible impressions. Rorty believes, contrary to Schick, that the given cannot be conceptually neutral without also being characterless, and that this leads to paradox. Schick believes, contrary to Rorty, that the given can be conceptually neutral without being characterless, and so Rorty's dilemma can be avoided. But, the assumption remains: the given is the object of our sensible impressions, albeit not an object in the everyday sense of this man or that horse.

Kant himself suggested that the given, or the raw material of the sensible impressions, is the manifold of sensible impressions themselves. He also suggested that to say that the material of sensible impressions is raw is to say something like this: the sensible impressions themselves are uncompared, uncombined, and unseparated, and so they are unordered. Examples of this are commonplace. For example, Socrates suspects that he has seen Theaetetus, but he isn't sure since it may have been Theodorus, or the whole episode may have been some sort of illusion. This episode is a sort of raw material, since it is uncompared, uncombined, and unseparated, and so it is unordered. In other words, this episode is raw, because it neither fits with the rest of Socrates' experience, nor does it fail to so fit. If this episode cannot be fit into the stream of Socrates' experience, it will be illusory; if this episode can be so fit, then not only did Socrates really see Theaetetus, what was once raw material will be an experience. This anticipates what is to come, however. The pivotal point is that this may provide an alternative to Rorty's and Schick's interpretations of the Kantian picture that itself may provide an exit from Rorty's dilemma, and that may also support his suggestion about how to make sense of the thesis that there are many actual worlds and truths. The idea turns on the distinction between providing raw material and being raw material. Let the given be the manifold of sensible impressions themselves, and let their being raw be equivalent to their being uncompared, uncombined, and unseparated, and consequently unordered. Then, the given could then be conceptually neutral without being characterless. So, Rorty's dilemma would be obviated, since conceptual neutrality would be compatible with the possession of a determinate character. But does this alternative account of the Kantian picture support a reconstruction of Rorty's suggestion about how there can be many actual worlds and truths? I will temporarily suspend this question, and I will turn to Rorty's claim that his suggested account of the multiplicity of actual worlds and truths fails because the Kantian picture upon which it depends itself depends on the untenable distinction between the analytic and the synthetic.

With respect to the distinction between analytic and synthetic, Rorty writes that

> [The] suggestion that [1] *the difference between a priori and empirical truth is merely that between the relatively difficult to give up and the relatively easy* brings in its train the notion that [2] *there is no clear distinction to be drawn between questions of meaning and questions of fact.* This, in turn, leaves us . . . with [3] *no distinction between questions about alternative 'theories' and questions about alternative 'frameworks.'*[14]

The efficacy of Rorty's remarks clearly depends on the power of Quine's criticism of the analytic-synthetic distinction. Although Quine

proffers many criticisms of this distinction, one important and fundamental reproach is this. If statements could be divided into the mutually exclusive and jointly exhaustive classes of analytic and synthetic,
there would be statements that are true no matter what happens. Every
statement is, according to Quine, revisable: "no statement is immune
to revision."[15] So, no statement is analytic, and the distinction lacks
point. How does this undercut Rorty's suggestion about how there can
be many actual worlds and truths? Quine's point about the analytic
and the synthetic can be made, *mutatis mutandis,* about the *a priori*
and the empirical. If statements could be divided into the mutually
exclusive and jointly exhaustive classes of those known *a priori* and
those known through empirical means, there would be statements that
are true no matter what course the stream of experience happened to
take. In short, every statement is revisable. So, no statement is known
a priori, and this distinction also lacks point.

As Rorty understands Quine, although the analytic-synthetic distinction cannot be made in terms of the impossibility and possibility of
revision, it can be made in terms of the degree to which it is difficult,
or easy, to revise a statement. An analytic statement is one that is
difficult to revise, and a synthetic statement is one that is easy to revise.
Within the context of fixing belief, the distinction between *a priori* and
empirical statements can be made in a similar manner. A statement
knowable *a priori* is one that is difficult to revise, and an empirical
statement is one that is easy to revise. So, criteria of objectivity or
ostensible logical truths are *a priori,* because they are difficult to revise;
any presumed empirical truth, such as *the cat is on the mat,* is empirical, because it is easy to revise. Moreover, if statements could be divided into the mutually exclusive and jointly exhaustive classes of
statements true by virtue of meaning and those true by virtue of facts,
there would be statements that are true no matter what happens. Since
every statement is revisable, no statement is true by virtue of meaning.
The distinction between statements true by virtue of meaning and
statements true by virtue of facts is, according to Rorty, also that
between what is difficult and what is easy to revise, and the same sorts
of examples apply. Rorty concludes that there is no distinction between
questions about alternative theories and questions about alternative
conceptual frameworks. What does this mean? How is this relevant to
Rorty's suggestion?

Rorty takes his own suggestion to rest on the premise that there can be many essentially different conceptual schemes. The basic idea of his objection is that the question whether one conceptual scheme is the same as, or different than, another scheme does not make sense without the notion of analyticity, or truth by virtue of meaning. Suppose that there were alternative conceptual schemes. There would then be at least two conceptual schemes, and so there would be at least two concepts, one drawn from each scheme. Consequently, there would be at least two expressions that didn't mean the same thing. Let these expressions be α and β. So, there would be an analytic truth, to wit, *α is not β,* or something like this. Moreover, this would be a statement that is immune from revision, but Rorty maintains, with Quine, that no statement is immune from revision. Therefore, there can be no alternative conceptual schemes, and so Rorty's suggestion fails.

Is Rorty right to take his own suggestion to rest on the premise that there can be many essentially different conceptual schemes? Is the notion of a conceptual scheme really the one that is operative in his suggestion? I have discussed his suggestion in terms of (1) the distinction between the empirical and the *a priori,* (2) the distinction between the intuitively given and conceptual molds, and (3) the distinction between the manifold of sensible intuitions and ways of ordering this manifold. Thus, Rorty's suggestion could be taken to rest on any one of the following three premises: (1) there can be alternative *a priorities* by means of which the empirical can be understood, (2) there can be many essentially different sets of conceptual molds into which the intuitively given can be cast, and (3) there can be alternative ways to order the manifold of sensible impressions. But does Rorty's objection apply to his suggestion when it is construed as based on any of these three different premises?

In the first case, does the question whether one *a priori* is the same as, or different than, another *a priori* make sense without the notion of analyticity? If there were an alternative *a priori,* there would be at least two *a priorities,* but would there be at least two expressions that didn't mean the same thing? This depends on how one construes *a priori.* If an *a priori* is construed as a repertoire of concepts, there would be at least two expressions that didn't mean the same thing. In the second case, does the question whether one repertoire of conceptual molds is the same as, or different than, another such repertoire make sense without the notion of analyticity? If there were alternative repertoires of conceptual molds, there would be at least two conceptual molds, but would there be at least two expressions that did not mean the same thing? This depends on how one construes the conceptual mold metaphor. For what could it be a metaphor, if not a metaphor for a conceptual scheme? But, then, if there were alternative repertoires of conceptual molds, there would be at least two conceptual schemes, and so there would be at least two expressions that didn't mean the same thing. In the third case, does the question whether one way of ordering the manifold is the same as, or different than, another way make sense without the notion of analyticity? Would there be at least two expressions that did not mean the same thing, if there were alternative ways of ordering the manifold? This depends on what a way of ordering the manifold is. Although this anticipates what it is to be developed below, a way of ordering the manifold is equivalent to an assortment of concepts. So, if there were alternative ways of ordering the manifold, there would be at least two such ways, and so there would be at least two expressions that did not mean the same thing.

Thus, for each way of construing Rorty's suggestion, there are at least two expressions that do not mean the same thing, and so the rest of Rorty's objection applies. Let these expressions be α and β. Et cetera. No matter the manner of its construal, it seems that Quine's criticism of the analytic-synthetic distinction shows, *mutatis mutandis*, that Rorty's suggestion fails. This is not the case. I think that the Quinean criticism is far from undermining Rorty's suggestion. The basic idea here is that the Quinean criticism supports Rorty's suggestion by showing us that Kant was wrong to think that there can only be one way to order the manifold, and by showing us how there can be many essentially different ways. To see this, suppose that the given is the manifold of sensible impressions themselves, and that their being raw is their being uncompared, uncombined, and unseparated, and consequently unordered. Or, in short, suppose that the given is the manifold of sensible impressions, and that their being raw is their being unordered. Then, Rorty's suggestion is this. There can be alternative ways of ordering the manifold of sensible impressions, and that experience is a product of this ordering. For each way of ordering the manifold, there is a different experience, and that a world is an ideal sum of what can be experienced. So, there can be many actual worlds. Et cetera. Given Rorty's objection, a pivotal problem is to show that it is possible for there to be alternative ways to order the manifold of sensible impressions. To paraphrase Quine, nothing is immune to revision in the face of a recalcitrant manifold of sensible impressions, and so it is possible to adopt alternative ways of ordering the manifold. Kant would have said that our ways of ordering the manifold are not subject to revision, and it is, therefore, impossible to adopt different ways. But, according to Quine's criticism, even our ways of ordering the manifold are subject to revision, and so it is possible for there to be alternative ways of ordering the manifold. Quine's point is that if the right sensible impressions came along, we might revise our ways of ordering the manifold. So, Rorty has, I think, misconstrued the import of the Quinean criticism of the analytic-synthetic distinction; it does not show that Rorty's suggestion fails, instead it shows why one of its pivotal premises is correct.

What, then, about Rorty's objection to his own suggestion? Once again, here is his objection. Suppose that (1) there were alternative conceptual schemes. Thus, (2) there would then be at least two conceptual schemes, and so (3) there would be at least two concepts, one drawn from each scheme. Consequently, (4) there would be at least two expressions that didn't mean the same thing. (5) Let these expressions be α and β. So, (6) there would be an analytic truth, to wit, α is not β, or something like this. Moreover, (7) this would be a statement that is immune from revision, but Rorty maintains, with Quine, that (8) no statement is immune from revision. Therefore, (9) there can be no alternative conceptual schemes, and so (10) Rorty's suggestion fails. Where does this fail? One place it fails, I think, is in the inference from (5) to (6). Doesn't this move beg the question? Part of the point of saying that there are alternative conceptual schemes is that concepts drawn from different schemes can't be constituents of the same judgments, and so a sentence such as α is not β is not meaningful. Just because one can write α is not β doesn't mean that one has written something that is either meaningful or grammatical.

If Rorty's Kantian suggestion doesn't succumb to his own objections, what of its other defects? Recall the questions that might be asked. Do we really intuit and think? There are questions that arise from the metaphorical character of some of the elements of Rorty's suggestion. What is to be made of the metaphorical characterization of thinking as the casting of the intuitively given into conceptual molds? Or the metaphorical characterization of experience as a product of the conceptual molding of the intuitively given? There are questions that arise from an ambiguity in the word *world*. Is a world an ideal sum of (i) what is experienced, or (ii) what is and can be experienced, or (iii) what is and can be experienced plus whatever may be connected by rules to what is and can be experienced? Is a world (i) that which imposes on the passive faculty of sensuous intuition, or (ii) that of which we are supposed to be conscious after the active faculty of thought has interpreted what the world, in the just-mentioned sense, has imposed on the passive faculty of intuition? There are questions that arise from some of the substantive assumptions of Rorty's suggestion. What reason is there for thinking that there can be essentially different sets of conceptual molds? Why should one think that the given can be cast into these molds? Lastly, there is a metaphilosophical question: By what means are the answers to such questions to be uncovered? The uncovering process will be, to some extent, arbitrary. I will begin by recalling, and reflecting on, the Protagorean vision. My aim is to uncover, and perhaps justify, a number of theses that are central to the Kantian world picture, and my method is to show that these theses emerge from a number of criticisms of the Protagorean world vision.

Protagoras maintained that the world of Socrates is the aggregate of whatever appears to him, and since perception is the principal mode of appearance, his world is the aggregate of what he perceives. More generally, the aggregate of what is perceived by an individual, or the aggregate of what appears to an individual, is her world. Since there are many perceiving individuals, there are many worlds. All of this is, or should be, familiar, but there is an additional dimension. According to Plato's reconstruction of the Protagorean vision, perception depends on the senses in such a way that what appears through perception is partitioned on the basis of an alignment between the senses and the *proper* objects of the senses. Plato writes:

> *Socrates:* And will you be willing to agree that if you perceive something by means of one power, it's impossible to perceive that same thing by means of another? For instance, you can't perceive

by means of sight what you perceive by means of hearing, or perceive by means of hearing what you perceive by means of sight?

Theaetetus: Of course.[16]

In other words, the ideal sum of perceptual appearances, which constitute a Protagorean world, is partitioned into the seen, the heard, et cetera. On the one hand, some characteristics, such as being red, stay within certain perceptual partitions, and other characteristics, such as the darker than relation, only seem to involve elements that themselves stay within the confines of specific partitions. In other words, not only does red lie within the perceptual partition of the seen, but if one thing is darker than another, these two things also lie within the perceptual partition of the seen. On the other hand, it is important to note that not only are some seen things different from other seen things, but some heard things are different from some seen things, and, of course, vice versa. The seen and the heard belong, according to the Protagorean hypothesis, to different partitions, but in this case, difference involves elements belonging to more than one partition. Thus, some characteristics, or features of a perceptual world, cross, so to speak, partitions. Moreover, there is a distinction between two types of characteristic to be made here: (1) there are the well-behaved characteristics, namely, those that do not cross perceptual partitions, and (2) there are the ill-behaved characteristics, that is, those that do cross perceptual partitions. The pivotal question is: Do ill-behaved characteristics have a place in a Protagorean world?

The answer to this last question must be, I think, negative. The reason is that if a Protagorean world is an ideal sum of what is perceived by some individual, and the perceived is partitioned into the seen, the heard, *et cetera,* then there could be no ill-behaved characteristics. This is an important criticism of the Protagorean vision. I also think that this implication shows that there is something missing from the Protagorean picture, and what is missing is an essential element of the Kantian picture that I am attempting to articulate in a manner that will enable me to me make sense of the theses that there are many actual worlds and truths.

Focus on the incompatibility that Plato noted, when he wrote the following:

Socrates: Now take a sound and a colour. First of all, you think just this about them: that they both *are?*

Theaetetus: Yes.

Socrates: And that each is *different from* the other and *the same as itself?*

Theaetetus: Of course.

Socrates: And that both together are *two* and each is *one?*

Theaetetus: Yes, that too.

Socrates: And you're able to raise the question whether they're *like* or *unlike* each other?

Theaetetus: I suppose so.

Socrates: Well now, by means of what do you think all those things about them? Because *it's impossible to get hold of what they have in common either by means of hearing or by means of sight.* Besides, here's another proof of the point we're talking about. If it were possible to raise the question whether both are salty or not, of course you'll be able to say what you'd investigate it with: it would clearly be neither sight nor hearing, but something else.

Theaetetus: Yes, of course: the power that's exercised by means of the tongue.

Socrates: Good. But what about *the power which makes clear to you that which is common to everything,* including these things: that to which you apply the words 'is', 'is not', and the others we used in our questions about them just now? What is that power exercised by means of? *What sort of instruments are you going to assign to all those things, by means of which the perceiving element in us perceives each of them?*

Theaetetus: You mean being and not being, likeness and unlikeness, the same and different, and also one and any other number applied to them. And it's clear that your question is also about odd and even, and everything else that goes with those. What you're asking is *by means of what part of the body we perceive them with our minds.*

Socrates: You follow me perfectly Theaetetus. That's exactly what I'm asking.

Theaetetus: Well, good heavens, Socrates, I couldn't say; except that I think *there simply isn't any instrument of that kind peculiar to those things,* as there is in the case of those others. On the contrary, it seems to me that *the mind itself, by means of itself, considers the things which apply in common to everything.*[17]

Theaetetus is confused in a way that Socrates—or Plato?—either does not notice, or does not note. A sound, a color and a taste are presumably apprehended by three different modes of perception, namely, those respectively associated with the ear, the eye, and the tongue. These three characteristics are well behaved, that is, they do not cross perceptual partitions. Consequently, the tongue can taste neither the color nor the sound, but then it cannot be used to determine whether they are salty. So, when Theaetetus asserts that it is by means of the tongue that he would investigate whether a color and a sound are salty or not, he has erred. But, this is an important error, since it shows that there are elements in a Protagorean world for which the Protagoreans cannot account.

Here are just three instances. First, there are relations that the elements of two partitions bear to an element of a third partition: neither color nor sound is salty. Second, there are relations that the elements of two partitions bear to each other: sound and color are different. Third, there are characteristics that belong to all partitions: both colors and sounds are, that is, exist. There is, of course, the question of the possible permutations, but I will not consider it here. Instead, I will merely note that although a Protagorean would not, I assume, want to deny any of this, it is, on Protagorean principles, unintelligible. *Is, isn't, difference, sameness, otherness, identity, oneness, twoness, likeness, unlikeness, et cetera,* are, it would seem, part of any world, and so they are part of every Protagorean world. Perception—understood as dependent on the senses in such a way that what appears through perception is partitioned on the basis of an alignment between the senses and the proper objects of the senses—cannot have any of these characteristics as its objects. Consequently, if Protagorean worlds are ideal sums of what is, or can be, perceived by some individual, then not only are they incomplete, but perception cannot be the only world constituting representation. Another sort of representation is required to account for ill-behaved characteristics, but Plato's

Theaetetus does not contain an account of the required sort of representation.[18]

In sum, Protagoras thought that for each sentient individual, there is a manifold of perceptions, and that the sum of the objects of these perceptions is a world. He concluded that since there are many sentient individuals, there must also be many worlds. The problem is that a Protagorean world evidently contains more than what can be given through, or constituted by, perception. So these worlds must be incomplete, and there must be, if a complete world is even possible, another kind of world constituting representation. In short, to return to the *leit motif* of Rorty's suggestion, it must be that we both perceive and think. This raises familiar questions. What is thought? How can thought constitute what perception cannot? Are many repertoires of world constituting thoughts possible? It is also necessary to say how it is that thought can constitute any segment of a world, what a world is, and what an object is. I think that Kant explains how thought or conception can be world constituting, and that he gives an account of what an object must consequently be. It might be better to say that he gives us an account of objectivity, but there will be more on this below. I also maintain that his story can be appropriated to show that there are many actual worlds. So it is to Kant's views on these matters that I must now turn.

There is a thesis that the foregoing critique of Protagoras renders discernible, and that is essential to the Kantian picture of what it is to be a world. What is this thesis? In short, it is this: If a manifold of perceptions has an object, it must also have a certain unity, and this unity cannot be given through perception. Kant thinks that the fact of this unity entails that every event follows another event according to a rule, and so on. Bracket this. I propose to follow up Rorty's suggestion, and to use the Kantian story of this unity to explain, and to argue for, the thesis that there are many actual worlds. So the pivotal question is: What is this unity?

In a way reminiscent of the just-discussed Platonic criticism of Protagoras, Franz Brentano remarks that many of us definitely recognize that sound and color are different, and so many of us are clearly capable of comparing color and sound. He inquires: "How would this presentation of their difference be possible if the presentations of color and sound belonged to a different reality?"[19] It cannot be that one simply looks, since this would exclude the sound that is to be compared with what is seen. It cannot be that one merely listens, since this would exclude the color that is to be compared with what is heard. It cannot be that one employs some third perceptual modality, since this would exclude both the color and the sound that are to be compared, unless, of course, one's auditory and visual perceptions were somehow united in it. This is the first hint of the unity that I seek to explicate.

In order to make the nature of this unity clearer, Brentano points out that this unity of visual and auditory perception is not at all like that of the mere juxtaposition of the auditory perceptions of a blind man and the visual perceptions of a deaf man. No matter how the two men may be juxtaposed, they cannot be aware of the relation between color and sound. Brentano thinks that

> the cognition which compares them [to wit, sound and color] is *a real objective unity*, but when we combine the acts of the blind and the deaf man, we always get *a mere collective* and never *a unitary real thing*.[20]

He continues:

> Obviously, it makes no difference whether the blind man and the deaf man are far apart or near one another. If they lived together permanently in the same house, indeed, even if they had grown up together as inseparably as Siamese twins or even more so it would not increase the possibility of the hypothesis one bit. Only if sound and color are presented jointly, *in one and the same reality*, is it conceivable that they can be compared with one another.[21]

An important point here is that our ability to compare such mundane things as colors and sounds, and our ability to be aware that they are different, both rest on some sort of unity of our visual and auditory perceptions. Moreover, an equally important point is that this unity is not that of the blind man and the deaf man in mere juxtaposition. Together, they do not form, or constitute, a unitary real thing, but instead they form a mere collective. Although Brentano may have shown us that there is a unity that needs to be explained, and that such a unity is importantly different from the mere collectivity illustrated by the juxtaposition of the blind man and the deaf man, he has not himself provided, at least in the passage under consideration, such an explanation. So, there remains the question of what this unity is.

The existence and essence of this unity is further illustrated by a thought experiment that was presented by William James. He wrote:

> Take a sentence of a dozen words, and take twelve men and tell to each one word. Then stand the men in a row or jam them in a bunch, and let each think of his word as intently as he will; nowhere will there be a consciousness of the whole sentence.[22]

It is unfortunate that James does not say more about this thought experiment, but one point is clear: James's twelve men are importantly analogous to Brentano's blind man and deaf man. Just as Brentano's pair cannot be conscious of the relation between color and sound, James's dozen can't be conscious of the whole sentence in question. If there were, in addition to Brentano's two men, a third man who could both hear and see, he would presumably be conscious of at least one relation between sound and color, namely, that color is not sound. The sounds that a blind man hears cannot be compared to the colors that a deaf man sees, because their perceptions do not, and presumably cannot, possess the unity of the visual and auditory perceptions of someone who both sees and hears. Analogously, if there were, in addition to James's dozen men, a thirteenth man who was told the entire dozen word sentence, he would presumably be conscious of the complete sentence of the thought experiment. A thirteenth man would be capable of being conscious of something of which the dozen were incapable of being conscious. The point of James's thought experiment is to get us to understand that the dozen word-perceptions of the man who has perceived the whole sentence are essentially different from the dozen word-perceptions of the twelve men who have not perceived the whole sentence. The former possess the unity required of perceptions through which a sentence—or, more generally, an object—may appear, whereas the latter do not. The dozen men cannot go through, take up, and connect into a single consciousness of a single sentence their dozen individual perceptions of one of a dozen words, since these perceptions fail to possess the unity of the perceptions of the man who has perceived the whole sentence.[23]

Brentano and James have proffered importantly different thought experiments, however. Brentano's point is that different perceptual modalities must be somehow united, if we are to be capable of comparing their contents. So, for example, our visual and auditory perceptions must somehow be united, if we are to be capable of comparing sounds and colors, and recognizing that sound is not color. James makes a similar and perhaps deeper point: even perceptions within the same modality must somehow be united, if one is to be capable of being aware of objects that have parts that are serially presented by means of these perceptions. This is, I think, what Kant meant, when he wrote: "It is only when we have . . . produced synthetic unity in the manifold of intuition that we are in a position to say that we know the object."[24] In other words, even perceptions within the same modality must somehow be united, if one is to be capable of being aware of an object that is composed of parts that are thereby perceived. So, for example, a dozen perceptions of a dozen words must somehow be united, if one is to be capable of being aware of a sentence that is composed of these words.

In the context of James's point that even perceptions within the same modality must possess some sort of unity, if one is to be capable of being aware of objects that are composed of parts that are serially presented by means of these perceptions, reconsider the above criticism of the Protagorean vision. A Protagorean world contains more than what can be given through, or constituted by, perception, namely, relations among the objects of different perceptual modalities. So such worlds must be incomplete. Et cetera. This makes it seem, however, that a Protagorean world could still contain the objects of the individual perceptual modalities, but in the light of James's thought experiment, this can be seen to be mistaken. The basic reason is that everything is, for the Protagorean, given through perception, but the unity of the manifold of perceptions can never be perceived, that is, can never be given through perception. As Kant wrote in an important passage of his first *Critique*: "the combination . . . of the manifold in general can never come to us through the senses."[25] In other words, the unity of the manifold of perceptions can never be given through perception. The fundamental mistake is that if every element of a Protagorean world comes through perception, and the unity in question cannot be given through, or constituted by, perception, then the unity that is necessary for there to be any awareness of objects must be absent, and so there cannot be any awareness of objects.

For example, even a Protagorean would admit, I think, that there is, and so there can be, an awareness of such objects as twelve-word sentences, but the problem is that this is, on Protagorean principles, impossible. A Protagorean has a place for a dozen perceptions of a dozen words, but he has no place for the unity that these perceptions must possess if there is to be an awareness of a twelve-word sentence, and so she cannot account for what is obvious: not only is such an awareness possible, it is actual. Indeed, since we are actually aware of objects such as twelve-word sentences, it must be possible for us to be aware of them. More generally, even the perceptions of a particular modality must possess a unity, which is as yet unexplained, if there is to be any awareness of objects. So the Protagorean must tell us that we cannot be conscious of the sentence of James's thought experiment, and consequently we cannot be aware of certain sorts of object of which we are certainly aware, but this would seem to refute it. In the light of James's thought experiment, it can be seen that a Protagorean world cannot even contain the objects of the individual perceptual modalities, and this too would seem to refute it. The Protagorean vision is refuted because perceptions, if they are to be perceptions of objects, require a unity that cannot come through perception. And, so, a Protagorean world depends on, if it is to contain such objects, a unity that its own defining principles deny it.

There are a pair of problems here, and I'm not sure what to say about them. First, if knowledge is to be intersubjective, and solipsism is to be avoided, must not what seem to be separate minds be unified in some way? Just as I can only know that color and sound are different if my visual and auditory perceptions are somehow unified, I can only know that your visual perceptions are different from my auditory perceptions if your visual perceptions and my auditory perceptions are somehow unified. What is wrong with this? This quickly leads to the conclusion that there is only one mind, or does it? Second, why cannot unity be given through perception? Why cannot the unity of the manifold of perceptions be perceived? Perhaps there is some unattested Protagorean doctrine according to which perception is able to constitute much more than is usually supposed. A contemporary neo-Protagorean, Maurice Merleau-Ponty, seems to find more in perception than Kant did. He writes: "One sees the hardness and brittleness of glass, and when, with a tinkling sound, it breaks, this sound is conveyed by the visible glass." [26] I will bracket these issues here.

Not only are the above-described thought experiments the basis of a number of powerful criticisms of the Protagorean vision, but they also establish the necessity of the unity of consciousness, and they provide a glimpse into what this unity is. However, they do not explain this unity, and they do not establish what follows from the fact of this unity. On the one hand, Kant attempted to both explain it, and divine its consequences. On the other hand, my aim is to show that the Kantian world picture, of which it is an essential element, supports the theses that there are many actual worlds, and that there are many truths. This is not a use to which Kant would happily see his vision put, I think, since some things that Kant writes in his first *Critique* suggest that he thought that the fact of the unity insinuated above entails that there is just one actual world. For example, Kant thinks that since the world, or nature, is merely an aggregate of appearances, and not a thing in itself, the fact of its conformity to law is entailed by the fact of the unity that I have been discussing, which Kant entitles the transcendental unity of apperception. It can, according to Kant, be known *a priori* both that the events, of which the world is composed, must conform to law, and that the world must be unitary, that is, unitary in the sense that the law to which its events conform imposes a unifying structure on them, and thereby on it. It is in this context that Kant writes about the necessary interconnection of events, and the universal unity of the world, or nature. [27] It is, moreover, difficult to understand how Kant could write in this manner, if he did not believe that the transcendental unity of apperception, which is, at this point, little more than a title, necessitates that there be one and only one actual world or nature.

The thesis that there are many actual worlds is not utterly alien to Kant's thought, however. At one point in his *Inaugural Dissertation*, however, Kant writes that "a plurality of actual worlds outside one another is not impossible by its very concept." [28] What I hope to show is that a more articulated account of the unity hinted at above can be used to define *world;* the basic idea is that a world is something like a sum of all that can be represented through the representations that can possess this unity. Moreover, there are many actual worlds just when

there are many sums of things that can be represented by many manifolds of representations each of which can possess this hitherto elusive
unity.

Let me elaborate this by using Kant's terms to give a rough account
of the point of Davidson's polemic against *conceptual relativism.* Davidson's insight might be paraphrased in the following manner: were
there to be a conceptual scheme that is alternative to ours, there would
be representations that could not be united with our representations.
These alternative representations would stand to ours as the blind
man's auditory perceptions stand to the deaf man's visual perceptions.
Just as the blind man's auditory perceptions can be nothing to the deaf
man, or just as the deaf man's visual perceptions can be nothing to the
blind man, the representations, which are associated with an alternative conceptual scheme, can be nothing to us. Moreover, just as the
sounds exhibited by means of the blind man's auditory perceptions can
be nothing to the deaf man, or just as the colors exhibited by means of
the deaf man's visual perceptions can be nothing to the blind man, the
objects exhibited by means of the representations, which are associated
with an alternative conceptual scheme, can be nothing to us. Consequently, the world of objects exhibited by means of alternative representations is different from the world of objects exhibited by means of
our representations, and so not only cannot we know it, but we must
also conclude that it is unreal. Presumably, a conceptual relativist
wants to say both that (1) there are other, and therefore different,
worlds of objects, and that (2) somehow they can be represented.
Davidson's point is that these two theses can't be put together. Simply
put, the intuition that underlies his point is that any object that we can
represent cannot belong to a world other than our own. The conceptual relativist must show, therefore, how it is that worlds of objects can
be both different and something to us. Moreover, there is the altogether
different requirement that she show that there are worlds of objects
that are both different and something to us.

An adequate answer to Davidson's objection, and an adequate
explication of the thesis that there are many actual worlds and truths,
require, I think, an alternative conception of what it is to be an object.
Protagoras offers us a paradigm of such an alternative conception.
Faced with the fact of conflict betwixt his peers, Protagoras conjectured that they perceive different objects. If, for example, Socrates and

Theaetetus are opposed over *the* character of *the* wind, they must be, according to Protagoras, perceiving different winds. If Socrates and Theaetetus perceive different winds, however, they cannot be perceiving *the* wind as it is in itself. What, then, are they perceiving? The Protagorean answer to this question depends on a reconceptualization of what it is to be an object. About this alternative conceptualization, Plato wrote:

> [B]lack, white, or any other colour will turn out to have come into being, from the collision of the eyes with the appropriate motion. What we say a given colour is will be neither the thing which collides, not the thing it collides with, but something which has come into being between them; something peculiar to each one.[29]

Perception involves, according to Protagoras, two elements. In the case of visual perception, these are (1) the eyes, and (2) something that Protagoras—or Plato?—entitles *motion*. Color is constituted by the collision, or interaction, of these two elements. Consequently, color itself is neither in the motion, nor in the eyes. As Plato puts it, color is something that is constituted, or comes into being, between the eyes and the motion. For each pair of eyes, therefore, there is a distinct point that is between them and the motion, and so there is a distinct color. So, color is peculiar to each pair of eyes, or, in other words, color is peculiar to each percipient. Moreover, I presume that this story applies, *mutatis mutandis,* to any other perceptible object, for example, tastes, sounds, or textures.

With this story, Protagoras provides us with an alternative conception of what it is to be an object. He also provides us with the key to explain what it means to say that objects are appearances, to wit: objects are neither merely subjective—in the eyes, for example—nor things in themselves—for example, some sort of motion in itself. To say that an object is an appearance is to say that it is between the merely subjective and things in themselves. One could object that this notion of being between the subjective and things in themselves is vague, but one could make the stronger objection that there is a way in which this story depends on essentially anti-Protagorean presuppositions: it depends on the supposition that there are eyes and motion that are themselves not between some eyes and motion, that is, eyes and motion in themselves. In other words, this story depends on the supposition of things of which man is not the measure. There is sense in the suggestion that man is the measure of all those things that are between eyes in themselves and motion in itself, since there is sense in the idea that eyes in themselves have some role in the constitution of this somewhat mysterious middle region. However, eyes in themselves do not, at least within the context of the story in question, have any role in their own constitution. If man were the measure of all things, he would be the measure of eyes and motion, and so they would seem to need to be between yet further eyes and motion. The Protagorean would seem to face, therefore, either an infinite regress, or entities for which he cannot account.

Let me place this problem aside, since it is not clear whether it is the result of authentic Protagorean doctrines, or Protagorean doctrines tainted with Platonic poison. Although it fails, Protagoras offers us a paradigm of an alternative conception of what it is to be an object. A Protagorean object is somehow between subject and object in itself, but a purified Protagorean world picture would, I presume, eliminate all things in themselves, whether they be subjects (eyes) or objects (motions). But, on the supposition of such a purge, what would things —subjects or objects—then be? One might continue to talk in the manner of the old story, and say that things would then be *appearances,* but this would not explain their curious status. To what, in the absence of the old story about eyes and motions, does saying that a thing is an appearance amount? An answer to this question is contained in the Protagorean thesis that the world of Theaetetus is the aggregate of whatever appears to him, and since perception is the principal mode of appearance, his world is the aggregate of what he perceives. According to Protagoras, I think, to say that objects are appearances is to say that objects are nothing more than objects of perception. However, as should be clear, there are several ways in which these aspects of the Protagorean vision are defective. So it cannot be followed here. In other words, although Protagoras offers us a paradigm of an alternative manner of conceiving what it is to be an object, since his alternative is based on a defective vision, we cannot decline or conjugate our Kantian alternative on the basis of his paradigm. The Kantian alternative has a grammar that is specific to it.

According to the Kantian world picture, what is it to be an object? The essential idea is that an object is an object of some representation that is somehow unified with other representations. Since it is not clear what this unity is, this idea is, at best, a suggestion about how to proceed, and it is, therefore, necessary to rethink what it is to be an object. Kant said as much as this, when he said that "we must make clear to ourselves what we mean by the expression 'an object of representations'."[30] One finds confirmation of Kant's intention in his claim that

> it is a question for deeper enquiry what the word 'object' ought to signify in respect of appearances when these are viewed not in so far as they are (as representations) objects, but only in so far as they stand for an object.[31]

By reflecting on Kant, I hope to sift out an account of what it is for object to be an appearance, and an account of the representations that constitute what perception cannot. I will begin with this question: What must an object be, if there are to be many actual worlds?

Kant's conception of what it is to be an object, which I want to appropriate for my cause, is part of his account of *a priori* knowledge. For example, he wanted to explain how, and show that, we can know *a priori* that every event must follow another event according to a rule. Bracket this aspect of his world picture. In a conceptually revolutionary passage, Kant wrote:

> Hitherto it has been assumed that *all our knowledge must conform to objects*. But all attempts to extend our knowledge of objects by establishing something in regard to them *a priori*, by means of concepts, have, on this assumption, ended in failure. We must therefore make trial whether we may not have more success in the task of metaphysics, if we suppose that *objects must conform to our knowledge*. This would agree better with what is *desired*, namely, that it should be possible to have knowledge of objects *a priori*, determining something in regard to them prior to their being given.[32]

Kant's explanation and argument begins with what he takes to be two mutually exclusive and jointly exhaustive possibilities: either (1) knowledge conforms to its object, or (2) objects somehow conform to knowledge. As I have noted, he thought that the former option entails skepticism. If knowledge conforms to its object, then there is an object that exists in itself, and knowing involves correctly representing this object as it is in itself. As he wrote in his *Prolegomena*: "Should nature signify the existence of things in themselves, we could never cognize it either *a priori* or *a posteriori*."[33] If knowledge is supposed to conform to a distinct and representation independent object, it must be possible for knowledge to fail to conform, and it is exactly this that is skepticism. Therefore, one must choose between an intuition about the essence of knowledge—namely, that it somehow conforms to preexistent objects in themselves—and an intuition about skepticism—namely, that it is utterly wrongheaded. Kant rejected skepticism, and so he opted to abandon the intuition that knowledge somehow conforms to preexistent objects in themselves. Kant prefers to reject skepticism, even if he must then affirm that in some manner objects conform to knowledge. What, then, are objects? The desire for *a priori* knowledge, not to mention knowledge *simpliciter*, can only be satisfied by renouncing the intuition that knowledge conforms to its object, and the affirming that objects somehow conform to knowledge. The idea is not that there is first an object, and then there is someone who knows, and finally the object changes so as to conform to this person's knowledge. For example, the idea is not that there is first an apple, and then Socrates knows that it is an orange, and finally the apple changes into an orange so as to conform to Socrates' knowledge. But, then, what is the idea? What can it possibly mean to say that objects conform to knowledge? What is Kant's conception of what it is to be an object?

There are a number of sites where Kant works out the details of his alternative conception of what it is to be an object. In my attempt to appropriate this conception, I will mainly draw from the *Transcendental Deduction in A*, or, more specifically, the *Subjective Deduction*, although I will also consider, in an incidental manner, the *Second Analogy*.[34] On the reading taken up here, these two sites contain Kant's justification for the thesis that, in the words of the *Subjective Deduction*, "all appearances stand in a thoroughgoing connection according to necessary laws."[35] Or, in the words of the principle of the first edition version of the *Second Analogy*: "Everything that happens, that is, begins to be, presupposes something upon which it follows according to a rule."[36] More generally, the conclusion of Kant's argument is that if there is a consciousness that possesses the unity described above, it must be possible for there to be authentic empirical knowledge. In other words, the conclusion is that the unity of consciousness is a sufficient condition for both the possibility and the actuality of empirical knowledge of objects in space and time. For my purposes, what is important about this argument is that it is intertwined with an account of what it is to be an object—or more accurately perhaps, an account of objectivity—and this is exactly what I hope to appropriate from Kant. In the following, I will attempt to disentangle the elements of his conception of what it is to be an object, and put them together in a way that I think supports the thesis that there are many actual worlds and truths. How do I plan to do this?

The elements of Kant's conception of what it is to be an object, not to mention the justification of this conception, are mostly to be found in the *Subjective Deduction*. This text is, or appears to be, an inconsistent muddle, however. One conjecture that has been offered to explain this is the historical thesis that Kant more or less capriciously arranged four groups of his writings—each of which dates from a different period, and each of which is incompatible with the other three—into the *Subjective Deduction*. This is, of course, the famous patchwork thesis.[37] Whereas the patchwork thesis explains the apparent muddle of the *Transcendental Deduction* by means of a thesis that concerns the manner of its composition, Wolff explains the ostensible disarray of Kant's text with a thesis that concerns the manner of its exposition. His idea is that since Kant could not be sure that the readers of the first *Critique* would have read his previous works, it was necessary for him to explain at least three previous stages of his thought. In other words, his strategy for explaining the doctrines of the *Subjective Deduction* was to begin by explaining a number of earlier accounts of the transcendental unity of apperception that he had considered, but rejected. It is only in the *Second Analogy*, which forms, so to speak, a fifth stage, that Kant presents his most fully developed position. For my purposes, what is important is that each of these five stages is intertwined with an account of what it is to be an object; and it is this account that I hope to appropriate in order to make sense of the theses that there are many actual worlds, and that there are many truths. Moreover, an important feature of the last four stages is that each includes a criticism of the doctrines, including the various conceptions of what it is to be an object, upon which the analysis of the preceding stage depends. By the fifth and last stage, namely, the *Second Analogy*, Kant has provided both an alternative conception of what it is to be an object, and a justification of this conception. Such a justification is obviously essential to any attempt to make sense of the theses that there are many actual worlds, and that there are many truths. So an important part of the task of making sense of these two theses can be accomplished by following Kant through the argument of the *Subjective Deduction,* and subsidiarily, the *Second Analogy.*

Although it might seem that good sense would now counsel me to turn to a discussion of the doctrines and argument of stage one, a preparatory discussion of two further premises of Kant's argument is necessary, that is, premises in addition to the already discussed premise that consciousness possesses the unity described in James's thought experiment. The first premise is that representations have two importantly different aspects. On the one hand, a representation is an episode in someone's conscious life. For example, my perception of a cat is an episode in my conscious life. As such, it has a date, and it has a place in a sequence of other such episodes. For example, it might be that I perceived the cat at 10:06 a.m., on September 6, 1993. Moreover, it might be that I perceived the tree before I perceived the cat, and that I perceived the cat before I perceived the dog. So I first perceived the tree, then secondly the cat, and finally the dog. On the other hand, representations refer to, or represent, objects that are not themselves representations. For example, my perception of a cat refers to, or represents, a cat that is not itself a perception. As Kant wrote in the *Subjective Deduction:* "All representations have, as representations, their object." [38] Wolff glosses this fragment of a passage in the following manner:

> [T]his referential function [of representations] exists whether or not there really is some object to be represented. It is precisely because the concept of a unicorn purports to represent that we can call it fictitious. [39]

Mutatis mutandis, Hamlet's perception of his father's ghost has a referential function, even if his father's ghost fails to exist; it is precisely because Hamlet's perception of his father's ghost purports to represent that we can all it an illusion. But Hamlet's perception does not purport. People purport, not their perceptions. So, although it might be that Hamlet purports, his perceptions do not. Moreover, it is far less than felicitous to say that there is something that is the object of Hamlet's perception, but it does not exist.

Although this cannot be made precise at this point in my discussion, there are good reasons to think that it is incorrect to say, as Wolff says that Kant says, that representations function referentially, when there is no object to be represented. First, this runs counter to the intuition that it is deeply wrongheaded to say that there is something that is the object of Hamlet's perception, but it does not exist. Second, it runs counter to a distinction that Kant is at pains to make in the *Second Analogy,* to wit, the distinction between *subjective representations,* which do not function referentially, and *objective representations,* which do so function. Note, however, that there is an intuition behind Wolff's gloss: it is precisely because Hamlet's perception seems to be a perception of his father's ghost that it can be said that it is an illusion. In other words, if Hamlet did not visually perceive anything at all, there would be little point to saying that he had been the victim of an illusion, as opposed to being unconscious. Perhaps this merely means that Hamlet's perception has a sense, but no reference, although this would require rethinking the notion of reference. So, when Kant claims that every representation has its object, this need mean no more than every representation, *qua* representation, has a sense. There is, then, no need to be saddled with the completely infelicitous thesis that there is something that is the object of Hamlet's perception, but it doesn't exist. A paradigm might be this: although the word *unicorn* has a sense, it has no reference. So, one can say, on Kant's behalf, that although Hamlet's perception has a sense, it has no reference. Moreover, this preserves the distinction, which is made in the *Second Analogy,* between subjective representations and objective representations. Both subjective and objective representations have a sense, but only the latter have a reference. The important Kantian move is to explain objective representations in terms of a certain sort of relation among representations, instead of a relation between a representation and a utterly distinct object. Thus, in addition to the premise that consciousness must possess the unity illustrated by James's thought experiment, there is this first important premise: representations have two aspects: (1) they are episodes in our conscious lives, and (2) they have, *qua* representations, a sense.[40]

The second premise concerns an essential feature of knowledge. It is an answer to the question: What characteristic distinguishes knowledge from imagination? In short, the pertinent characteristic is, according to Kant, necessity. Now, there are a number of analyses of the relevant form of necessity, but let me prescind from them here. The premise in question only concerns the deep relation between knowledge, imagination, and necessity, not the nature of this necessity. The basic intuition here is that since not all assertions are true, if I assert something, I have not *ipso facto* asserted something true. Similarly, if I assert something, I do not *ipso facto* assert something that I know. For example, if I assert that the cat is blue, it is not *ipso facto* true that the cat is blue; similarly, if I assert that the cat is blue, I do not *ipso facto* know that the cat is blue. This is related to, if not the same as, the *belief constraint,* which I have discussed above: to say or believe something is not *ipso facto* to say or believe something true. In imagining a cat, there is a certain amount of free play. I can imagine a black cat, but I can also imagine a blue cat, a green cat, and even a grue cat, which would be a cool cat indeed. This free play and the necessity in question here are opposites. There is little, if anything at all, about an imagined cat that constrains the imaginative ascription of color to it; in the case of a real cat, however, there is something that constrains the true and faithful ascription of color to it, namely, the cat itself, or so one might presume. In the latter case, the act of forming a true judgment about the cat, or knowing the cat, would seem to be constrained by the existence and essence of the cat. This begs an important question, however, to wit: How is the necessity or constraint in question here to be explained? To describe such a necessity in terms of the existence and essence of some cat in itself is to foreclose the possibility of describing and explaining it in terms of something else, for example, some relation among representations. This latter explanation can only be, however, a forethought of what is to come. The point, which needs to be made at this juncture, is that an essential characteristic of knowledge is necessity or constraint, but it is also important to prescind from any specific explanation of this necessity. In other words, at this point, it is necessary to prescind from explaining or describing this necessity in terms of some relation between the relevant representations and some object in itself, or in terms of some relation among representations *simpliciter.*

Before I proceed to my discussion of the first stage of the *Subjective Deduction,* I will first note that and why I have articulated the second premise in a way that is partly different from the manner in which Wolff has put it. He writes:

> What is the defining mark of knowledge that sets it off from mere subjective fancy? The answer . . . is *necessity.* Knowledge is the assertion of a necessary connection between the subject and the predicate of a judgment. . . . [When I know] . . . I . . . [assert] . . . that there is an objective connection among these properties [which are presumably denoted by the aforementioned subject and predicate], such that I *must* connect them in my judgment.[41]

I presume that Wolff would also want to assert that there are cases in which when one knows, one asserts that there is an objective connection between some thing and some property; for example, when I know that the cat is black, I assert that there is an objective connection between the cat and the property of being black. Be this as it may, this is somewhat misleading. It is important to note that this necessity, or this *must,* is not the necessity of analyticity. In other words, it is not necessary to connect the relevant subject with the relevant predicate because there is some sort of logical or semantic connection between them. Moreover, in this case, the necessity in question cannot be explicated in terms of truth in all possible worlds. For example, given a black cat, the necessity of connecting *the cat* with *is black* is not to be understood in terms of the cat's being black in all possible worlds. This is a mistake; the cat's being black is—I suppose—a contingent matter. So I suspect that Wolff has made the point of the second premise in a somewhat misleading way, that is, misleading relative to an audience that is euphoric with a certain view of necessity. In sum, the second premise might be put this way: when I know, not only must I assert that there is a connection among certain properties, or among some thing and some property, et cetera, but this connection must be such that I must connect them in my judgment. However, the second premise might also be put this way: to assert something is not *ipso facto* to assert something that one knows. With these two premises in hand, it is now possible to turn to stage one of the *Subjective Deduction.*

Kant desires to show that empirical knowledge of objects in space and time is not only a possibility, but it is an actuality. One version of

Kant's argument rests on the premise that a manifold of perceptions of objects must possess the unity depicted in the above thought experiments, especially that of James. It is, moreover, mixed with an account of this unity. His strategy is to explain the nature of this unity by explaining why it is that the manifold of perceptions possess it. At this stage of things, the conjecture is that the manifold of perceptions is unified because each perception is directed to a unitary object that is both distinct from, and independent of, perception. In the case of James's thought experiment, for example, the reader's dozen perceptions of a dozen words are unified because each perception is also directed to a unitary and distinct sentence. However, a perception that is directed to an object cannot fail to be empirical knowledge. There are two reasons for this. First, a perception that fails to be directed to an object also fails to be knowledge. In the case of James's thought experiment, any perception that is directed to the sentence in question is inevitably an empirical knowledge of it. Second, since a representation that is directed to an object is constrained or necessitated by this object, it is knowledge. Recall that a pivotal premise of Kant's argument is that an essential characteristic of knowledge is necessity or constraint. When one knows, not only must one assert that there is a connection among certain properties, or among some thing and some property, et cetera, but this connection must be such that one *must* connect them in one's judgment. In sum, a representation that is directed to a constraining object is *ipso facto* knowledge. Therefore, given the premise that the manifold of perceptions possesses the unity described in James's thought experiment, and given the above described explanation of this unity, it follows that empirical knowledge is actual, and so it is possible. The essential idea here is that the mere fact of the unity of consciousness implies that the contents of consciousness are directed to objects, which itself implies both the actuality and the possibility of empirical knowledge.

Prescinding from the question of the merits of this argument, it is clear that it is intertwined with an account of what it is to be an object. Since this account rests on the assumption that there is a distinct and unique object that is representation independent, it is obviously inconsistent with the thesis that there are many actual worlds, and so it is obviously not useful to the advocate of this sort of plurality. Notwithstanding, this account has a problem that is independent of the thesis that there are many actual worlds, and that an advocate of this plurality can exploit to motivate Kant's conception of an object, which he must do, since he can't appeal, as Kant does, to the presumably desirable result of a unique *a priori* knowledge. As Kant himself points out:

> [I]t is easily seen that this object must be thought only as something in general = x, since outside our knowledge we have nothing which we could set over against this knowledge as corresponding to it.[42]

The *explanandum* is the unity of our perceptions, and the *explanans* is, at least at this stage of things, the distinct, unitary, and perception-independent object of these perceptions.[43] The essential point of the aforementioned problem is that if it should turn out that no content can be given to the concept of this object, it will be unable to play any role in the suggested explanation of the unity of consciousness. Now, this is exactly what Kant, not to mention this advocate of a multiplicity of actual worlds, thinks: "this object must be thought only as something in general = x."[44] It is thought that the concept of a distinct and representation independent object, that is, an object = x, must remain contentless, but why think this? Because, Kant answers, "outside our knowledge we have nothing which we could set over against this knowledge as corresponding to it."[45] It might seem that Kant's answer here is the mere tautology that we know nothing outside of what we know that is (1) other than what we know, and (2) could be the object = x. Of course, we know nothing outside of what we know, not to mention that we know nothing that is both outside of what we know, and that has any specifiable feature whatsoever, including these two. What, then, is the point of this tautology? Does Kant think that the above-discussed account of the unity of consciousness is, in some manner, incompatible with this tautology? Does he think that this tautology is incompatible with the conception of what it is to be an object that is concomitant with this account? In what manner is this tautology related to the pivotal thesis that this conception of what it is to be an object is necessarily empty? Does Kant even think that the last quoted remark *is* a tautology? In short, why think that the concept of a distinct and representation-independent object is necessarily empty?

The essential point here is that if the concept of the utterly distinct object, or the object = x, must be empty, then one can't explain the unity of representations by virtue of their directedness to such an object. Why this conditional? Because if no content can be given to the concept of something, there is nothing to be said about it, and so it cannot figure in any explanation of anything. Once again, in giving an explanation, one tells a story about something that makes it clear why the thing to be explained is the way that it happens to be; telling a story about something involves asserting that something has certain characteristics, which are somehow related to the thing to be explained. So, if the concept of this thing is to have any explanatory power, it must not be necessarily empty. So, if the concept of the object $= x$ must be empty, it cannot explain anything. Although written in the context of his discussion of private languages, this is, I think, Wittgenstein's point, when he wrote: "Here I should like to say: a wheel that can be turned though nothing else moves with it, is not part of the mechanism."[46] Be this as it may, Kant's reason for this antecedent—the concept of the utterly distinct object must be empty—is, at best, cryptically expressed. He wrote:

> [O]utside our knowledge we have nothing which we could set over against this knowledge as corresponding to it.[47]
>
> [W]e have to deal only with the manifold of our representations.[48]
>
> [T]hat x (the object) which corresponds to them [our representations] is nothing to us [that is, has none of the properties of a knowable object]—being, as it is, something that has to be distinct from all our representations.[49]

It is unclear how any of this gets one to the conclusion that the concept of a distinct and perception unifying object is necessarily empty. The fundamental idea is, I am conjecturing, this: if it were possible to give content to the conception of the object $= x$, it would be possible to compare a situation in which some instance of this conception is represented with a situation in which some instance of this conception is not represented. And it is clearly impossible to make this sort of comparison. In other words, to give content to this concept, one must compare situations in which the distinct object is and is not represented, but it is impossible to do this.

Ralph Barton Perry has expressed this point better than any other thinker that I know:

To determine roughly whether *a* is a function of *b,* it is convenient [necessary?] to . . . compare situations in which *b* is and is not present. But where *b* is 'I know,' it is evidently impossible to obtain a situation in which it is not present without destroying the conditions of observation.[50]

To give content to the conception of the object = *x*, that is, the conception of the distinct and representation independent object that unifies the manifold of consciousness, it must be possible to compare the represented object with the unrepresented object. This is impossible, since comparison is a form of representation. Suppose that Socrates wants to compare a situation in which some stone is represented with a situation in which the stone in question is not represented. So, he sets up the following three step experiment. First, he sets up a situation in which the stone is represented. Perhaps he gives it an intent stare. Second, he sets up a situation in which the stone is not represented. Perhaps he locks it away in a box that is impervious to even the stares of the gods. Third, he compares the stone in the first situation with the stone in the second situation. On the one hand, because of the design of the experiment, to wit, the second step, the stone in the second situation cannot be, and so is not, represented. On the other hand, because of the design of the experiment, to wit, the third step, the stone in the second situation must be, and so is, represented. In other words, according to the third step of the experiment, Socrates compares the stone in the first situation with the stone in the second situation; thus, the stone in the second situation is compared, and so it is represented. Thus, the design of the experiment is contradictory, and so Socrates cannot get what he wants. In other words, it shows that it is impossible to compare an object *qua* represented with the same object *qua* unrepresented, and so it is impossible to give content to the concept of an utterly distinct object. The conception of the unique and distinct object to which all of our representations are directed, and which is supposed to explain the unity of consciousness, is, therefore, necessarily empty. It can only be the concept of an object = *x*. There is a necessary incompleteness, emptiness or vacuity here, since it is, so to speak, impossible to solve for *x*. Recall that if the concept of the utterly distinct object, or the object = *x*, must be empty, the transcendental unity of apperception can't be explained by means of the supposition that every act of consciousness—perceptual or otherwise—is directed to a unitary, distinct and representation-independent object. Consequently, such a conception cannot explain the unity of consciousness.

There is another way to make this point about the necessary emptiness of the concept of the unique and representation-independent object. Henry E. Allison has contrived the idea of an *epistemic condition,* which he defines as a condition that is "necessary for the representation of an object or an objective state of affairs." [51] To extend Allison's idea, let me define an *epistemic property* as a property that is necessitated by representability. So the set of epistemic properties may be defined as the set of all properties, F, such that it must be the case that if x is representable, or knowable, x has F. I suspect that this is the sort of idea that Kant was attempting to bring to his reader's attention, when he wrote that "the representation is a priori determinate of an object, if it be the case that only through the representation is it possible to *know* anything as an *object.*" [52] The idea here is, I think, that it can be known *a priori* that something has some property, F, just when it is necessarily the case that if it is knowable, or representable, it has F. Suppose that a knowable or representable object must be capable of being both intuited and thought. Then, it can be known *a priori* that something has some property, F, if it is necessarily the case that if it can be intuited or thought, it has F. For example, Kant maintains that since every outwardly intuitable object must have location in space, and since Euclid's geometry describes the structure of space, it can be known *a priori* that its axioms must describe all outwardly intuitable objects. [53] For similar reasons, we can know *a priori* that every intuitable object will be temporal, and we can know *a priori* that every event must follow another event according to a rule. This is what Kant desired to show, but it follows, moreover, that the concept of the distinct object, to which representations are assumed to correspond, is necessarily contentless, and this is what I desire to show.

In the light of this idea of an epistemic property, a distinct and representation independent object may be defined as a knowable or representable object minus its epistemic properties. Now, the pivotal point is that the concept of such an object must be empty. Since an utterly distinct object does not possess the properties necessary for its representation, it is obviously unrepresentable. It is, however, only by representing an object that I can give content to its concept. Therefore, the concept of the utterly distinct object, that is, the concept of the object minus its epistemic properties, must be empty. In other words, the concept of the unique and distinct object to which all my representations correspond, and by which they are unified, must remain empty, therefore. So, since the concept of an utterly distinct object must be contentless, it can play no explanatory role in accounting for the unity of consciousness.

Let me put this pivotal point in yet a third manner. The essence of the idea of the essential emptiness of the concept of the distinct and representation independent object appears to be made manifest by an intuitive metaphor for the Kantian world picture. As H. J. Paton has written:

> It is impossible to invent any exact parallel for this revolutionary doctrine [that is, the doctrine that space and time are imposed on objects by the nature of our sensibility], but if we looked at everything through blue spectacles, we could say that the blueness of things, as they appeared to us, was due, not to the things, but to our spectacles. In that case the spectacles offer a very rough analogy to human sensibility in Kant's doctrine.[54]

A. C. Ewing approvingly cites this metaphor:

> Space and time . . . are those factors in our sense-experience which are due to ourselves and not to things-in-themselves acting on us. Because they are contributed by ourselves we can tell *a priori* that all objects which we experience will conform to them, just as when we use blue spectacles we can tell *a priori* that everything we see will look blue. This account of the *a priori* carries with it the implication that we can have *a priori* knowledge only of appearances not of reality, just as from the premiss that I wear blue spectacles I could infer not that all the physical objects I see really will be blue, but that they will look blue to me.[55]

If this were a good metaphor, it would certainly help to make sense of the thesis that there are many actual worlds and truths. If there were many pairs of differently colored spectacles, and an actual world were some sort of sum of all the things that could be seen through such a pair of spectacles, then there would be many actual worlds. Moreover, if each had a complete description, there would be many truths. There are, however, a number of ways in which the blue spectacles metaphor fails. Here are four. It falsely presupposes that (1) the only sense is sight, and that (2) blueness is as universal as space or time. It also wrongly presupposes that just as it is impossible to imagine something that is neither spatial nor temporal, (3) it must be impossible to imagine something that fails to be at least some shade of blue. Moreover, it mistakenly presupposes that (4) it must be, in effect, impossible to remove the blue tinted spectacles.

Paton also thinks that the blue tinted spectacles metaphor fails. He continues:

> By abstraction we could think the concept of blueness, but we could never intuit the one infinite blue of which all blues are necessarily parts; yet unless we can do so, blue is not really analogous to space. ... We could see no necessity why every blue area as such should be a part of a wider blue area. We could indeed see the necessity why every area should be part of a wider area, but this would have nothing to do with its blueness.[56]

What is Paton's criticism here? An essential premise of Kant's argument for the conclusion that space is an *a priori* intuition is the thesis that what we might take to be diverse spaces are necessarily parts of one all encompassing space. In the case of the blue tinted spectacles, however, what we might take to be diverse patches of blue are not necessarily parts of one all encompassing blue. This is another way in which the metaphor of the blue tinted spectacles falters. It fails to snare the quiddity of the Kantian analysis of *a priori* concepts such as the category of causality. Since space and time are, in the Kantian scheme of things, intuitions, space and time are passive, and so it takes no cognitive effort, such as judgment, to impose them on the manifold. So they are much like the blue tint of the spectacles, that is, the blue tint is imposed on the manifold without any effort—cognitive or otherwise —of the subject who wears them. To be imposed on the manifold, a category, such as causality, does require cognitive effort on the part of the subject, that is, a subject must judge. So, even if the blue spectacles metaphor did capture the Kantian doctrines about space and time, it would get something quite wrong about the categorial contribution of the subject. Now, I will pursue none of these criticisms here. Instead, I will suspend the disanalogies, and I will attempt to show that the concept of the unique, utterly distinct, and representation-independent object is, on the weak and fragile understanding provided by this metaphor, necessarily empty.

As I have already noted, if the blue-tinted spectacles metaphor is to have any force, sight must be the only sense. Moreover, since it must be impossible to remove the blue spectacles, blueness must be universal as space or time. Such suppositions are, however, false, but suspend this. Focus instead on the fact that the force of the blue spectacles metaphor also depends on the concept of the far-side object, that is, the concept of the object on the eyeless side of the blue spectacles. In other words, the force of the blue spectacles metaphor depends on there being a distinct and spectacles independent object. I can imagine the actuality of the just cited conditions, but I cannot imagine this without there being a far-side object, or, in other words, I cannot imagine this without there being a distinct and spectacles-independent object. Within the context of this metaphor, however, it can be seen that it is consequently impossible to give any content to the concept of the far-side object, or the concept of the distinct and spectacles-independent object. To be able to give content to the concept of the far-side object, it must be possible to remove the blue spectacles. *Ex hypothesi,* however, it is impossible to remove the blue spectacles, and no content can be given, therefore, to the concept of the far-side object. In short, the concept of the far-side object, that is, the concept of the distinct and the spectacles-independent object, is necessarily empty. So, to the extent that the blue spectacles metaphor captures the essence of the Kantian world picture, it is clear that the concept of the distinct and representation-independent object is itself necessarily empty, and therefore incapable of explaining the unity of consciousness.

According to the Kantian world picture, our representational capacities are our only paths to what there is, and these capacities are necessarily invariant. In terms of the metaphor of the blue-tinted spectacles, it is only by means of, or through, such spectacles that we have access to what there is, and they are invariant in the sense that they cannot, by assumption, be removed. Objects must, according to Kant, be representable, and the world is an ideal sum of representable objects. As Kant expressed this idea in a work subsequent to his first *Critique*, " 'nature' [or: the world] is . . . the sum total of all things insofar as they *can* be objects of our senses and hence objects of experience."⁵⁷ To extend the metaphor, the world is the sum of all things insofar as they can be seen through the blue-tinted spectacles. Moreover, every representable object must be, if it is to be represented, represented through such capacities. There are, consequently, strictly universal and necessary features of every representable object, namely, the epistemic properties, and so it is impossible to know or represent an object that did not possess these epistemic properties. To extend the metaphor further, every visible object must be, if it is to be seen, seen through the blue-tinted spectacles. There is, consequently, a strictly universal and necessary feature of every visible object, namely, being some shade of blue, which is analogous to any one of the epistemic properties, and so it is impossible to see an object that is not blue. Thus, the parallel between the blue spectacles and the Kantian *a priori* goes this far, and it goes a bit further. It is impossible to give any content to the concept of the far-side object. To give content to this concept, it is necessary to access the far-side object without the mediation of the blue-tinted spectacles. *Ex hypothesi*, however, such access is impossible, and so no content can be given to the concept of this object. In short, the concept of the far-side object is necessarily empty. In terms of the Kantian world picture, no content can be given to the concept of the distinct and representation-independent object. If it were possible to give content to this concept, it would be possible to access this object without in any way representing it. Such access is impossible, and so no content can be given to this concept. In short, the concept of the distinct and representation-independent object is necessarily empty.

There is another way in which the first version of Kant's argument fails, which reinforces the point just made. It might also be said that the idea of an object, which is opposed by both Kant and those who affirm that there are many actual worlds, is the idea of a distinct and representation-independent thing that necessitates the order and consistency of our representations or perceptions. Such an utterly distinct object is supposed to necessitate this order and consistency by being the orderly and consistent thing to which our experience corresponds. As Kant wrote:

> Now we find that our thought of the relation of all knowledge to its object carries with it an element of necessity; the object is viewed as that which [1] *prevents our modes of knowledge from being haphazard or arbitrary,* and which [2] *determines them* a priori *in some definite fashion.* For in so far as they are to relate to an object, they must [3] *necessarily agree with one another,* that is, must [4] *possess that unity which constitutes the concept of an object.*[58]

According to this idea, an object has at least two essential features. An object is (1) that which is distinct from and independent of our representations, and (2) that to which our representations correspond. An object consequently has four additional features. An object is (3) that which prevents our representations from being haphazard or arbitrary, (4) that which determines our representations (*a priori*) in some definite fashion, (5) that by virtue of which our representations cohere or agree with one another, and (6) that by virtue of which our representations possess that unity which constitutes the concept of an object, or directed to an object. How is it that such an account of what it is to be an object explains the order and consistency of the stream of consciousness? The essential idea of the realist's answer is that if our perceptions are perceptions of orderly, consistent, distinct, and perception-independent objects, they must themselves be orderly and consistent. On the one hand, there is an intuition to be had here, but this is, according to the stricter standard of logical validity, just a *non sequitur.* Why? Because, suppose that our perceptions are perceptions of orderly, consistent, distinct, and perception-independent things; not only does it not follow that our perceptions are themselves perception distinct, but it does not follow that our perceptions are themselves perception independent. It is not clear what sense can be made of the thesis that our perceptions are independent of our perceptions. *Mutatis mutandis,* it does not follow that our perceptions must themselves be orderly and consistent. It might be that the intuition can be developed in a manner that ameliorates the transgression of the logical standard in question, but I will not pursue this possibility here. On the other hand, the essential reason why this answer is wrongheaded is that it presupposes as much as it attempts to explain, to wit, that the objects that are distinct from our perceptions are themselves orderly and consistent. Let me explain this.

Consider, in the style of James's thought experiment, an ordinary object such as a book. Such an object is discovered through a series of perceptions over a period of time. An important fact of our common experience is that the turning of a page never precedes, or, at least, it has not yet preceded, the discovery that one's book is, after a long history of booklike behavior, a hippogryph or chimera. In other words, our perceptions of ordinary objects such as books are both orderly and consistent. What explains this? According to the answer in question here, it is because that which is discovered, or perceived, on the turning of each page, is a book that is both distinct from, and independent of, our perceptions of it. Perceptions are orderly and consistent, because they are directed to an orderly, consistent and distinct and representation-independent object. This, however, is hardly an explanation. If one's perceptions of a book could go awry, even the distinct and representation independent book in itself could go awry. In other words, if the turning of a page could precede the perception of something entirely fantastic, the book in itself might be such that its page aspects precede its fantastic aspects. Certain apparently chaotic trains of perceptions cannot be ruled out by appealing to an orderly and consistent book in itself, since this presupposes that such a book cannot conduct itself in chaotic manner. More generally, any reason to suspect the order and consistency of the stream of perception is, *mutatis mutandis*, a reason to suspect the order and consistency of supposedly distinct and representation-independent objects.

A similar point can be made about the unity of consciousness and the unity of the object. The essential idea is that if one is puzzled about the oneness of consciousness, one should also be puzzled about the oneness of the object. Both Kant and those who affirm that there are many actual worlds oppose the conception of what it is to be an object that underpins the supposition that the unity of consciousness is explained in terms of a unitary and representation-independent thing. Such an object is supposed to necessitate this unity by being the unitary thing to which our representations or perceptions correspond. The pivotal question is: How does such a conception of what it is to be an object explain the unity of the stream of consciousness? The realist answers that: Were our perceptions directed to some unitary thing,

they would themselves be unitary in the manner made clear—I hope—
by James's thought experiment. Although there is an intuition here,
this is just a *non sequitur.* As I noted above, even if our perceptions
were directed to perception-independent things, it would not follow
that our perceptions themselves would be perception-independent.
Mutatis mutandis, it does not follow from the premise that our perceptions are directed to a unitary thing that our perceptions must themselves be unitary. I will ignore the possibility that the relevant intuition
could be developed in a manner that ameliorates the *non sequitur.*
Instead, I will focus on the reason why this answer is wrongheaded,
namely, it presupposes as much as it attempts to explain, to wit, that
representation-independent objects are themselves unitary. Let me explain this.

In the case of James's thought experiment, an object, to wit, a
sentence, is discovered through a series of perceptions over a period of
time. The point of James's thought experiment is that these perceptions
possess a certain kind of unity. This raises two questions: (1) What is
this unity? and (2) What explains it? In the first stage of Kant's argument, the premise is that the nature of this unity is best understood in
terms of its explanation, and the essential idea is that there is a unitary
and perception-independent object, and the manifold of consciousness
is directed to it. In short, our perceptions possess the unity of James's
thought experiment because they are directed to an unitary and representation-independent object. In the context of the above-discussed
explanation of the presumed order and consistency of consciousness, I
noted that postulating an orderly and consistent object was hardly
an explanation. Similarly, postulating a unitary object is hardly an
explanation of the unity of consciousness. If the unity of our representations needs to be explained, the unity of the representation-
independent thing in itself also needs to be explained. In other words,
if the unity of our perceptions of the various aspects of some object
needs to be explained, the unity of these aspects also needs to be
explained. For example, if the unity of our perceptions of the various
words of some sentence needs to be explained, the unity of these words
also needs to be explained. The disunity of our perceptions cannot be
ruled out by appealing to the unity of an object in itself, since this
presupposes both that such an object is unified, and that it is obvious
what the object's unity is. Neither of these is obvious, however. Any

reason to think that the unity of consciousness needs to be explained is, *mutatis mutandis,* also a reason to think that the unity of objects in themselves needs to be explained.

Kant's alternative account of the order and consistency of the stream of perceptions, which he entitles the *transcendental unity of apperception,* shifts the conceptual focus from the concept of the *object* as it is in itself to the concept of *objectivity.* The basic idea is that an objective representation is one that stands in rule governed relations with other representations, and that objects are what objective representations represent. To say that representations are objective is to say that they are subject to a rule, and so it is necessary to connect them in some one definite manner; to say that representations necessarily stand in certain temporal relations is to say that they are objective. As Kant wrote:

> If we enquire what new character *relation to an object* confers upon our representations, what dignity they thereby acquire, we find that it results only in subjecting the representations to a rule, and so in necessitating us to connect them in some one specific manner; and conversely, that only in so far as our representations are necessitated in a certain order as regards their time relations do they acquire objective meaning [Bedeutung].[59]

Kant maintains, moreover, that objects must, on this analysis, have the third through the sixth of the features cited above, yet it need not be supposed that objects are either distinct, or that they are that to which our representations correspond. Although this shift is perhaps the most remarkable aspect of Kant's concept of an object, it is precisely this that I hope to appropriate in order to give sense to the thesis that there are many actual worlds.

The fact of the necessary emptiness of the concept of the utterly distinct and representation independent object provides the advocate of a plurality of actual worlds with at least a partial justification of Kant's alternative conception of what it is to be an object. Kant believed that his conception of what it is to be an object is justified because it delivers the desideratum of unique *a priori* knowledge, but the advocates of a plurality of actual worlds maintain that there is no unique *a priori,* or, in other words, there are many sets of categories. So, what motivates their acceptance of the Kantian conception of what it is to be an object? Here is one answer: it is the only coherent alternative to what is a necessarily empty account of what it is to be an object. What, however, is the Kantian alternative to conceiving of objects as distinct and representation-independent? Kant begins to answer this question in the second stage of the argument of the *Subjective Deduction*.

The argument of the first stage is, in short, flawed, and it is the aim of the subsequent stage to ameliorate it. In fact, the aim of each of the last three stages—or last four stages, if the *Second Analogy* is counted as a stage—is to both correct some flaw in the doctrine and the argument of the preceding stage, and to advance to a more adequate doctrine and argument. Be this as it may, at this point, I will assume that what has been said is sufficient to secure the thesis that the concept of the unique, utterly distinct, and representation-independent object is necessarily empty. Not only does the conception of such an object have no explanatory value, but there are then no unique, distinct and representation-independent objects. This is, I suppose, what Kant meant, when he wrote:

> That a concept, although itself neither contained in the concept of possible experience nor consisting of elements of a possible experience, should be produced completely *a priori* and should relate to an object, is altogether contradictory and impossible. For it would then have no content, since no intuition corresponds to it; and intuitions in general, through which objects can be given to us, constitute the field, the whole object, of possible experience.[60]

The importance of this is situated in its providing the advocate of a plurality of actual worlds with a justification for accepting Kant's alternative conception of what it is to be an object: it is the only coherent alternative to what is a necessarily empty account of what it is to be an object. This once again raises the question of what this alternative account is, and this, in turn, brings me back to my project of disentangling the Kantian account of what it is to be an object from the last three stages of the *Subjective Deduction*, and this brings me to the argument and doctrines of the second stage of this text.

There is an ambiguity in the explanation of the unity of consciousness that is offered in the first stage of the text at hand. First: one might say that the manifold of representations is unified because each representation is directed to an unique, distinct, and representation-independent object. Second: one might say that the manifold of representations is unified because each representation can be subsumed under a concept, namely, the concept of being directed to a unique, distinct, and representation-independent object. In other words, one might say that the manifold is unified because each of its elements can be subsumed under the concept of being of a unique and utterly distinct object. This is equivalent to saying the manifold of representations is unified because the concept of a unique and utterly distinct object applies to each of its elements, that is, each element of the manifold is a representation of a unique and utterly distinct object. Therefore, there are two incompatible explanations of the unity of the manifold: (1) because each representation is directed to a utterly distinct object, or (2) because each representation can be subsumed under a concept, namely, the concept of being directed to a utterly distinct object. These are two essentially different explanations. The difference here is between explaining the unity of the manifold of representations (1) in terms of something that is not itself a representation, namely, some utterly distinct object $= x$, and (2) in terms of something that is itself a representation, namely, the concept of being directed to some utterly distinct object. The second explanation contains the essence of the explanation of unity that is proffered in the second stage of the *Subjective Deduction*: the manifold of representations is unified because there is a concept that applies to every representation.

With just the addition of this as yet undeveloped account of unity, however, there is enough conceptual stuff to articulate and construct the argument of the second stage of the *Subjective Deduction*. A pivotal premise of this argument is that consciousness is one. Another premise is that there is only one alternative to explaining the unity of consciousness in terms of the transcendental object $= x$, to wit: the contents of consciousness are unified because they can be subsumed under a concept, namely, the concept of being directed to some object $= x$. In other words, consciousness is one because the manifold of representations can be subsumed under the concept of an object $= x$. Yet another premise is that the categories define the concept of an object $= x$, that is, they define the concept of being directed to an object. Moreover, since any representation that is directed to an object is *ipso facto* knowledge, any representation to which the categories apply is knowledge. So, since consciousness is one, the elements of the manifold of representations can be subsumed under the categories. Therefore, the contents of my consciousness constitute knowledge.

It is not clear what conception of an object is at work in this argument. Since the unity of the manifold of representations is explained in terms of something that is itself a representation, namely, the concept of being directed to some object, that is, the categories, it might seem that objects—transcendental or otherwise—become irrelevant or superfluous. This is not true. Although objects do not figure in the explanation of the oneness of consciousness, they do not thereby become irrelevant, but they do become secondary in the sense that what it is to be an object comes to be understood in terms of the manifold of representations that can be subsumed under the categories. This is the fundamental shift that I have hitherto sought. Instead of thinking of the unity of consciousness in terms of an utterly distinct object in itself, Kant thinks of the unity of consciousness in terms of the subsumption of our representations under the categories, and he thinks of objects in terms of what such representations represent.

There is a crude analogy between this and two ways of understanding the conceptual relationship between truth and reality. According to one understanding of the conceptual relationship between truth and reality, reality is conceptually prior to truth, and a true statement is a statement that corresponds to some segment of a representation independent reality. This is realism. According to an essentially different understanding of the conceptual relationship between truth and reality, truth is conceptually prior to reality, and reality is that to which all the true statements correspond. Analogously, although we intuitively think that time and space are conceptually prior to clocks and rulers, and that clocks and rulers measure some preexistent time and space, we might invert this conceptual relation, and think of clocks and rulers as conceptually prior to time and space. We might come to think that time and space are what clocks and rulers measure. In other words, we might think that time and space are defined in terms of clocks and rulers, and not vice versa.

There is, however, little or no reason to think that the categories define the concept of being directed to an object. So there is virtually no reason to believe that the categories define objectivity, that is, the concept of being directed to an object, and there is, in effect, no reason to believe that the second-stage explanation of the unity of consciousness succeeds. Most importantly, there is little or no reason to accept the conception of an object with which the argument of the second stage is entangled. Not much sense can be given to the idea of the fundamental shift of the second stage, and its concomitant conception of what it is to be an object, unless it is clear how subsumption under the categories unifies the manifold of representations. It cannot be the mere fact that there is a concept that applies to every element of the manifold, since there would then be many concepts that would unify the manifold, for example, the concept of being a representation. It seems clear that Kant would not have wanted to say that the manifold is unified because each of its elements is a representation. Here, to pursue the relevant conception of what it is to be an object, and to pursue the third stage of the *Subjective Deduction,* it is necessary to introduce an additional premise, which is the basis of Kant's analysis of the unity of consciousness. This most important premise is, as Kant wrote, that "a concept is always, as regards its form, something universal which serves as a rule."[61] In short, *a concept is a rule.*

The plan is to explain the unity of consciousness in terms of the notion of a rule and several notable features of rule-directed activities. If an activity is rule-directed, then (1) it proceeds, vis-à-vis some rule, correctly or incorrectly, (2) it has stages that are determined by some rule, and (3) it has stages that belong together by virtue of some rule, and that are set off from other events that may be accidentally conjoined with it. In other words, rule-directed activities (1) proceed correctly or incorrectly, (2) have stages, and (3) cohere. The last characteristic is the most important: rule-directed activities have stages that belong together, and that are set off from events with which they may be fortuitously federated. As Wolff writes:

> The third significant characteristic of a regulated activity is its coherence. All the parts or stages of the activity *belong together* by virtue of the rule, and are *set off* from other activities which may be accidentally associated with it, for example by occurring at the same time.[62]

Consider counting. It is a rule-directed activity that proceeds correctly or incorrectly. It has stages. Most importantly, there is a way that the activity of counting coheres, and is thereby one. In other words, counting has stages that belong together by virtue of a rule, namely, adding one, and that are set off from other events that may be accidentally associated with it, for example, tapping one's foot as one adds one.

The above-noted facts about rules are not sufficient to remedy the defects of the argument of the second stage, and so to develop that of the third stage. It is also necessary to distinguish two kinds of activity: there are activities that yield rules, and there are activities that yield something other than a rule. In the latter case, the activity is first-order. In the former case, if the activity yields a rule that directs a first-order activity, it is a second-order activity. More generally, if an activity yields a rule that directs an activity of the n-th order, it is an activity of the $n + 1$-th order. Corresponding to this hierarchy of activities, there is a hierarchy of rules. First-order rules direct first-order activities; second-order rules direct second-order activities; et cetera. I will, and need, only focus on first- and second-order rules. The pivotal point here is that this distinction between these first two orders of rules corresponds, or is identical with, Kant's distinction between empirical concepts and the categories. The distinction between first and second order rules is the distinction between empirical concepts and categories. In other words, empirical concepts are first-order rules, and the categories are second-order rules. It is now possible to give an account of the unity of consciousness upon which the argument of the third stage of the *Subjective Deduction* depends, and that will facilitate the explication of Kant's conception of what it is to be an object. Its basic idea is quite simple: the manifold of consciousness is one because its elements can be subsumed under a rule that unifies them.

As with the arguments of the first two stages of the *Subjective Deduction,* a pivotal premise of the argument of the third stage is that consciousness is one. Another premise is that consciousness is one because its elements—representations—can be subsumed under a rule that unifies them. Yet another premise is that the categories are, given the above analysis of the categories and rules, the rules for making the rules under which the manifold is subsumed. So the manifold of representations can be subsumed under the categories. Moreover, representations that can be subsumed under the categories, which are rules, stand in necessary relations with other representations. Thus, the manifold of representations stand in necessary relations with one other. Further, given the above analysis of knowledge, representations that stand in necessary relations with other representations are objective, that is, they are knowledge. So the manifold of representations are objective, that is, they are knowledge.

Kant ends the *Subjective Deduction* with a fourth argument that he thinks establishes the above-cited conclusion that "all appearances stand in a thoroughgoing connection according to necessary laws."[63] In short, the argument is this. Consciousness is one, and it is one because its elements can be subsumed under a rule. So the manifold of contents of my consciousness must be subsumable under a rule. By definition, however, a law just is a rule under which a manifold must be subsumed. Therefore, the contents of consciousness, that is, appearances, are connected by a necessary law. Be this as it may, given my aim of making sense of the thesis that there are many actual worlds and truths, it is more important to extract and articulate the Kantian conceptions of what it is to be an object and what it is to be a world that are intertwined with this argument.

What is an object? An object is not an utterly distinct thing in itself. The concept of such an object is necessarily empty, and so it can do no philosophical work. Moreover, if the objects of knowledge were utterly distinct, not only could there be no *a priori* knowledge, but there could be no empirical knowledge. As Kant wrote: "Should nature [the world] signify the existence of things in themselves, we could never cognize it either *a priori* or *a posteriori*."[64] Most importantly, given my aim in this work, utterly distinct objects don't help to make sense of the thesis that there are many actual worlds and truths. There are really two issues here. First, there is the question of what it is for a mental content to represent an object; second, there is the question of what it is to be an object. With respect to the former, Wolff writes:

> To say that mental content R represents object O is to say that R is one of a variety (= manifold) of mental contents which has been, or can be, reproduced in imagination according to the rule which is the concept of O.[65]

This is only a somewhat less lucid paraphrase of Kant's words, when he wrote:

> If we enquire what new character *relation to an object* confers upon our representations, what dignity they thereby acquire, we find that it results only in subjecting the representations to a rule, and so in necessitating us to connect them in some one specific manner.[66]

The idea here is simple: a representation refers to an object just when it can be subsumed under a rule—that itself conforms to the rules for rules, namely, the categories—that necessarily connects it with other representations. What, then, is an object? Let an objective representation be a representation that refers to an object, that is, a representation that can be subsumed under a rule—that conforms to the categories— that necessarily connects it with other representations. Then: something is an object just when it is represented by an objective representation. Now, it is just a short step to the relevant Kantian conception of a world: a world is just a sum of all objects, that is, a sum of all that is represented by some manifold of objective representations.

The pivotal question is this: How does this contribute to my project of making sense of the thesis that there are many actual worlds? To answer this question, I must introduce two additional premises. First: every representation is tensed. In other words, time is the form of consciousness. Second: every representing being is a practical being. These are not, I think, dubious premises. First, consider the import of the first. In conjunction with the conclusion of the fourth stage of the *Subjective Deduction,* it has an important consequence, namely, a world consists of a series of causally related events. In short, a world is necessarily temporal. This is the conclusion of the *Second Analogy.*

The argument of the *Second Analogy* has three premises: consciousness is one, consciousness is one because its elements can be subsumed under rules, and objective representations are exactly those that are, or can be, subsumed under rules. Obviously, then, the elements of the manifold of consciousness can be subsumed under rules. Now, since representations are tensed, the rules under which they are subsumed are themselves tensed, that is, they state that representations of one type temporally follow representations of some other type. Consequently, the elements of the manifold of consciousness have a temporal order that is imposed on them by virtue of their subsumption of tensed rules. In other words, since time is the form of consciousness, the elements of the manifold of my consciousness must possess a rule-determined temporal order. Now, an element of the manifold of consciousness is objective just when it falls under a rule that determines its place in a temporal sequence of representations. So, since objects, or events, are what objective representations represent, every event temporally follows another event according to a rule.

One consequence of this is that a world consists of all the events that possess an order that is imposed by tensed rules. Another consequence of this is that a time is a sequence of events that possesses an order that is imposed by tensed rules. To see the relevance of the second of the two premises that I noted above, it is necessary to distinguish between two kinds of time. This is the distinction between *isotropic* and *anisotropic* time. The former might be best explained by contrasting time with space. Disregarding the obvious empirical questions, space itself has no direction. North and south are but local directions, and the same is true for up and down. Although these oppositions may be defined in terms of the earth and its physical properties, they have no meaning outside the framework they can provide. To say that space is isotropic is to say that the contents of the universe and their physical properties do not define a spatial direction. To say that space is isotropic is to say that it has in and of itself no direction.

As space is isotropic, time is isotropic. To say that time is isotropic is to say that it has in itself no direction, that is, the contents of the universe and their physical properties do not provide a physical correlate for temporal direction. Thus, time is isotropic just when no criterion—physical or otherwise—can be given for the proposition that one event is before another. Although the quantity of chocolate is—in principle, I suppose—measurable, it is not true to say that one event, *A,* is earlier than another event, *B,* just when the quantity of chocolate at the time of *A* is less than the quantity of chocolate at the time of *B.* More generally, to say that time is isotropic is to say that there is no measurable feature of the world which is such that one event, *A,* is before another event, *B,* just when its quantity at the time of *A* is less than its quantity at the time of *B.* Now, time is anisotropic just when there is a correlate for the later than relation.

Let me make the following aside. It might seem that entropy is an essential part of the definition of the later than relation. It is not difficult to suppose that entropy is, at least in principle, a measurable feature of the world. So one might conjecture that one event, *A,* is later than another event, *B,* just when the quantity of entropy at the time of *A* is greater than the quantity of entropy at the time of *B.* Presumably, this is based on the second law of thermodynamics, to wit: "No change occurring in an isolated system can result in a decrease in the entropy of the system."[67] There are two problems with this. First, the above conjecture requires the space of events to be the entire universe, but it is not clear that the universe is an isolated system. The second problem is that the above is a crude version of the second law that has been supplanted by a statistical version, to wit: "A change occurring in an isolated system will most probably lead to a state of greater or equal entropy."[68] As Van Fraassen concludes, "we cannot simply define *later than* as the direction of change to higher entropy in most cases."[69] I do not know whether this is right. My aim is to note the issues raised by these considerations. Since they transcend the scope of this work, I will not pursue them here.

Now, time is anisotropic just when there is a determinable correlate for the *later than* relation. Even if physics cannot provide a correlate for this relation, it doesn't follow that there is no such correlate. Dilthey suggests that there is a determinable correlate for the temporal direction of human events. He wrote:

> [T]he parts of filled time are not only qualitatively different from each other but, quite apart from their content, have a different character according to whether we look from the present back to the past or forward to the future.[70]

The past can be regretted, but it cannot be the object of intention or purpose. The future can be the object of intention or purpose, but it cannot be regretted. Consequently, human events are such that there is a difference between past and future, and so there is a determinable correlate for the *later than* relation. To say this, however, is to say that human time, that is, the sequence of human events, is anisotropic.

Although Dilthey's observation establishes the fact that human time is anisotropic, it does not explain this fact. This is where the second premise, which I noted above, becomes relevant. Recall that this is the premise that every representing being is a practical being. Or, in other words, every representing being is a purposive being. Crudely put, the idea here is that purposes impose an anisotropic structure on time.[71] A purposive being sets out to get things done, and there is, therefore, always a distinction between things done and things to be done. Consequently, when a purposive being represents itself, its representation will always be asymmetrically divisible into at least two parts. A world consists of all the temporally ordered sequences of events that are the senses of some manifold of objective representations. Moreover, a time just is such a sequence of events. Thus, since a representing being is a purposive being, the time within which a representing being exists is anisotropic.

To draw my conclusion that there are many actual worlds, it is necessary to add one last premise: Not all representing beings have the same purposes. If different representative beings set out to get different things done, the times within which they exist will be asymmetrically divided in different ways. Consequently, since each time will be structurally different, they will not be congruent, and so they will not be the same. In other words, since there are many purposes, there are many times. Since a world is a sum of what is in a time, there are many actual worlds. Now, since each such world is the sum of what is represented by some manifold of objective representations, each such world has a complete description, and so there are many truths.

The preceding argument has taken my reader down a long and tortuous road. So, it may serve my readers well, if I repeat the summary that I presented at the beginning of this essay.

1. There are many representing beings. [Premise]

2. The set of representing beings partitions into many non-empty classes. [Premise]

3. For each such class of representing beings, there is a set of purposes, and each set of purposes is incompatible with every other such set. [Premise]

4. For each class of representing beings, there is an ideal sum of representations that has an asymmetric structure that is imposed by the set of purposes that is associated with the class of representing beings in question. [Premise]

5. There is no ideal sum of representations that includes or subsumes all the ideal sums of representations that are associated with the various classes of representing beings. [3,4]

6. There are many ideal sums of representations. [2,4,5]

7. For each ideal sum of representations, there is an actual world. [Premise]

8. There are many actual worlds. [6,7]

9. There are many truths. [6,8]

With this, I can now turn to social theoretic concerns.

V
Toward the Social Theoretic

There are many actual worlds, and there are many truths. A world is a structure of objects, and an object is what a manifold of objective representations represents. Objectivity is a temporal relation among representations, and representations are collectively produced by groups of subjects that share purposes that impose an asymmetry on this relation.[1] There is a very basic problem with this picture. It entails that objects are representation dependent, and this seems empirically falsifiable. It seems that there is just one world, and it seems that the world consists of objects that are independent of our perceptions, thoughts, and desires, our representations. If we bracket the question of the reality of the world of everyday life, and if we focus on the way it presents itself in experience, we will discern just this. Berger and Luckmann described it well:

> I apprehend the reality of everyday life as an ordered reality. Its phenomena are prearranged in patterns that seem to be independent of my apprehension of them and that impose themselves upon the latter. The reality of everyday life appears already objectified, that is, constituted by an order of objects that have been designated as objects before my appearance on the scene.[2]

The employment of the first person singular, which is the result, I think, of their commitment to the phenomenological method, is not necessary. The point, which I assume to be equivalent to this description, is that we experience our worlds as *the* world, as disarticulated, as independent of our representations, as constraining our representations, as having existed before us, and as something that will continue to exist after us. In other words, we experience the objects of our worlds as the only objects, as making the world's disarticulation manifest, as independent of our beliefs and desires, as preventing belief from being sufficient for truth, as having existed before us, and things that will continue to exist after us. Since my picture entails that objects are representation-dependent, there is clearly something wrong with my picture.

The problem at hand is analogous to the problem with the astronomical version of the Copernican revolution: Since the cosmological theory requires the earth to move, and we experience the earth as stationary, or what is the same, the earth appears to be unmoving, there must be something wrong with the astronomy. The metaphysical problem is that since my picture requires objects to be representation-dependent, and they are experienced as representation-independent, there is something wrong with this picture. In the physical case, the response to the objection is that the appearance of the earth as unmoving is an illusion, and in the metaphysical case, the answer is, I think, that the appearance of the objects within our worlds as representation-independent is likewise an illusion, which I shall call *metaphysical illusion*. If there were, within the framework of my picture, a way to explain metaphysical illusion, that is, a way to explain why representation-dependent objects seem to be representation-independent, there would also be a solution to the problem in question.

To begin to see my solution to this problem, consider that since objectivity is a temporal relation among representations, and representations are collectively produced by classes of subjects that share purposes that impose an asymmetry on this relation, every object is a social object. Thus, the apparently purely metaphysical problem above is identical with the following. Social objects are constructed in the sense that each is identical with what is represented by a manifold of objective and collectively produced representations. However, most social objects are such that belief is not sufficient for truth, that is, they are experienced as if they are representation-independent, that is, socially constructed objects are experienced as if they are not social constructs. In short, social objects have the ontological status that I maintain every object has, and yet they are experienced as representation-independent.[3] Thus, my view of the ontological status of social objects, that is, all objects, is also empirically refuted. Moreover, the above metaphysical problem is a social-theoretic problem, and a solution to the social-theoretic problem is available just when there is a solution to the metaphysical problem. In other words, since all objects are social, there are two questions. (1) Why are socially constructed objects experienced as unconstructed? (2) Why are representation-dependent things experienced as representation-independent? An answer to either is an answer to the other. From this perspective, there is also an illusion, which I designate by *social illusion,* and which is identical with metaphysical illusion. More importantly, if there were, from the standpoint of my picture, a way to explain social illusion, that is, a way to explain why social constructs are experienced as if they are not constructed, there would not only be a solution to the problem at hand, but there would be a solution to this problem in both its forms. Here is an answer that focuses on the social-theoretic form.

On the one hand, Berger and Luckmann forthrightly tell us that "reality is socially constructed."[4] On the other hand, they unquestionably maintain that socially constructed realities are experienced by their constructors as unconstructed. They have written that "man is capable of producing a world that he then experiences as something other than a human product."[5] What explains this? A fundamental premise of Berger and Luckmann's explanation is that when two agents interact, each forms habits with respect to the other's behavior. They explain this sort of formation in terms of the conservation of the energy that would otherwise be required to decide what to do, and the reduction of the tension that would result in not being able to anticipate what will be done. Whatever may be the case with this reduction of habit to the economies of energy and tension, they maintain that such habits are the basis of the social construction of reality. In the case of habits formed in the context of such interactions, the resulting institutions or social realities exist in a merely nascent state, and it is only when others are initiated into such habituated behaviors, or when these habits are passed on to others, that institutions exist in a fully developed form. This distinction between the nascent and the fully developed leads Berger and Luckmann to a trichotomy that is the framework of their explanation of the apparently unconstructed character of social constructs. They maintain that there is a distinction between the ways that institutions are experienced by those who originate them and those who are initiated into them, and that there is also a distinction between the ways institutions are experienced by their originators before and after they initiate others. Thus, there are three cases, and it is in their analysis that Berger and Luckmann's account of the apparently unconstructed character of social constructs emerges.

First, there are those who can remember engaging in various behaviors until some subset of them became habitual. For these persons, the nascent institutions that are constituted by these habitual behaviors are experienced for what they are, namely, contingent constructs.[6] Berger and Luckmann write:

> Although the routines, once established, carry within them a tendency to persist, the possibility of changing them or even abolishing them remains at hand in consciousness. . . . [S]ince they themselves have shaped this world in the course of a shared biography which they can remember, the world thus shaped appears fully transparent to them.[7]

There is, in this case, a conflict between memory and habit, and the force of habit essentially fails to overcome the power of memory to reveal routinized behavior as a contingent construct, and they are, therefore, transparent. Consequently, habitual behaviors will be experienced as contingent, and they will only be, at most, nascent social realities. Second, there are the children of these same persons. For them, the behaviors in question have never been otherwise. Consequently, there are no memories that can reveal the contingency of routinized behaviors, and there are no memories that the force of habit can fail to overcome. So, the children experience their habituated behaviors as necessary and unconstructed, and they are, therefore, opaque. Third, there are the persons of the first case after they have parented the children of the second case. Parenting increases the power of habit in such a way that it can now overcome the power of memory to reveal the contingency of routinized behavior. What was once transparent becomes opaque. Berger and Luckmann write: "The objectivity of the institutional world 'thickens' and 'hardens,' not only for the children, but (by a mirror effect) for the parents as well."[8] They also remark that "the process of transmission simply strengthens the parent's sense of reality if only because, to put it crudely, if one says, 'This is how these things are done,' often enough one believes it oneself."[9] These persons of the third kind, parents, now experience these routinized behaviors as necessary and unconstructed, even though they were once experienced as contingent constructs.

In sum, when habits can be checked by sufficiently strong memories, social realities are experienced as contingent constructs; when habits cannot be checked by memories, because there are none or because they are too weak, social realities are experienced as necessary and unconstructed. Berger and Luckmann conclude that the basic mechanism that explains the unconstructed or necessary character of social constructs is habit unchecked by memory. I think that there are four reasons to doubt the adequacy of this explanation. (1) Habit cannot do the work that Berger and Luckmann want it to do. (2) It conflicts with Berger and Luckmann's view of the ontological status of social realities. (3) It is a *non sequitur.* (4) It does not work within the framework of their ontology.

First, habit cannot do the work that Berger and Luckmann want it to do. To see this, consider language. A fundamental fact about our use of language is that it is creative. Noam Chomsky traces this notion to the ostensibly Cartesian idea that we have the "ability to form new statements which express new thoughts and which are appropriate to new situations."[10] That is, we continuously produce and understand sentences that have meanings and grammatical structures that differ from those of any sentence that we have ever heard. If habit is to explain some instance of our creative use of language, we must have previously heard many sentences that have its meaning or grammatical structure. Given the very essence of the creative use of language, however, we cannot have heard such sentences. So, habit cannot explain creative linguistic behavior. Thus, the explanatory scope of habit is somewhat limited. Berger and Luckmann do not make a case for the explanatory applicability of habit in the case of the unconstructed character of social constructs, and so there is some reason to doubt their explanation, but not much. However, there is a more direct reason to doubt that habit can explain this character.

A fundamental fact about our social behavior is that it is also creative. We constantly engage in unprecedented social behaviors. If this does not seem evident, consider that the effective paradigm of social behavior is the creative use of language. Moreover, since social behaviors are constituted by creative linguistic representations, and given the metaphysical apparatus of the above discussion, social behaviors are themselves creative. Given that social behavior is creative, however, we cannot have previously engaged in such behaviors, and, therefore, habit cannot explain it. Thus, there is more reason to doubt Berger and Luckmann's explanation of the unconstructed character of social constructs. But, it does not follow that habit cannot explain this character of social realities, unless creative social behaviors, and so social realities, are both constructed and experienced as unconstructed. What reasons are there to believe that this condition obtains? One is that social realities are constructs, and that their phenomenology reveals that not only are they experienced as unconstructed, but they are also unprecedented and, consequently, creative. Another is that the social realities that are experienced as unconstructed are constructed by creative linguistic representations. So, this condition obtains, and habit cannot explain the unconstructed character of social constructs.

Second, Berger and Luckmann's explanation of the unconstructed character of social objects conflicts with their view of the ontological status of these objects. With regard to the latter, they maintain that not only are social realities constructed by collective behavior, but they will continue to exist only if the collective behaviors that construct them continues. If we were to stop doing the things that constitute some social object, it would cease to exist; that is, social objects lack ontological inertia. They write:

> [S]ocial order is a human product, or, more precisely, an ongoing human production. . . . Social order is not part of the "nature of things," and it cannot be derived from the "laws of nature." Social order exists *only* as a product of human activity. No other ontological status may be ascribed to it without hopelessly obfuscating its empirical manifestations. Both in its genesis (social order is the result of past human activity) and its existence in any instant of time (social order exists only and insofar as human activity continues to produce it) it is a human product.[11]

This view about the ontological status of social realities conflicts with Berger and Luckmann's conclusion that the mechanism that explains the unconstructed or necessary character of social constructs is habit unchecked by memory. On the one hand, when habit can be checked by sufficiently strong memories of the construction of some social reality, this reality will be experienced as a contingent construct. On the other hand, however, a socially constructed reality will seem to be unconstructed, when habit cannot be checked by memory. Moreover, there are at least two ways in which habit can go unchecked by memory: either when (i) memory is too weak or when (ii) there is no memory. To see the conflict, consider that: if social reality is a human product, and it continues to exist only and insofar as the members of some group continue to produce it, then there are no moments when there is no memory of its production.

For example, suppose that I was a part of the process of working out how the children should enter the local grammar school, and that it was decided that there should be one line for each of seven grades, and that the line of kindergartners should enter through the main door first, the first graders should be the second group to pass through, and so on. Berger and Luckmann would expect that since I can remember its construction, I will experience this door-entering institution as a contingent construct. However, if my son comes to attend this school, which is now partly composed of the door-entering institution that I had part in constructing, they would expect that since he did not participate in the construction of this institution, he cannot remember its construction, and so he will experience it as unconstructed and necessary, as if it were a part of the natural world. But, given their view of the ontological status of this institution, if my son experiences this door-entering institution at all, he must have been present at its construction, which in this case must be a reconstruction. So he did participate in the construction of the institution that he experiences as unconstructed. So he is not in a cognitive state that is relevantly different from mine, and that necessitates that his experience of the door-entering institution will be fundamentally different from mine, that is, as necessary and unconstructed. It is not that Berger and Luckmann's general principle—those who are absent from the construction of a social reality will experience it as an unconstructed necessity—is false. Instead, it is otiose, and it cannot explain why social constructs seem unconstructed. Since social realities must be continuously constructed, lest they cease to exist, the only social realities that one can experience, and so the only social realities that can seem to be unconstructed necessities, are exactly the social realities whose production one must have been able to witness. Social objects do not possess ontological inertia, that is, it is not that once a social object is constructed, it continues to exist independently of the actions and efforts of social agents. Therefore, if one experiences a social reality as an unconstructed necessity, one must be present at its construction, because if one were not so present, the putative social reality would not be an experienced social reality. Thus, I must have witnessed the construction of any social reality that I experienced as an unconstructed necessity, and so Berger and Luckmann's explanation of the social-theoretic illusion at hand fails.

Third, Berger and Luckmann's explanation of the social illusion that social constructs seem unconstructed is a *non sequitur.* They maintain that if we do not experience the production of a social reality, the habit that constructs it cannot be mnemonically checked, and so we will experience it as unconstructed. Why should habit unchecked by memory necessitate this kind of experience? There is a gap between unchecked habit and this particular quality of the experience of social constructs. Why is it that if one is absent from the construction of some social reality, then one will experience this reality as if it were not socially constructed? Why must one experience habit constituted artifacts as necessary? Why does not one experience them as arbitrary and contingent? To continue the above example of our grammar school, the children enter the building in an order that was determined by actions that were performed years before any child in question was born, and yet, *pace* Berger and Luckmann, some children are utterly amazed at the arbitrariness of this procedure, and consequently they do not experience this part of the institution as objective or necessary. There are, I think, many examples of habitual behaviors that are not experienced as necessary, unconstructed or natural. Instead, they are experienced as boring, contingent, and in need of being bested. Thus, since the quality of our experience of social constructs is variable, we ought not to infer that we will experience some social reality as either necessary or contingent from the premise that it was formed before our births. Therefore, Berger and Luckmann have not explained the unconstructed character of socially constructed realities.

Last, Berger and Luckmann's explanation of social or metaphysical illusion does not rest on their insight into the ontological status of the social, and consequently, it needlessly appeals to psychological mechanisms that are doubtful with respect to their theoretical efficacy. My explanation of metaphysical or social illusion has the virtue that it does work within the framework of what I take to be the ontological status of all objects, that is, all objects are what is represented by an ideally completable manifold of objective and collectively producible representations.

The case in which the earth seems to be unmoving provides a context in which to explain what a general account of metaphysical or social illusion must do. The Copernican theory entails that even though the earth appears to be unmoving, it moves. In order to adequately respond to the ostensible empirical refutation of the theory by this appearance, it is necessary to establish two things. First, it is necessary to show that the earth does move, and second, it is necessary to show that given both the facts of the matter and the relevant physical theory, the earth must appear to be unmoving. Similarly, current theory about light and color entails that even though the sky appears to be blue, it is not blue. Why should not one take this to be an empirical refutation of this theory? If the theory entails that the sky is not blue, and when one looks, it is blue, then one should conclude that the theory is false. The proponent of such a theory of color and light must do two things to adequately respond to this sort of objection. First, she must show that the sky is not blue, and second she must establish that given some assumed facts about color perception and the composition of the sky, the sky must seem to be blue. Now, in the case of a social theory that entails that social objects are constructed, even when they are experienced as if they are not constructed, it is necessary to do two similar things, if it is to adequately respond to the charge that this theory is empirically refuted. First, it is necessary to show that social objects are constructed, and second, it is necessary to show that given the relevant facts about social construction, social objects must appear as if they were not constructed. The relevant fact here, which Berger and Luckmann fail to utilize, is that an object, that is, a social object, is identical with a manifold of collectively produced and objective representations.

Most of the preceding text has aimed at showing that objects are, in short, constructed.[12] This is not, therefore, the unfulfilled part of responding to the charge that constructivist theories of social objects are empirically refuted by the fact that these objects are experienced as representation-independent or unconstructed. The lacking part of this task lies in showing that if social objects, that is, objects *simpliciter,* have the ontological status that I have ascribed to them, then they must appear as if they were not socially constructed. A necessary foretask is to describe this appearance, and to some extent, this has already been done. I have already pointed out that the experience of the unconstructed character of social objects amounts to the following: we experience the objects of our worlds as the only objects, as making the world's disarticulation manifest, as independent of our beliefs and desires, as preventing assertion from being sufficient for truth, as having existed before us, and things that will continue to exist after us. Thus, the experience of the unconstructed character of social objects is made manifest in at least four ways. First, it seems that they are the only objects. Second, it seems that they are the way that the world's disarticulation is made manifest. As Plato suggested, the way that the world divides into objects is the way that it is *cut at the joints,* that is, the way that the world is disarticulated. In his *Phaedrus,* Plato has Socrates assert that we do two things about the nature of which it would be good to have a systematic knowledge or art. The first is "seeing together things that are scattered about everywhere and collecting them into one kind."[13] The second is "to be able to cut up each kind according to its species along its natural joints, and to try not to splinter any part, as a bad butcher might do."[14] Plato has kinds, species and genera, in mind here, and I am thinking of objects, but given a sufficiently wide conception of *object,* this second desideratum amounts to a possession of a systematic grasp of the nature of the way that the world can be divided into objects that corresponds to transcendentally real cuts, that is, that corresponds to the world's joints, and not to splinter the world, as a bad butcher might do. Of course, I do not accept the idea that there is a unique world that has transcendentally real cuts. My point is that each apparently unique world also appears to be transcendentally cut. Objects seem to be divided from one another as a matter of the representation independent way of a world that appears to be the world. Third, objects seem to be independent of our beliefs and desires, that is, belief is not sufficient for truth. Fourth, objects seem to have existed before us, and it seems that they will exist after us. The task of showing that given the relevant account of the constructive social processes, social objects must seem to be unconstructed, is equivalent to the task of showing that given that social objects have the ontological status that I have ascribed to them, they will appear in these four ways.

Consider, then, the first way that socially constructed objects are experienced, that is, as if they are the only objects. The premise here is that these objects are identical with what a manifold of collectively produced representations represent, and the conclusion is that they must seem to be the only objects. How does this conclusion follow from this premise? Suppose that something seemed to be an object that could not be represented by any class of objective representations. In other words, suppose that something was the object of a representation, a thought or a perception, that could not be synthesized with at least some representations that are taken to be objective. This representation would not be objective. It would be subjective. Insofar as it would fail to be veridical, its putative object would be no object at all, and this contradicts the above supposition. Thus, anything that appears to be an object must seem to be among the only objects.

Now, consider the second way in which social objects seem to be unconstructed, that is, it seems that these objects are the way in which the world's disarticulation is made manifest, that is, such objects are experienced as divided from one another. This man is experienced as something that is different from that horse. *Ex hypothesi,* both this man and that horse are what is represented by a manifold of objective representations. Now, in this work, I have assumed that every object constituting representation has a structure that is captured by the first-order predicate calculus. In the case of perceptions, such a representation corresponds to a perceptual judgment, and in the case of a thought, it also corresponds to a judgment. In either case, however, I assume that the relevant structure is captured by this logic. This is a revisable assumption, but I shall not here consider how it might be revised. It follows, I think, that something is an object of an objective representation just when it quantifies over it. This quantificational apparatus only works in a context in which there are identity conditions for the objects that are taken to be the values of the tacitly supposed bound variables. If a representation is objective, what it represents, its entities, must have identities.[15] Where there are such identity conditions, however, the objects that are supposed to be the values of the bound variables will appear to be distinct from one another. Thus, any socially constructed object will appear to be distinct from every other socially constructed object, and any socially constructed object will make the world's disarticulation manifest.

There is a third way in which socially constructed objects seem to be unconstructed, that is, merely asserting one of them to be some way is not sufficient for its being this way. In other words, one of the ways in which socially constructed objects seem to be unconstructed is that with regard to them, mere assertion is not sufficient for truth. In other words, socially constructed objects are experienced as unconstructed, if they seem to constrain assertion. I have already discussed this above, when I discussed Protagoras. Protagoras maintained that the world of Socrates is, for example, the aggregate of whatever appears to him, and since perception is the principal mode of appearance, his world is the aggregate of what he perceives. Moreover, the assertion *the wind is cold* is true for Socrates just when the wind that appears to Socrates is cold, or the wind perceived by Socrates is cold. So, if the wind that appears to Socrates is cold, the assertion that the wind is not cold is not sufficient for it to be true for him. In other words, to assert something is not *ipso facto* to assert something true. Now, a world's objects are, I maintain, all the things that would be represented by an ideal manifold of objective representations, and a representation is objective just when it stands in rule governed relations with other representations. To continue the above example, the wind is what is represented by a manifold of collectively produced and objective representations. The assertion *the wind is cold* is true for some member of this collective just when the wind that is the object of some manifold of objective representations is represented as cold. Thus, if someone merely asserts that the wind is not cold, then since this assertion need not be among the manifold of objective representations that constitutes the wind, it need not be true. Socially constructed objects constrain assertion, and given the ontological status that I think they possess, they should be experienced as representation independent in this third way in which the experience of independence is made manifest.

Fourthly and lastly, a way in which socially constructed objects seem to be unconstructed is that they seem to have existed before us, and it seems that they will exist after us. Once again, the premise is that an object is what is represented by a manifold of collectively produced and objective representations. Given the additional and already mentioned premise that representations are tensed, and that some representations are tensed in such a manner that they represent objects as existing when we do not, it follows directly that some socially constructed objects will seem to exist when we do not. In order for an object to seem to exist when we do not, it is sufficient for there to be an objective representation that is tensed or dated with a time when we do not exist, and since objectivity is a relation among representations, it is obvious how there could be such a representation. This completes the task of showing that given that social objects have the ontological status that I have ascribed to them, they will appear in the four ways just described. However, given the identity between this task and the task of showing that given the relevant account of the social construction of reality, especially the often-repeated premise about their ontological status, social objects must seem to be unconstructed, the latter task is also completed. This, moreover, not only shows that constructivist views of social objects are not subject to empirical refutation by virtue of the experience of them as unconstructed, but it also constitutes an explanation of social or metaphysical illusion.

Some of the further significance of the analogy with which I began this discussion of social or metaphysical illusion should now be more perspicuous. Such illusion is analogous to the illusion associated with the astronomical version of the Copernican revolution that the relevant cosmological theory requires the earth to move, and yet we experience the earth as unmoving. Insofar as this experience is the basis of an objection to this physical theory, the correct response is that the appearance of the earth as unmoving is an illusion, and that in the metaphysical case, the response is, I think, that the appearance of objects within our worlds as representation independent is likewise an illusion. Now, this analogy not only functions to introduce a difficult problem with my explanation of my thesis that there are many actual worlds and truths, but it also functions to bring out the more general character of my solution or explanation of this problem. In general terms, metaphysical illusion is the phenomenon that an object, which is identical with what an ideally complete manifold of objective representations represents, is experienced as if it is representation-independent. That is, representation-dependent objects are experienced as representation-independent. Metaphysical illusion is social-theoretic illusion, because since every object is a social object, it is the phenomenon that socially constructed objects are experienced as if they are not social constructs. The earth seems to be unmoving because of a relation between it, its motion and us. I will not attempt to articulate the details of this explanation here, but in general, it is clear that the earth appears to be unmoving because of a relation that it bears to other things. Generally, the representation-independent character of objects that are constituted by some manifold of objective representations is an artifact of the relation that these representations must bear to one another by virtue of their being objective, and they must stand in these relations, if they are to constitute any objects whatsoever. Such an analogy does not explain social or metaphysical illusion, but it does serve to make my explanation more comprehensible. To add to this intelligibility, I will now turn to a case that illustrates my broadly sketched explanation.

There is an extraordinary and remarkable case of social or metaphysical illusion in Foucault's *The Order of Things*.[16] That is, it is a paradigm of representation-dependent objects seeming to be representation-independent.[17] Foucault tells us about the Italian naturalist, Aldrovandi, who wrote a treatise called *Historia serpentum et draconum*. This treatise contained a chapter entitled "On the Serpent in General." It included the following headings:

> equivocation (which means the various meanings of the word *serpent*), synonyms and etymologies, differences, form and description, anatomy, nature and habits, temperature, coitus and generation, voice, movements, places, diet, physiognomy, antipathy, sympathy, modes of capture, death and wounds caused by the serpent, modes and signs of poisoning, remedies, epithets, denominations, prodigies and presages, monsters, mythology, gods to which it is dedicated, fables, allegories and mysteries, hieroglyphics, emblems and symbols, proverbs, coinage, miracles, riddles, devices, heraldic signs, historical facts, dreams, simulacra and statues, use in human diet, use in medicine, miscellaneous uses.[18]

To us, this mixture seems capricious and unnecessary. To Buffon, an eighteenth-century French natural historian, it seemed similarly unnecessary. About this passage, he remarked: "Let it be judged after that what proportion of natural history is to be found in such a hotch-potch of writing. There is no description here, only legend."[19] Thus, in Aldrovandi's world, a veridical expression of the knowledge of the serpent *überhaupt* must include some three dozen or more divisions, and in Buffon's world, such a fanciful mélange just is not knowledge.

Although Aldrovandi saw his divisions as a necessary part of what it is to know the serpent, and Buffon saw them as an arbitrary and contingent hotch-potch that could not be knowledge, they had something in common. Both Aldrovandi and Buffon experienced these divisions as having a modality, and although the modality experienced by the former is not the modality experienced by the latter, each experienced his respective modality as representation-independent. Moreover, these modalities are representation-dependent in the sense that each is an artifact of the ideally completable manifold of objective representations that constitutes the known or knowable objects of their respective worlds.[20] Thus, since Aldrovandi and Buffon experienced their respective representation-dependent modalities as representation-independent, they both suffered from social or metaphysical illusion. In what follows, I will focus on Aldrovandi's and Buffon's modal perceptions as instances of metaphysical illusion, and I will offer an account of just these perceptions, or, in other words, of just the phenomenon of these transcendentally ideal modalities seeming to be transcendentally real, which I expect to be able to serve as a paradigm for accounting for other instances in which constituted objects are experienced as if they are not constituted. As I display my account, which employs the metaphysical apparatus of my preceding chapters, I will present more of the detail of the case of Aldrovandi and Buffon as described by Foucault. My aim will be to provide a systematic *misreading* of Foucault's description that shows how the representations that constitute the objects of the worlds of Aldrovandi and Buffon differ in such a way that what seemed necessary to Aldrovandi seemed arbitrary and contingent to Buffon, or, what is the same, what seemed contingent to Buffon seemed necessary to Aldrovandi. As with my readings of Kant, Quine, and others, my aim is not to get Foucault right, but to get a more secure grasp on what I think is right.[21]

Foucault's account of the differences between Aldrovandi and Buffon depends on his well-known theoretical concept of an *episteme*. He thought that what it is to be knowledge varies with historical period. This is not the quotidian claim that what people think they know varies with historical period. Foucault's point is not that at different times, people take different things to be known, although I think that he would have thought this to be true; instead his point is that at different times, what it is to know is fundamentally different, and consequently, over time, the things that seem to be known are themselves fundamentally different. Foucault maintained that what it is to be knowledge during each historical period depends on three conceptions. It depends on (i) a conception of the basic ways in which things are ordered, and on (ii) a conception of the signs used to express various known truths. Since the signs used to articulate these truths are linguistic, what knowledge is during a historical period also depends on (iii) a conception of language. Three such conceptions together constitute an *episteme*. Now, according to Foucault, the inevitability that Aldrovandi perceived in his subdivisions, and the contingency that Buffon perceived in them, are artifacts of their respective epistemes. Thus, his archaeological explanation of the relevant modalities depends on what he took their epistemes to be. What are their epistemes? How do they account for these modalities?

According to Foucault's account of the episteme in which Aldrovandi participated, which extended over the sixteenth and seventeenth centuries, the most fundamental way in which things are ordered is resemblance, and moreover it assumes four principal forms, namely, convenience, emulation, analogy, and sympathy. With regard to convenience, Foucault quotes Porta:

> As with respect to its vegetation the plant stands convenient to the brute beast, so through feeling does the brutish animal to man, who is conformable to the rest of the stars by his intelligence; these links proceed so strictly that they appear as a rope stretched from the first cause as far as the lowest and smallest of things, by a reciprocal and continuous connection; in such wise that the superior virtue, spreading its beams, reaches so far that if we touch one extremity of that cord it will make tremble and move all the rest.[22]

What could Porta have had in mind here? We get a glimpse of his meaning, if we take into account the fundamental conception of the order of things that is at work in this passage. Things are ordered by resemblance, and the particular form that is pertinent here is convenience, which is explained in terms of spatial proximity. Two things resemble one another in the mode of convenience insofar as they occupy the same region, and vice versa. In this passage, Porta is telling us that since plants and beasts are spatially proximate, that is, one is located next to the other, they resemble one another in the mode of convenience. Moreover, since the beasts and man occupy the same taxonomic space, that is, they both feel, they too resemble one another in this mode. And, since man and the stars also occupy the same space in the sense that his intellect is in a way the stars, they too resemble one another in the mode of convenience. Thus, the plants, the beasts, man, and the stars are all connected by virtue of this form of resemblance, namely, convenience. Thus, convenience relates everything to everything else, and so it is as if a rope or cord or string bound all to all; to tug any one end is to tug at everything else in the universe.

In asking the initial question of the preceding paragraph, and in pursuing Porta's meaning, I am intentionally ignoring Foucault's methodological supposition that the focus of his archaeological digs is neither some mental content, nor the meanings of various statements. The focus is a manifold of statements that are the product of what might be described as an archaeological reduction, which is analogous to or extends Husserl's phenomenological reduction of the existential import or truth of statements in that it also brackets their meaning. Foucault intended to treat Porta's statement as a move in a game, and he intended to discover the rules that rendered this move legitimate, or, in other words, that make it possible, not to discover what subjective suspicions may have motivated the move. My intention *per se* is not to discover the move legitimating rules of Porta's game, or that of Aldrovandi. My aim is to find the categories, the objectivity conferring relations among representations, that enable us to have a sense of the way that Porta and Aldrovandi experienced their world. Foucault's archaeology is a means to this end, even though it may be incompatible with it. That these categories are not Buffon's categories is rooted, I think, in a difference in their respective purposes, but here I need not pursue my analysis to this depth, since my goal is to display the manner in which Porta, *et alia*, may have experienced a world that is fundamentally other than the world experienced by Buffon and his peers. An analysis that merely discloses their epistemic differences is sufficient for this. Again, my aim is to make sense of metaphysical illusion, and in a world in which there is neither existential import or truth, nor meaning, it might seem that there couldn't be any such illusion. However, even in a world that purports to be *sans* existence and *sans* essence, it must seem that Aldrovandi's moves are vis-à-vis Buffon arbitrary or contingent, and Buffon's moves vis-à-vis Aldrovandi are also impossible insofar as they are unimaginable. To each, these modalities must seem to be a part of the world as it is in itself, and not the result of various methodological decisions. Thus, even in an archaeological world, there is social or metaphysical illusion, and there is, with respect to it, the problem of what explains it. My version of this explanation depends on my appropriation of Foucault's description of the differences between Aldrovandi and Buffon.

A second mode of resemblance is emulation, which is unlike convenience in that it does not depend on proximity. One example of emulation is the relation that a face bears to its mirror image; this is easy to understand. Other examples are the relations between the human face and the sky, and our eyes and the moon and the sun. What emulates what here? Inquiries into the direction of any number of pairs of such items undoubtedly made up the substance of many renaissance research proposals. Foucault quotes Crollius:

> The stars are the matrix of all the plants and every star in the sky is only the spiritual prefiguration of a plant, such that it represents that plant, and just as each herb or plant is a terrestrial star looking up at the sky, so also each star is a celestial plant in spiritual form, which differs from the terrestrial plants in matter alone . . . , the celestial plants and herbs are turned towards the earth and look directly down upon the plants they have procreated, imbuing them with some particular virtue.[23]

As with Porta, we begin to understand Crollius, when we read him in the light of the fundamental conception of the order of things that structures this passage, and in particular, in the light of the conception of emulation. It is not clear when one thing emulates another, but part of the relation involves the possibility of thinking of one in terms of the other. So, the stars and the plants resemble one another in such a way that one can think of each plant as a terrestrial star that looks up to the sky, and one can think of each star as a celestial plant that has a spiritual form and that differs from the terrestrial plants only in regard to the matter out of which it is composed. This is only part of it. It is not clear whether the terrestrial stars are to be thought of as turned up to the sky and looking upon the stars that they have procreated, and imbuing them with some virtue. Foucault only succeeds in revealing a fragment of Aldrovandi's episteme.

Analogy is a third form of resemblance, and it differs from convenience and emulation in that it is not a relation between objects. Instead, it is a relation among relations. It is like emulation since what it relates need not be proximate; it is like convenience since what it relates is thereby joined or bonded together. Whole series of relations may be related by analogy. Foucault tells us that "the relation of the stars to the sky in which they shine may also be found: between plants and the earth, between living beings and the globe they inhabit, between minerals such as diamonds and the rocks in which they are buried, between sense organs and the face they animate, between skin moles and the body of which they are the secret marks."[24] Moreover, there was one thing whose parts were related in such a way that this relation served as an analogy for all other relations, namely, man. In a way that mimics a move in the episteme he was out to uncover, and yet at the same time illustrates analogy, Foucault wrote that: "Man's body is always the possible half of a universal atlas."[25] This mode of resemblance, analogy, made it possible for Belon to draw the first comparative illustration of the human skeleton and the skeletons of birds. Belon wrote:

> [T]he pinion called the appendix which is in proportion to the wing and in the same place as the thumb on the hand; the extremity of the pinion which is like the fingers in us . . . ; the bone given as legs to the bird corresponds to our heel; just as we have four toes on our feet, so the birds have four fingers of which the one behind is proportionate to the big toe in us.[26]

As with Porta and Crollius, we begin to discern what Belon was doing, when we see that his comparisons were an obvious move in a game that was in part ruled by the conception of an analogical ordering of things. If the relation among any parts of any thing is analogous to some relation among at least some parts of man, then the relations among the parts of various animals must be analogous to some relations among some parts of man. Thus, for anyone working within the framework of the episteme of the sixteenth and seventeenth centuries, it was possible to embark on the research program of finding the analogy between the relations among the parts of some particular species and the relations among some set of human parts. This illustrates as well as anything else Foucault's notion that an episteme makes various statements possible. Belon picked the birds, and the result was something that might appear to us as comparative anatomy. Note well that Foucault opposed reading Belon's work in the light of this appearance.

One can see Belon's comparisons as comparative anatomy, only if one sees it from the perspective of a later episteme. Foucault maintained that it may seem like comparative anatomy because: "the grid through which we permit the figures of resemblance to enter our knowledge happens to coincide at this point (and at almost no other) with that which sixteenth-century learning had laid over things." [27] Belon's comparisons and those of comparative anatomy are importantly different even though they seem to overlap. The former are possible by virtue of the Renaissance conceptions of order, and the latter are possible by virtue of a later conception of order. Perhaps it is easiest to see this by noting that the episteme that lead to Belon's comparisons, and that would come to seem to his successors like the form of knowledge that they called comparative anatomy, also lead to comparisons that would come to seem to them to be nothing at all like knowledge. The same episteme, by virtue of its inclusion of a conception of order that itself included the notion that things are analogically related, made it possible for Aldrovandi to compare "man's baser parts to the fouler parts of the world, to Hell, to the darkness of Hell, to the damned souls who are like the excrement of the Universe." [28] Belon's and Aldrovandi's comparisons belonged to the same "analogical cosmography" as the comparison between apoplexy and tempests. Foucault describes it thus:

> [T]he storm begins when the air becomes heavy and agitated, the apoplectic attack at the moment when our thoughts become heavy and disturbed; then the clouds pile up, the belly swells, the thunder explodes and the bladder bursts; the lightening flashes and the eyes glitter with a terrible brightness, the rain falls, the mouth foams, the thunderbolt is unleashed and the spirits burst open breaches in the skin; but then the sky becomes clear again, and in the sick man reason regains ascendancy. [29]

Neither this comparison, nor the just mentioned one by Aldrovandi, seem to us to be knowledge. They may make entertaining poetry, but they are not knowledges. This pair of comparisons and Belon's comparison of men and birds are statements that are made possible by that part of the sixteenth- and seventeenth-century episteme that delimits the modes in which things are fundamentally ordered, to wit, this mode of resemblance, analogy. Analogy makes these comparisons possible in the way that a grammar or syntax makes possible any number of well-formed formulas; cognition may result in there being two grammatical and meaningful sentences in two different languages that seem to be points at which these languages coincide, but this would be a mistake, since two different grammars would be the grounds of the possibility of these sentences. Be this as it may, insofar as these comparisons are made possible by this episteme, they are structurally different from the comparisons of later comparative anatomists, and so although it appears that the work of Belon and others coincides with this later work, it does not. This later work is itself made possible by an essentially different set of conceptions of order, signs and language.

There is a fourth mode of order in things, which is also a mode of resemblance, namely, sympathy. Sympathy is more than a relation among things; the things that stand in this relation may be moved just by virtue of this standing. Given that some heavy thing stands in this relation to the heavy earth, it may come to move toward the earth; given that some light thing stands in this relation to the weightless ether, it may move up toward the ether. A particularly lucid example is, as Foucault writes, that "sympathy . . . makes the great yellow disk of the sunflower turn to follow the curving path of the sun." [30] Moreover, sympathetically related things become the same:

> [F]ire, because it is warm and light, rises up into the air, towards which its flames untiringly strive; but in doing so it loses its dryness (which make it akin to the earth) and so acquires humidity (which links it to water and air); it disappears therefore into light vapour, into blue smoke, into clouds: it has become air. [31]

Consequently, lest all become one, sympathy must be countered by antipathy. Antipathetically related things intensify their differences, and so although various species tend, by virtue of their being sympathetically related, toward assimilation, their being antipathetically related results in their maintaining their differences. Having seen that sympathy and antipathy are two additional ways in which the things of the Renaissance world can be ordered, we can at least partly see what Cardan was doing, when he wrote:

> It is fairly widely known that the plants have hatreds between themselves. . . . [I]t is said that the olive and the vine hate the cabbage; the cucumber flies from the olive. . . . Since they grow by means of the sun's warmth and the earth's humour, it is inevitable that any thick and opaque tree should be pernicious to the others, and also the tree that has several roots.[32]

Sympathy and antipathy explain everything including the resemblances of convenience, emulation, and analogy. Together they formed the core of the Renaissance theory of everything.

In part, at least, these four modes of resemblance also formed the core conception of the order of things in the episteme of the sixteenth and seventeenth centuries. An episteme, as I noted above, involves more than a conception of the most fundamental ways in which things are ordered. It must also include a conception of signs and language. It must include the former, since what it is to be knowledge depends on a conception of the signs used to express known truths about things that are ordered in these most fundamental ways; it must also include the latter, since the signs used to express such truths are linguistic. The episteme in which Aldrovandi, *et alia,* participated is not lacking here. The Renaissance conception of the order of things entails that the world consists of things that form endless chains of resemblances; but this picture of the world needs to be supplemented with an account of how resemblances may be recognized, since it is possible to coexist with all these resemblances and yet fail to apprehend the order that they induce on things.

Foucault provides this example: "In order that we may know that . . . ground walnut mixed with spirits of wine will ease headache, there must of course be some mark that will make us aware of these things: otherwise, the secret would remain indefinitely dormant."[33] For metaphysics, there is nothing worse than an indefinitely dormant secret. Thus, the epistemological viability of the episteme of Aldrovandi, *et alia,* depends on things possessing marks that indicate their resemblances to other things. In short, it depends on signs. Paracelsus explained this in terms of the will of God:

> It is not God's will that what he creates for man's benefit and what
> he has given us should remain hidden. . . . And even though he has
> hidden certain things, he has allowed nothing to remain without
> exterior and visible signs in the form of special marks—just as a man
> who has buried a hoard of treasure marks the spot that he may find
> it again.[34]

Thus, the resemblances that constitute the order of things can be discovered, only if one can uncover and learn to read their signs or signatures. It has already been suggested that this aspect of the Renaissance episteme renders intelligible certain medical practices. Thus, given this episteme, it is possible for there to be an affinity between the walnut and the human head, and so it is also possible that "what cures 'wounds of the pericranium' is the thick green rind covering the bones —the shell—of the fruit; but internal head ailments may be prevented by use of the nut itself 'which is exactly like the brain in appearance'."[35] Here, an analogy is a signature or a sign for a sympathy. The relation between the shell of the walnut and its fruit is analogous to the relation between the skull and the brain, and so wounds of the skull may be cured by means of the application of the shell, because there is, I presume, a sympathetic relation between shell and skull, which is discovered by learning to read the analogy as a sign or signature for this sympathetic relation, and by introducing the shell, the skull will come to be like the shell, that is to say, whole, hard, and consequently healed. Moreover, a convenience can be a sign for an emulation, and an emulation can be a sign for an analogy, and an analogy can be, as we have just seen, a sign for a sympathy, and so on. This is generalizable: each mode of resemblance can be a sign for every other mode of resemblance, and insofar as the world is a web whose nodes are things, and whose strands are resemblances, and each thing resembles every other thing including perhaps itself, the world is also a world of signs, and knowing is reading these signs.

Just this fragment of the Renaissance episteme makes it possible to explain what is for us a peculiar fact about what passed for knowledge during this period, to wit, the fact that both what we can see as products of scientific rationality *and* magic should count as knowledge. As Gary Gutting has noted: "Even in as late a figure as Newton, we find enduring achievements in mechanics and optics disconcertingly side by side with the serious pursuit of alchemy and bizarre scriptural exegesis." [36] During the Renaissance, mechanics and magic are epistemological peers. How could this have been? The answer to this question depends on a conception of language. According to the Renaissance episteme, language is a part of the world, that is, it is a part of an endless network of things that resemble one another. Consequently, it must be studied and known as any other thing. As Foucault writes: "Language partakes of the worldwide dissemination of similitudes and signatures. It must, therefore, be studied itself as a thing in nature." [37]

More importantly, if linguistic signs are things, they too are ordered with other things in all the relations of resemblance. However, if linguistic signs resemble, they stand in sympathetic and antipathetic relations to other things, but then it makes complete sense to think— that is, it is possible—that there are strings of words that repel snakes, and that there are strings of words that transform lead into gold. Think of the way that someone in the grip of the Renaissance episteme would have understood the medicinal effects of the walnut, and substitute words for walnut shells, lead for a wounded skull, and gold for a healed skull. Given the proper sympathetic resemblance relation between gold and some string of words, muttering the words in the vicinity of the lead will transform it into gold. Such a transformation will be analogous to the way that the walnut shell heals the skull, or at least this is the theory. The same sort of story can be told about snakes and their repulsion, except that the words and the snakes would stand in an antipathetic resemblance relation. In short, given the Renaissance episteme, magic makes sense, that is, anyone in its grip will experience magic as possible. For reasons to which I have already alluded, and to which I will return in order to expand, Foucault might think it better to say that given the Renaissance episteme, magic is possible, for example, given this episteme, it is possible to say that there must be a string of words that will transform lead into gold when spoken in the presence of the lead. Thus, as Foucault writes:

> The project of elucidating the "Natural Magics," which occupies an
> important place at the end of the sixteenth century and survives into

the middle of the seventeenth, is not a vestigial phenomenon in the European consciousness; it was revived . . . and for contemporary reasons: because the fundamental configuration of knowledge consisted of the reciprocal cross-reference of signs and similitudes. The form of magic was inherent in this way of knowing.[38]

Here, the problem has been to explain how magic could have made sense, but one wonders how mechanics fits into the Renaissance episteme, an issue that Foucault does not address. Foucault may have explained how what does not make sense to us—magic—made sense to Aldrovandi and his peers, but it is another matter to explain how what makes sense to us—mechanics—fits in with what made sense to them. Be this as it may, what we have here is a paradigm that the explanation of Aldrovandi's perceived necessity and Buffon's perceived contingency can mimic. The strategy is to show that just as the possibility of magic is an artifact of Aldrovandi's episteme, so are his perceived necessity and Buffon's perceived contingency artifacts of their respective epistemes.

Recall Buffon's remark about Aldrovandi's divisions: "Let it be judged after that [series of divisions] what proportion of natural history is to be found in such a hotch-potch of writing. There is no description here, only legend."[39] Foucault begins his explanation of these divisions by noting the irony of this remark: "indeed, for Aldrovandi and his contemporaries, it was all *legenda*—things to be read."[40] Again, according to the Renaissance episteme, the world consists of a manifold of things that are ordered by their resemblances to one another, the various features of things are our clues to these resemblances, and in coming to know things, one learns to see or read these features as signs, marks or signatures of their resemblances to other things. The irony of Buffon's remark rests on this last and strictly epistemological thesis. Knowing something, for example, the serpent, is being able to see its various features as signs or signatures of its resemblances to other things, that is, it is being able to read these features. Now, since knowing is reading, a report of what there is to know about something is a list of its readable features, even though in practice such a list could only be, at best, partial. Moreover, among the readable features of the serpent are, according to Aldrovandi, the items listed in his divisions. Each element of Aldrovandi's divisions corresponds to a sign or signature that must be read in order to know the serpent. The presence of these divisions is not, therefore, the result of a hyperbolic imagination; their presence is an artifact of, is determined by, the Renaissance episteme. The conjunction of a conception of order and a conception of signs, linguistic or otherwise, yields a conception of what the serpent is, how the serpent is to be known, and what form the expression of this serpentine knowledge must assume. Consequently, given the Renaissance episteme, and given that the elements of Aldrovandi's divisions are readable features of the serpent, his divisions are necessary, and just as someone in the grip of his episteme will experience magic as a possibility, someone in its grip will also experience these divisions as inevitable or necessary. The perceived necessity is, therefore, an artifact of the episteme.

Thus, on the one hand, that was the Renaissance, its episteme, Aldrovandi, his divisions, and most centrally, his modal perception of his divisions. On the other hand, however, Buffon perceived Aldrovandi's divisions as contingent and arbitrary, and according to Foucault, this perceived contingency is an artifact of the classical episteme. What was the classical episteme? How did it determine Buffon's perceptions of these divisions? One can begin to grasp the sense of the classical episteme by considering its two step emergence from the Renaissance episteme. The first step toward the classical episteme was taken by Bacon. He noted that resemblances have a propensity to proliferate, and that they do not generally result in a knowledge of how to determine the relations among things. In other words, he saw that there are no principled limits on the pairs of items whose elements can be asserted to resemble one another, and that such assertions rarely concern similitudes that enable one to have any deliberate effect on the environment. Bacon knew that there is a superficial way in which the meat of the walnut resembles the brain, but he also knew that after consuming ground walnut mixed with spirits of wine, he still has his headache. According to Foucault, Bacon could see that although the procedures for investigating the world that are built into the Renaissance episteme may occasionally lead to some practical result, they don't do so in any methodological manner. This was a problem in Bacon's eyes, but he did not provide the conceptions of order, signs, and language that are necessary for the classical episteme that would ostensibly overcome it. In another idiom, Bacon would seem to have

been in the curious position of having had classical purposes without
having had classical categories.

The second step into the classical episteme was, according to Foucault, taken by Descartes. *Pace* the mind-body problem, he realized
that one could find cures for headaches, only if one could analyze
things into their parts in such a manner that one could know how
these parts interact to do the things that one desires to determine. So,
for example, if one wants to end headaches, one must analyze the head
in such a way that one comes to know which movements of which of
its parts make it ache, and then, and only then, will one be in a position
to know what plant one needs to mix with what drink to end the pain
in question—assuming, of course, that one has worked out similar
analyses of the plants and the relevant fluids. In another idiom, Descartes' purposes and categories were both classical. Now, Foucault
thinks that a central part of the classical episteme was well expressed
by Descartes, when he stated that all knowledge is either intuition or
deduction. As Descartes wrote, "the actions of the intellect by means
of which we are able to arrive at a knowledge of things with no fear of
being mistaken . . . [are] . . . intuition and deduction." [41] In regard to
this well-known thesis, Foucault points out that Descartes explains
deduction in terms of the classical notion of order. Descartes writes, as
Foucault reminds us, that "all knowledge whatever . . . save knowledge
obtained through simple and pure intuition of a single, solitary thing
. . . [results] . . . from a comparison between two or more things." [42]
That Descartes meant to include deduction under knowledge is indicated by his choice of example: "in all reasoning it is only by means of
comparison that we attain an exact knowledge of the truth. Consider,
for example, the inference: all A is B, all B is C, therefore all A is C. In
this case, the thing sought and the thing given, A and C, are compared
with respect to their both being B, etc." [43] What is comparison? How
is it related to the classical conception of order? How does it function
in Foucault's account of Buffon's experience of Aldrovandi's divisions?

Foucault tells us that during the classical age, comparison was
thought to have two forms. One is the result of *measuring* things, and
the other is the result of *classifying* them. The former itself has two
forms, namely, measurement of sizes and measurement of multiplicities. In both cases, one begins with a unit, for example, the cubic inch
or the goat. In the case of a size, one divides or analyzes the size in

question into some number of units, for example, one divides a sphere into some number of cubic inches; in the case of a multiplicity, one analyzes or divides it into some number of items, for example, one divides the herd into some number of goats. In general, this sort of analysis or division can be done in many ways for any thing or multiplicity. Consequently, things and multiplicities are ordered according to relations of arithmetic equality (identity) or inequality (difference). Given the classical episteme, not only are things ordered according to their possession of certain quantities of various measurable features, but multiplicities are ordered according to the number of their elements. Jointly, they make up the order that results from measurement, but there is also the order that results from classification. This is somewhat self-evident. A classification imposes an order on the things that it classifies, for example, classifying the items within the animal kingdom into various phyla, classes, orders, families, genera, and species imposes an order on them. For example, since the goats are classified under the mammals, there exists a transitive, antisymmetric, and reflexive relation between the former and the latter. Foucault maintains that the order due to measurement is reducible to the order due to classification. He writes, "relations between beings are indeed to be conceived in the form of order and measurement, but with this fundamental imbalance, that it is always possible to reduce problems of measurement to problems of [classificatory] order."[44] The idea is, I suppose, that things and multiplicities can be ordered according to arithmetic relations, precisely because the quantities associated with measured things and counted multiplicities are themselves arithmetically classified in a way that imposes an order on these quantities, and so the order of measurement is reducible to the order of classification.

This conception of order makes it possible to elaborate the point that if one observes that the meat of the walnut resembles the brain, and yet this resemblance resists reduction to some form of classical order, one's observation cannot be knowledge. The resemblance in question would have to resist reduction to an identity of two quantities of some unit, an identity of the numerical sizes of two multiplicities, or an identity of the class memberships of two things. The point is that if the meat of the walnut and the brain are not identical in at least one of these three ways, then from the perspective of the classical episteme, neither is *really* related to the other, and since the putative recognition of their resemblance is consequently not a recognition of something that is, it is not knowledge. It is not that the concept of resemblance is completely absent during the classical age, instead it just is not the concept of the fundamental way in which things are ordered. Consequently, although knowledge may begin with the recognition of resemblance, when an ostensible instance of resemblance cannot be elucidated in terms of at least one of the fundamental forms of classical order, its recognition cannot count as knowledge. From the perspective of the classical episteme, therefore, there is a principled limit on the seemingly never ending proliferation of resemblances that vexed Bacon, or, in other words, that there is also a principled way of distinguishing apparent resemblances from real resemblances. This, note well, is the beginning of Foucault's account of Buffon's modal perception of Aldrovandi's divisions.

Since the classical conception of order puts a principled limit on the proliferation of resemblances, it also puts a principled limit on the corresponding proliferation of signs. From the perspective of the Renaissance episteme, signs are a part of the world, and it is the resemblance relation that metaphysically underwrites the semiotic relationship. One thing is a sign for another thing just when it resembles this other thing, and in a world where all resembles all, everything is a sign for every other thing. Therefore, since the classical episteme undercuts the universality of the resemblance relation, it also undercuts the universality of the semiotic relation. In the context of the classical episteme, for any two things, it is not necessary for one to resemble the other, and consequently it is not necessary for one to be a sign for the other.

Buffon would distinguish between reports about and observations of an object, for example, the serpent. Within the framework of the classical episteme, the two sources of knowledge are intuition and deduction, and since reports are neither, neither counts as a source of knowledge. As Descartes wrote in his third rule for the direction of the mind:

> Concerning objects proposed for study, we ought to investigate what we can clearly and evidently intuit or deduce with certainty, and not what other people have thought or what we ourselves conjecture. For knowledge can be attained in no other way.[45]

Consequently, when Buffon examined Aldrovandi's list of divisions, he found that some were included on the basis of observation or intuition, for example, anatomy, temperature, and diet, and he found that some were included on the basis of report, for example, hieroglyphics, coinage, riddles, and heraldic signs. Buffon might have admitted that the former are related to the serpent in a way that can be reduced to some form of classical order. I do not know. Be this as it may, he would have seen the inclusion of the latter items on Aldrovandi's list as arbitrary and unnecessary. Thus, he could and would see Aldrovandi's divisions as a hotch-potch, that is, as an assemblage that is unmotivated by the classical conception of the fundamental order of things, and that is consequently unnecessary and contingent. Anyone caught in the Renaissance episteme, to wit, Aldrovandi, would have thought that since all resembles all, all is a sign for all, and so what anyone caught in the classical episteme, to wit, Buffon, would have thought of as irrelevant reports must be included in Aldrovandi's divisions of what there is to know about the serpent. Given Buffon's epistemic position, he had to think that some does not resemble some, and so some are not signs for some, and so it is not necessary to include reports about the serpent in one's divisions of what there is to know about the serpent. Buffon could not perceive Aldrovandi's divisions in any way other than as a hotch-potch, that is, as unmotivated, unnecessary, and contingent. It is not that within the context of the classical episteme, reports—hieroglyphics, coinage and riddles—cannot be signs of the serpent, instead it's just that within the classical episteme, such reports are not necessarily signs for serpent, and that within the Renaissance episteme, what would come to be classified as reports must be signs for the serpent.

Let me put this in other words. From the perspective of the Renaissance episteme, all resembles all, and since resemblance is the metaphysical foundation of the semiotic relation, all is a sign for all. Given the classical conception of order, however, since it is possible for one thing to fail to resemble another thing, it is possible for one thing to fail to be a sign for another thing. This implies that Aldrovandi's divisions are a hotch-potch. Why? From the perspective of the classical episteme, since intuition and deduction are the only two sources of knowledge, and reports are neither intuitions nor deductions, and observations are a kind of intuition, reports and observations are distinct.

From the classical perspective, therefore, Aldrovandi's divisions can be divided into two distinct groups, namely, those based on reports and those based on observations. Aldrovandi included among his divisions what Buffon saw as reports, because he thought that they were signs for the serpent, and he thought this because he thought that the semiotic relation is a form of the all pervasive resemblance relation. The clue to Foucault's account of Buffon's modal perception of Aldrovandi's divisions lies in the fact that once the pervasiveness of the resemblance relation is undermined, so is the necessity of the pervasiveness of the semiotic relation. Buffon had to see Aldrovandi's divisions as arbitrary and contingent, because he could not see the inclusion of what he had to think of as reports as having a necessary place among the divisions of what could be known about the serpent. Buffon's modal perception is a product of two vectors, so to speak. One is the necessity for dividing Aldrovandi's divisions into reports and observations, and the second is the necessity for seeing the reports as contingent signs for the serpent. If the reports may not be signs for the serpent, they do not have to be included in a list of things that have to be read in order to know the serpent, and so their presence among Aldrovandi's divisions makes these divisions seem contingent to Buffon.

Before I end this chapter, and this book, I will address one more issue, to wit, the question of what distinguishes my account of Aldrovandi and Buffon from Foucault's account. In short, the answer is that Foucault *qua* archaeologist is necessarily blind to the phenomenon of metaphysical illusion, and since he cannot see it, he cannot explain it. Let me explain.

Note well that in the above exposition of Foucault's account of Aldrovandi and Buffon, two fundamentally opposed modes of explanation have been mixed. As I read Foucault, he explains the necessity of Aldrovandi's use of his divisions *qua* statement in terms of the Renaissance episteme, and he explains the necessity of Buffon's reaction to these divisions *qua* statement in terms of the classical episteme. In brief, his idea is that Aldrovandi's use of his divisions is necessitated by his episteme, and that Buffon's reaction is necessitated by his episteme. Now, I have added the anti-Foucaultian ideas that Aldrovandi's *experience* of his divisions as necessary is an artifact of the Renaissance episteme, and that Buffon's *experience* of these divisions as contingent and arbitrary is an artifact of the classical episteme. To clarify what I have added, it is helpful to consider Gutting's reading of Foucault on this matter.

According to Gutting's reading, Foucault maintained that when Buffon read Aldrovandi's treatise, he thought that Aldrovandi was incapable of distinguishing between what he firmly knew on the basis of observation *and* what he indefinitely believed on the basis of the unreliable reports of ancient authorities. Moreover, since Buffon thought that Aldrovandi could not distinguish between "what is seen and what is read,"[46] he had no choice aside from concluding that his work is "an inextricable mixture of exact description, reported quotations, fables without commentary."[47] Thus, Buffon had no choice but to judge that Aldrovandi's divisions are a hotch-potch. According to Gutting, Foucault contended that Buffon reasoned that since synonyms, etymologies, epithets, mythology, gods to which the serpent is dedicated, coinage, riddles, simulacra, and statues are all to be classed with *what is read,* or what is reported, and since knowledge rests on *what is seen,* only a proper part of what is included under Aldrovandi's divisions is or could be knowledge, and, consequently, Buffon took these divisions to be an arbitrary hotch-potch.

Now, Gutting supposes that Foucault explained Aldrovandi's use of these divisions in terms of the fact that the distinction, on which Buffon's judgment is founded, had little or no significance for him. That is, Foucault is supposed to have thought that Aldrovandi's divisions are a consequence of the fact that the above distinction did not have the weight that it would come to have for subsequent naturalists such as Buffon. Gutting writes:

> Renaissance naturalists were certainly capable of understanding the distinction in question; but, because of their subsumption of both observations and myths to the category of written [sic] signs, they had no reason to give it any special weight.[48]

It is illuminating to note the similarity that this bears to Goodman's remark that in some cases, some of the significant kinds of one world are not to be found in another world, but in other cases, it might be more accurate to say that

two worlds contain just the same classes sorted differently into relevant and irrelevant kinds. Some relevant kinds of the one world,
rather than being absent from the other, are present as irrelevant
kinds; some differences among worlds are not so much in entities
comprised as in emphasis or accent, and these differences are no less
consequential.[49]

This suggests the following extension: two worlds might contain the
same distinctions sorted differently into relevant and irrelevant. Thus,
one may say that on Gutting's reading, Foucault thought that what
Goodman suggests might be the case was the case in the worlds of
Aldrovandi and Buffon. The worlds of Aldrovandi and Buffon both
contained the distinction between the observed and the reported, and
although it was important to the latter, it had little or no significance
for the former. Gutting thinks that part of Foucault's conclusion is
that for Aldrovandi, "there is no particular reason to emphasize the
differences between . . . the fact that an animal has a certain color skin
and the fact that it figures in certain myths."[50] Thus, Aldrovandi used
his divisions because he did not give sufficient weight to the distinction
that would have made their use seem incongruous. In other words,
since the distinction that speaks against his divisions was insignificant
to him, there was then no reason not to employ them, and so he
embraced and utilized them. Moreover, since Buffon gave substantial
weight to this distinction that conflicts with Aldrovandi's divisions, he
rejected them as useless.

On Gutting's reading, Foucault's argument seems to be a *non sequitur*: just as no one believes all of the logical consequences of what
she in fact believes, no one utilizes every conception that conflicts with
some other conception that is insignificant relative to her. The idea
presupposes an absurd omniscience. However this may be, it is more
pertinent to focus on the fact that given the way in which weighting
functions in this argument, it is especially anti-Foucaultian. As Gutting
has formulated Foucault's account of Aldrovandi's divisions, it essentially depends on the premise that Aldrovandi and Buffon had different
attitudes toward the distinction between the seen and the read, which
entails, note well, that Aldrovandi was able to make or comprehend
this distinction. I think that Foucault would have rejected Gutting's
reading, because he would have denied that the account that he im-

putes to him is archaeologically adequate. Moreover, he would have denied that this imputed account is adequate just because it rests on this premise. Let me focus on why this premise would have given Foucault reason to deny the adequacy of the imputed account, and consequently why it would have given him reason to reject Gutting's reading. I will then proffer some remarks about the entailment.

The account that Gutting imputes to Foucault depends on the ascription of a subjective state to Aldrovandi, and since a pivotal element of Foucault's conception of archaeology is the suspension of such ascriptions, he would have denied that it is an archaeologically adequate explanation. To see that accounts that depend on the ascription of subjective states are fundamentally incompatible with a central archaeological principle, consider some of the implications of Foucault's self-chosen methodological metaphor, namely, the archaeological dig. An archaeologist digs through the earth in order to discover a level over which various objects are dispersed, and then she attempts to discover the principles of the disparate relations among these objects that unite them and that bestow upon them their character as objects of this or that level. Foucault maintained that since the archaeologist uncovers objects that have had their meanings effaced by the passage of time, the very methodology of archaeology necessitates that its objects be uninterpreted, and this leaves the archaeologist with virtually nothing to do apart from discovering the rules that order its objects. The idea of an inquiry into uninterpreted objects and their rules can seem impenetrable, and so it may be instructive to briefly note the parallel between archaeology thus conceived and David Hilbert's *formalism* in the philosophy of mathematics. Just as Hilbert regarded mathematics as the rule-governed manipulation of methodically uninterpreted sequences of marks, Foucault regards archaeology as the production of the rules that define the specific character of meaning-effaced objects.

Whereas, in archaeology, the suspension of the truth and the meaning of its objects is imposed by the passage of time, in his historical inquiries, Foucault proposes, as a matter of methodological principle, to suspend the truth and the meaning of statements. In a Foucaultian archaeology, one digs through an archive in order to discover some group of texts through which a manifold of statements is dispersed, and as a consequence of this methodological principle, one then attempts to find the principles of the relations among such statements that unite them and that bestow upon them their character as statements of these very texts. Foucault writes:

> There was a time when archaeology, as a discipline devoted to silent monuments, inert traces, objects without context, and things left by the past, aspired to the condition of history, and attained meaning only through the restitution of a historical discourse; it might be said, to play on words a little, that in our time history aspires to the condition of archaeology, to the intrinsic description of the monument.[51]

Given this distinction between documents—the interpreted—and monuments—the uninterpreted—there are at least two possible projects. First, there is a project that begins with a mixture of documents and monuments, and being based on the assumption that a mere acquaintance with the uninterpreted is, historically speaking, epistemologically insufficient, it goes on to attempt to rethink the thoughts of the agents that produced these monuments, that is, it attempts to interpret or, as Foucault put it, *memorize* them, and thereby transforms these monuments into documents. The goal is to possess nothing but documents.[52]

Second, there is Foucault's archaeological project that begins with a mixture of monuments and documents, and that continues by bracketing any meaning that the documents may have had for the agents who produced them, which thereby transforms these documents into monuments. Foucault's project goes on to attempt to discover the rules that make these statements possible, that is, to discover their episteme. The goal is to possess nothing but monuments, and the rules that define the relations that unify them and that confer upon them their character as statements of this or that discourse.[53] That the ascription of subjective states is held in abeyance is, therefore, a result of a methodological decision to treat statements in the way that Foucault presumes that the archaeologist must treat her objects as uninterpreted monuments. The important consequence here is that the possibility, necessity, impossibility, or contingency of a statement is not determined by any subjective attitude of any individual, and so such modalities are not determined by the way some individual weighs some distinction. Therefore, the necessity or contingency of Aldrovandi's divisions is not archaeologically explained in terms of his or Buffon's attitude toward the distinction between the seen and the read. Such attitudes are not part of Foucault's archaeological project. He writes, "discourse is not the majestically unfolding manifestation of a thinking, knowing, speaking subject."[54] Moreover, "it is neither by recourse to a transcendental subject nor by recourse to a psychological subjectivity that the regulation of its [discourse's] enunciations should be defined."[55] What defines the sphere of possible statements, what regulates the modalities of a discourse's enunciations is very complicated indeed, but Foucault is clear that the subjective contents of this or that head have no part in it. Therefore, insofar as the account of Aldrovandi's divisions that Gutting imputes to Foucault turns on the ascription of subjective states, to wit, that Aldrovandi gave the distinction between the seen and the read far less weight than it would be given by later classical naturalists, and that Buffon gave this distinction far more weight, Gutting's reading is anti-Foucaultian. Moreover, Foucault would have denied the archaeological adequacy of the imputed account, and so he would have rejected Gutting's reading.

Before considering a way that Gutting could respond to this criticism, it is important to note that the above-mentioned *entailment—* that since Aldrovandi had an attitude toward the distinction between the seen and the read, it would have been intelligible to him— also renders the account that Gutting imputes to Foucault anti-archaeological. According to this account, the Renaissance naturalists were able to understand the classical distinction between the seen and the read. Indeed, since this account rests on the supposition that Aldrovandi gave this distinction little weight, and it is difficult, if not impossible, to see how he could have done this without being able to understand it, it must have been intelligible to him. Leaving aside the point that considerations of subjective states, to wit, considerations of intelligibility, have no place in Foucaultian archaeologies, is this right? Could Aldrovandi have made sense of the classical distinction? Here is a reason to answer in the negative. As I have argued, the Renaissance episteme necessitates conceptions of what it is to be a serpent, what it is to know the serpent, and the form that the enunciation of serpentine knowledge must assume. The necessitating of such conceptions is a part of the way that an episteme functions in a Foucaultian archaeology. Thus, given both the Renaissance episteme and what Aldrovandi

claimed to know about the serpent, his divisions were necessary. However, since these divisions and the classical distinction are not compossible, the distinction could not have been possible for Aldrovandi. In
other words, since the classical distinction conflicts with Aldrovandi's
divisions, and these divisions were, in the context of the Renaissance
episteme, a necessity, if Aldrovandi had considered the classical distinction, it would have seemed to him to have been a category mistake,
meaningless, nonsense, and impossible. In short, the classical distinction could not have been intelligible to Aldrovandi, and consequently,
insofar as the account that Gutting imputes to Foucault depends on
the supposition that this distinction could be understood by him, this
account is anti-archaeological.

Here, then, are three reasons to doubt the archaeological adequacy
of the account of Aldrovandi's use of his divisions and the account of
Buffon's inability to use them that Gutting imputes to Foucault: (i) it
depends on the ascription of subjective states, (ii) it is a *non sequitur,*
and (iii) it assumes to be intelligible what could only be nonsense, a
category mistake. These are also three reasons for thinking that Foucault would have for rejecting Gutting's reading of his account of
Aldrovandi's divisions.

It is somewhat obvious that Gutting could begin to respond to
these criticisms by saying that the presumed weighting functions belong to the Renaissance episteme, not to Aldrovandi, and to the classical episteme, not Buffon. That is, the Renaissance episteme itself
weighs the classical distinction in such a manner that this episteme
classifies it with the irrelevant distinctions, and the classical episteme
weighs its own distinction in such a way that it classifies it with the
imperative distinctions, the distinctions that cannot be ignored. Part of
the modified account of the modality of Aldrovandi's divisions that
Gutting could then impute to Foucault would be that since the Renaissance episteme did not give the classical distinction the weight that
would make Aldrovandi's use of his divisions *qua* statement impossible, this statement was possible. From a weightless point of view, if the
seen and the read are not the same, or the observed is not the reported,
and Aldrovandi, in using his divisions, conflates them, then not only
do this distinction and these divisions conflict, but insofar as Aldrovandi's use of them is a statement, it is impossible. However, from the
point of view of the weights that may be distributed over various

statements by the Renaissance episteme, if the Renaissance episteme assigns a sufficiently small weight to the classical distinction, then Aldrovandi's use of his divisions will be possible, even if the classical distinction and his divisions conflict, and the distinction is taken as necessary.

In other words, if the classical distinction between the read and the seen is taken to be incompatible with Aldrovandi's divisions, and this distinction is taken to be necessary, then from a weightless point of view, these divisions would have to be impossible. The explanation of the possibility of Aldrovandi's divisions begins with the supposition that the Renaissance episteme distributes various weights to statements, and that it assigns an especially low weight to the classical distinction. Then, the explanation of the possibility of Aldrovandi's divisions is that even though they are incompatible with the classical distinction, which is necessary, since the classical distinction is given little weight by the Renaissance episteme, the divisions are consequently possible. Moreover, the explanation of Buffon's statement that Aldrovandi's divisions are arbitrary or a hotch-potch proceeds similarly. It begins with the supposition that the classical episteme itself distributes various weights over the manifold of possible statements, and the further supposition that it assigns a substantially heavier weight to the dichotomy between the seen and the read, between the observed and the reported. The explanation of the impossibility of Aldrovandi's use of his divisions, *qua* statement, is that since it conflicts with this heavily weighted distinction, it is *ipso facto* impossible.

This modified account, which Gutting could impute to Foucault, would not be subject to the criticism that it is anti-archaeological because it essentially depends on the ascription of subjective states, and it might not be subject to the criticism that it is a *non sequitur*. It is clear that by shifting the conjectured weighting functions from Aldrovandi to the Renaissance episteme, and from Buffon to the classical episteme, Aldrovandi and Buffon, as the subjects of subjective states, and these very states themselves are not part of this account. Thus, since it does not involve the ascription of subjective states, it doesn't conflict with the archaeological suspension of such ascriptions. However, it is not clear that the part of this modified account that deals with Aldrovandi is not a *non sequitur*. Why should it be that Aldrovandi's use of his divisions *qua* statement is possible just because the classical distinction with which it conflicts is given a relatively insignificant weight by the Renaissance episteme? Even if the classical distinction is not given great weight by the Renaissance episteme, it is still necessary, and even if it is consequently irrelevant in the context of this episteme, if it conflicts with Aldrovandi's divisions, they fail to be possible. If it is true that the seen is not the read, it is, I suppose, a conceptual truth. So, the classical distinction is, vis-à-vis the Renaissance episteme, an irrelevant conceptual truth. In other words, it is an irrelevant necessity, but it is, notwithstanding, still a necessity. Thus, since this classical distinction and Aldrovandi's divisions are not compossible, the conclusion that his divisions are possible seems to be the wrong conclusion. Why not conclude that they are impossible? If this is not the right conclusion, it is at least a gratuitous conclusion. Why not conclude that they are a moderately weighted impossibility?

It is more important that this modified account does not explain part of what I think Foucault was out to explain, namely, that given the Renaissance episteme, Aldrovandi's divisions are necessary. Given what Aldrovandi had discovered about the serpent, namely, the equivocation of *serpent*, the gods to which the serpent is dedicated, its role in riddles, et cetera, his use of his divisions was necessitated by his episteme, not only made possible. The Renaissance episteme necessitates a conception of what it is to be a serpent, a conception of what it is to know the serpent, and a precise form in which Aldrovandi's knowledge of the serpent must be expressed. The modified account might explain the possibility of Aldrovandi's divisions, but given that the classical distinction is itself possible in the Renaissance episteme, even though it is, relative to this episteme, insignificant, and his divisions conflict with the classical distinction, these divisions are contingent, and so they are not necessary. The modified version of the account that Gutting might want to impute to Foucault is, consequently, an *ignoratio elenchi*. Now, not only does this modified version of Gutting's imputed account fail to capture this necessity, but there is a way in which it too is anti-archaeological.[56] It is not that the classical distinction was merely assigned an insignificant weight by the Renaissance episteme, instead this distinction just is not possible within its context. Analogously, it is not that one merely does not get any points for a checkmate in backgammon, instead checkmate is not possible in backgammon. Similarly, a formula of predicate logic is not a formula of sentential logic because it gives it a low weight. $\exists x(\phi x)$ is not a well-formed formula of sentential logic, but not because this logic assigns it an insignificant weight. This is not a well-formed formula of sentential logic because it does not satisfy the conditions for being a well-formed formula of sentential logic. From the archaeological perspective, a statement is possible relative to some episteme just when it is compatible with the episteme's conceptions of order, the sign, and language; a statement is necessary in the context of some episteme just when it is necessitated by one or all of its conceptions of order, the sign, and language. Thus, this modified version of the account that Gutting imputes to Foucault suffers from the defect of assuming that the classical distinction is possible within the context of the episteme, when it could only be something like an ill-formed formula or a category mistake. Thus, even if Gutting imputes to Foucault an account that places the weighting function in the Renaissance episteme, instead of Aldrovandi, or in the classical episteme, instead of Buffon, it still is not archaeologically adequate, Foucault would have had reason to reject it as a reading of his project.

My reconstruction of Gutting's reading is closer to Foucault's archaeology than his actual reading, but this reconstruction is, I think, inadequate as an account of metaphysical illusion. Given Foucault's archaeological proscription against the ascription of subjective states, his archaeology is incapable of describing the very phenomenon of metaphysical illusion, not to mention accounting for it. Its social theoretic counterpart consists of the phenomenon that socially constructed objects are *experienced* as if they are not constructed, and it is the phenomenon that representation-dependent worlds *appear* to be representation-independent, that is, what is experienced from a given perspective *seems* to be nonperspectival. The very ideas of these three forms of illusion depend respectively on the ideas of experiencing, appearing, and seeming. Metaphysical illusion, therefore, essentially involves the ways in which worlds are experienced, and this instance of experience is a subjective state.[57] Thus, insofar as Foucault's archaeology is methodologically committed to the suspension of subjective states, not only is it incapable of admitting the very phenomenon of metaphysical illusion, and its social-theoretic counterpart, but it is, by virtue of this very incapacity, also incapable of accounting for the phenomenon of metaphysical illusion. A theoretical position cannot explain what it cannot recognize, and since archaeology methodologically brackets the subjective states that are essential to metaphysical illusion, it thereby also brackets metaphysical illusion, and so since it cannot then recognize this illusion, it cannot account for this illusion. A theoretical position cannot explain what it cannot recognize.

Quod erat faciendum.

Notes

Introduction

1. Otto Neurath, "Protocol Sentences," in *Logical Positivism*, edited by A. J. Ayer (Glencoe, Ill.: The Free Press, 1959), 201.

2. Thomas Hobbes, "Elements of Philosophy," in *The English Works of Thomas Hobbes of Malmesbury*, first collected and edited by Sir William Molesworth, Bart., vol. 1, reprint of the edition of 1839, (London: Scientia Aalen, 1962), 136–37.

3. Donald Davidson, "On the Very Idea of a Conceptual Scheme," in *Inquiries into Truth and Interpretation*, reprinted with corrections, (Oxford: Clarendon Press, 1986), 184. There is an earlier and perhaps significantly different version of this essay in *Proceedings and Addresses of the American Philosophical Association* 47 (1974): 5–20.

4. Ibid., 183.

5. Christopher Marlowe, *Doctor Faustus*, edited and introduced by Sylvan Barnet (New York: Signet, 1969), 33.

6. Immanuel Kant, *Critique of Pure Reason*, translated by Norman Kemp Smith, (New York: St. Martin's Press, 1965); Robert Paul Wolff, "Narrative Time: The Inherently Perspectival Structure of the Human World," in *Midwest Studies in Philosophy*, volume 15: *The Philosophy of the Human Sciences*, edited by Peter A. French, Theodore E. Uehling Jr., and Howard

K. Wettstein (Notre Dame, Ind.: University of Notre Dame Press, 1990), 214.

Chapter 1. The Worlds of Protogoras

1. Hilary Putnam, "A Defense of Internal Realism," in *Realism with a Human Face*, edited by James Conant (Cambridge, Mass.: Harvard University Press, 1990), 30. Compare Hilary Putnam, *Reason, Truth and History* (Cambridge: Cambridge University Press, 1981), 49. I shall occasionally refer to the view summarized by Putnam's three theses as *realism;* he refers to this view as *metaphysical realism.* The theses that there are many actual worlds, and there are many truths, I shall, on various occasions, refer to as *relativism.* Note both that I prescind from ascribing to Putnam any attitude toward the two theses under consideration here, and that he rejects metaphysical realism.

2. Cf. D. J. O'Connor, *The Correspondence Theory of Truth* (London: Hutchinson University Library, 1975), 64–65. I should note that my point is, at this stage, that the correspondence theory of truth has various problems, and so it cannot be taken as given. I do not mean that the problem of negative facts is irresolvable. I just mean that it requires a proponent of the sort of realism expressed by Putnam's three theses to have more than an intuitive understanding of the notion of truth as correspondence. I return to this issue in chapter 3.

3. Michael Devitt, *Realism and Truth* (Princeton: Princeton University Press, 1984), 27. Italics added.

4. Putnam, *Reason, Truth and History,* 1–21. At this point in this text, I am only attempting to get my readers to have an intuitive grasp of the space of my central idea, and so I will not here define *skepticism.* I agree with Kant that philosophy might end with definitions, but it is wrongheaded to think that it must begin with them.

5. Putnam has presented this argument in the following: "Realism and Reason," *Proceedings and Addresses of the American Philosophical Association* 50 (1977): 483–97; "Models and Reality," *Journal of Symbolic Logic* 45 (1980): 464–82; and "Model Theory and the 'Factuality' of Semantics," in *Reflections on Chomsky,* edited by Alexander George (Oxford: Basil Blackwell, 1989): 213–32. In this work, I will not return to this argument, because a fair examination of it would require an excursion

into a number of the deeper technicalities of model theory, which are beyond the scope of this work. It seems clear that Putnam's model theoretic argument shows that Devitt should not simply assume that the referential notions that are assumed by his account of truth are unproblematic. A similar point about these notions holds for Putnam's so-called brains-in-a-vat argument, which I will discuss in chapter 3.

6. Yes, strings are deeply absurd, and I suppose them to be. This is the point. Metaphysical realism, of which correspondence truth is a part, is absurd, and my image is meant to reveal this.

7. Note the following. For the sake of exposition, I ignore relations, negations, conditionals, universally quantified elements, *et cetera,* of the complete and true description, since they can be *recursively* specified using what I give as a base. Moreover, I shall primarily disregard the possibility of the actuality of worlds that cannot be completely represented by a language that has a structure that is fully specified by first-order logic. This is partly motivated by my aim to construct a response to Davidson's aforementioned critique that works within the confines of his unexpressed assumption that whatever the world, or *a world,* is like, it can be represented by a language that can be specified by first-order logic. Davidson makes this assumption throughout his writings, but it is particularly evident in his "The Method of Truth in Metaphysics," which is in his *Inquiries into Truth and Interpretation,* (Oxford: Clarendon Press, 1986): 199–214. Thus, within the scope of this work, I generally suspend the possibility of the actuality of worlds that can only be represented, or constituted, by languages that have, for example, a structure of the sort that Ferdinand de Saussure attributes to languages. Compare Ferdinand de Saussure, *Course in General Linguistics,* edited by Charles Bally and Albert Sechehaye with the collaboration of Albert Riedlinger, translated and annotated by Roy Harris (La Salle, Ill.: Open Court, 1986). The point of writing in terms of representations, as opposed to propositions, or sentences, et cetera, which have a specific sort of structure, is to write with a generality that leaves open the possibility of extending my argument to these possibilities. Moreover, I wish not to be taken as being overly optimistic about first order languages. My point here is exactly that one should not be, but not because there are, for example, second order languages, but because there are totally different conceptions of language, for example, that of Ferdinand de Saussure.

8. Putnam, "Defense of Internal Realism," 30–31.

9. Devitt, *Realism and Truth*, 56. Italics added. Lynne Baker has pointed out to me that it is not obvious what it means to say that belief is constrained by the world, and consequently it is not obvious what a belief constraining world is. The next few paragraphs are the result of my reflections on her query.

10. One might object that realism is not motivated by the fact that it yields the result that belief is not sufficient for truth, instead it is motivated by the further fact that it explains this fact. However, realism explains this fact, only insofar as it yields it. In other words, realism explains it, only if realism entails it.

11. Hartry Field, "Realism and Relativism," *Journal of Philosophy* 79 (1982): 553.

12. One might think that my argument begs some important question, that my argument assumes that Field's multiplicity of predicates does not yield a multiplicity of truths. Why would anyone think this? Perhaps because I suppose that the parts of language must match up with the parts of the world. I do suppose this. But I suppose it because if Field has something to say about multiple truths, it is to be said within the context of the realist's assumption that the world is, so to speak, cut at the joints, and that a truth must respect these joints. So, when I assume this in my writing, it is not me talking, instead it is the realist with whom Field takes himself to be partly in agreement, at least within the context of his argument about the possibility of a plurality of truths. Again, the realist maintains that the world, or nature, is cut at the joints, and that a truth, and so the truth, about the world must reflect these cuts, and that any representation that does not respect the world's order just cannot be said to be true, that is, in a model-theoretic sense, which has been amply exploited by Putnam in his so-called model-theoretic argument against realism.

13. This needs argument, of course, and the argument is the text to come.

14. Cf. Ludwig Wittgenstein, *Tractatus Logico-Philosophicus*, translated by D. F. Pears and B. F. McGuinness, and with an introduction by Bertrand Russell (London: Routledge & Kegan Paul, 1961), 151, sect. 6.54.

15. Plato, *Theaetetus*, translated with notes by John McDowell (Oxford: Clarendon Press, 1973), 16, 152a.

16. One might think that a fourth question lurks here: Why does the constraint go in one direction instead of the other? that is, from mind to world as opposed to from world to mind? Yes, there are many more

questions that could be asked, but I think that my project of attempting to answer just these is a sufficiently large project as it stands.

17. How would Protagoras answer: Can something appear that cannot be described?

18. Plato, *Theaetetus*, 46, 171a–b. This passage is the *locus classicus* for the thesis that relativism is self-refuting.

19. Ibid., 46, 171a.

20. M. F. Burnyeat, "Protagoras and Self-Refutation in Plato's Theaetetus," *Philosophical Review* 85 (1976): 182–83. Italics added.

21. The literature on this subject divides along an admittedly artificial line. There are formally oriented pieces, and there are historically oriented pieces. The line is artificial since some involve both. The number of times the self-refutation objection is merely asserted to be the decisive refutation of relativism is far greater than the number of times it comes even close to being made formally clear. For discussions that try to be formally clear, compare the following: J. L. Mackie, "Self-Refutation—A Formal Analysis," *Philosophical Quarterly* 14 (1964): 193–203; Jonathan Bennett, "Review of J. L. Mackie, Self-Refutation—A Formal Analysis," *Journal of Symbolic Logic* 30 (1965): 365–66; John Passmore, *Philosophical Reasoning* (New York: Basic Books, 1969), 58–80; F. C. White, "Self-Refuting Propositions and Relativism," *Metaphilosophy* 20 (1989): 84–92; Peter Davson-Galle, "Self-Refuting Propositions and Relativism," *Metaphilosophy* 22 (1991): 175–78. Understanding the self-refutation argument has also benefited from various historical investigations. The activity has mostly centered around the interpretation of Plato's *Theaetetus*. The literature on this is immense. I have mostly drawn on the following: M. F. Burnyeat, "Protagoras and Self-Refutation in Plato's Theaetetus," *Philosophical Review* 85 (1976): 172–95; Jack W. Meiland, "Is Protagorean Relativism Self-Refuting?" *Grazer Philosophische Studien* 9 (1979): 51–68; Mohan Matthen, "Perception, Relativism, and Truth: Reflections on Plato's *Theaetetus* 152–160," *Dialogue* 24 (1985): 33–58. *Nota Bene*: Semantic self-refutation is not, I think, the same as pragmatic self-refutation. So, even if relativism is not semantically self-refuting, it could be pragmatically self-refuting. In this chapter, I shall only focus on the former, since I have not yet found a version of the latter that has been formulated with the degree of clarity required for critical evaluation.

22. Passmore, *Philosophical Reasoning*, 60.

23. White, "Self-Refuting Propositions," 84.

24. Putnam, *Reason, Truth and History,* 7.

25. Cf. Susan Haack, *Philosophy of Logics* (Cambridge: Cambridge University Press, 1978): 135–51. Peter Davson-Galle, in his recent response to White's version of the thesis that relativism about truth is self-refuting, suggests that "relativism about truth would seem to be able to spawn quasi-Tarskian variants that escape White's argument." Davson-Galle, "Self-Refuting Propositions," 178.

26. Nelson Goodman, "The New Riddle of Induction," in *Fact, Fiction, and Forecast,* 4th ed. (Cambridge, Mass.: Harvard University Press, 1983), 64.

27. There have been a number of controversies wherein it has been suggested that instead of augmenting our physics, logic itself should be changed. For a discussion of when there could be reasons for revising classical logic, compare Susan Haack, *Deviant Logic: Some Philosophical Issues,* (London: Cambridge University Press, 1974). For a recent example of the suggestion that logic be revised, compare the controversy surrounding the following: Patrick Grim, "There Is No Set of All Truths," *Analysis* 44, (1984): 206–8; Selmer Bringsjord, "Are There Set-Theoretic Possible Worlds?" *Analysis* 45 (1985): 64; Christopher Menzel, "On Set-Theoretic Possible Worlds," *Analysis* 46 (1986): 68–72; Patrick Grim, "On Sets and Worlds: A Reply to Menzel," *Analysis* 46 (1986): 186–91. Menzel claims that "the world-story theorist can have either his world stories [the ontology he needs to do his semantics] or an iterative understanding of sets that includes the power set axiom [his logic], but not both." Menzel, "On Set-Theoretic Possible Worlds," 71–72.

28. Passmore, *Philosophical Reasoning,* 58–80; Mackie, "Self-Refutation," 193–203.

Chapter 2. Updating Protagoras

1. Benjamin Lee Whorf, "The Punctual and Segmentative Aspects of Verbs in Hopi," in *Language, Thought, and Reality,* edited and with an introduction by John B. Carroll, foreword by Stuart Chase (Cambridge, Mass.: MIT Press, 1956) 55.

2. Benjamin Lee Whorf, "An American Indian Model of the Universe," in ibid., 58.

3. Ibid.

4. Ibid., 60.

5. Whorf, "Verbs in Hopi," 55.

6. Benjamin Lee Whorf, "Science and Linguistics," in *Language, Thought, and Reality,* 214, 213.

7. Devitt, *Realism and Truth,* 140.

8. Benjamin Lee Whorf, "Gestalt Technique of Stem Composition in Shawnee," in *Language, Thought, and Reality,* 162. Italics added.

9. Roger Trigg, *Reason and Commitment* (Cambridge: Cambridge University Press, 1973), 163.

10. Benjamin Lee Whorf, "Languages and Logic," in *Language, Thought, and Reality,* 235.

11. Compare Arthur Fine, "The Natural Ontological Attitude," in *Scientific Realism,* edited with an introduction by Jarrett Leplin (Berkeley, Calif.: University of California Press, 1984), 83–107. I only mean to borrow this phrase from Fine for the purpose of calling up my reader's realist intuitions, which I suspect are not in need of resurrection.

12. It may make the structure of my reconstruction of Whorf's suggestion more clear, if I number the relevant theses, and state the various problems and what I take to be their solutions in a much more abstract form: (1) experience is ordered by language, (2) different languages order experience differently, (3) there is just one actual world, (4) different languages have different resources for picking preexisting and language-independent patterns among preexisting and language-independent objects, (5) the actual world is ordered by language, (6) different languages order the world differently, and (7) there are many actual worlds. Now, 1, 2, 3, and 4 are supported by either reflection on common experience, or most people's natural ontological attitude. It is necessary to make a case for 5, 6 and 7. The first problem is that Whorf says that 5 is the result of 1, but there is a logical gap between 1 and 5. The solution is that the idea that there is a gap between 1 and 5 presupposes a nonrelativist conception of what it is to be a world. Given a relativist conception of what it is to be a world, there is no gap. The second problem is that 5 would seem to be the only support for 6, but the best motivation for 5 is 1, and 1 does not at all seem to support 5. The solution is that given a relativist conception of what it is to be a world, this problem also disappears. The third

problem is that even if there were support for 6, presumably from 5, which comes dubiously from 1, 6 only seems plausible if it is read as 4. But, when 6 is interpreted as saying 4, it offers no support for 7, and there is, therefore, no support for denying 3. The solution is that given a relativist conception of what it is to be a world, 6 has another reading, and on this reading, 6 supports 7, and 6 gives reason to deny 3. Now the last problem is: What premise in conjunction with 1 entails 7? I would say that it is this: a world is an ideal sum of the objects of a manifold of linguistically shaped experiences, but this is the basis of the solution of all these problems.

13. John B. Carroll, "Introduction," in Benjamin Lee Whorf, *Language, Thought, and Reality,* 7.

14. George Lakoff, *Women, Fire, and Dangerous Things: What Categories Reveal about the Mind* (Chicago: University of Chicago Press, 1987), 324.

15. Emily A. Schultz, *Dialogue at the Margins: Whorf, Bakhtin, and Linguistic Relativity* (Madison: University of Wisconsin Press, 1990), 7.

16. Note the similarity of Whorf's resolution of the science-religion conflict with Kant's resolution of the science-morality conflict. It was by reflection on the latter that I came to conjecture the form of the former, but I will not here provide any discussion of Kant's position on the science-morality conflict.

17. Cf. Whorf, "Science and Linguistics," 216. Cf. Geoffrey K. Pullum, "The Great Eskimo Vocabulary Hoax," in *The Great Eskimo Vocabulary Hoax and Other Irreverent Essays on the Study of Language* (Chicago: University of Chicago Press, 1991), 159–71. Also compare Laura Martin, " 'Eskimo Words for Snow': A Case Study in the Genesis and Decay of an Anthropological Example," *American Anthropologist* 88 (1986): 418–23. Moreover, compare Stephen O. Murray, "Snowing Canonical Texts," *American Anthropologist* 89 (1987): 443–44.

18. Davidson, "On the Very Idea of a Conceptual Scheme," in *Inquiries into Truth and Interpretation* (Oxford: Clarendon Press, 1986), 184. Davidson tells us that Whorf's phrase is to be found in his "Verbs in Hopi" (pp. 51–56). This is not correct. This phrase occurs in Whorf's "Science and Linguistics," 207–19. In this piece, Whorf writes: "We are . . . introduced to a new principle of relativity, which holds that all observers are not led by the same physical evidence to the same picture of the universe, unless

their linguistic backgrounds are similar, or can in some way *be calibrated"* (Whorf, "Science and Linguistics," 214, italics added).

19. Davidson, "Conceptual Schemes," 185.

20. Ibid.

21. Ibid., 185–86.

22. Cf. David Hume, *Enquiries Concerning the Human Understanding and Concerning the Principles of Morals*, edited by L. A. Selby-Bigge, 2nd ed. (Oxford: Clarendon Press, 1902), 109–31.

23. Willard Van Orman Quine, "On What There Is," in *From a Logical Point of View: Nine Logico-Philosophical Essays*, rev. 2nd ed. (Cambridge, Mass.: Harvard University Press, 1980), 1.

24. Ibid., 15.

25. Ibid., 13–14.

26. Willard Van Orman Quine, "Two Dogmas of Empiricism," in *From a Logical Point of View*, 45.

27. Charles Sanders Peirce, "The Fixation of Belief," in *Philosophical Writings of Peirce*, selected and edited with an introduction by Justus Buchler (New York: Dover, 1955), 38.

28. Willard Van Orman Quine, *Word and Object* (Cambridge, Mass.: MIT Press, 1960), 22. Italics added.

29. This example comes from Carl G. Hemple, *Philosophy of Natural Science* (Englewood Cliffs, NJ: Prentice Hall, 1966), 41.

30. Quine, *Word and Object*, 23. I will accept without question Quine's promiscuous employment of the concepts of *all the possible data* and *total theory*.

31. W. V. Quine, "To Chomsky," in *Words and Objections: Essays on the Work of W. V. Quine* (Dordrecht, North Holland: Reidel, 1969), 302.

32. W. V. Quine, "On the Reasons for Indeterminacy of Translation," *Journal of Philosophy* 67 (1970): 179.

33. W. V. Quine, "On Empirically Equivalent Systems of the World," *Erkenntnis* 9 (1975): 313.

34. Quine, *Word and Object*, 23.

35. Quoted from Roger F. Gibson Jr., *Enlightened Empiricism: An Examination of W. V. Quine's Theory of Knowledge* (Tampa: University of South

Florida Press, 1988), 115. The remark in this quote is Gibson's. Quine came to substantially change this passage. Compare W. V. Quine, "Empirical Content," in *Theories and Things* (Cambridge, Mass.: Harvard University Press, 1981), 29. The expression *observational categorical* may require explanation. An occasion sentence is a sentence that is true on some occasions and false on others. An observation sentence is an occasion sentence to which everyone in a speech community would assent on the occasion of the like stimulation of their sensory receptors. An observational categorical is a sentence of the form *whenever this, that,* where *this* and *that* are observation sentences. (Cf. page 4 of the above-mentioned work by Gibson.)

36. W. V. Quine, "Things and Their Place in Theories," in *Theories and Things* (Cambridge, Mass.: Harvard University Press, 1981), 21.

37. W. V. Quine, "Epistemology Naturalized," in *Ontological Relativity and Other Essays* (New York: Columbia University Press, 1969), 75.

38. W. V. Quine, "Reply to Roger F. Gibson Jr.," in *The Philosophy of W. V. Quine,* edited by Lewis Edwin Hahn and Paul Arthur Schilpp (La Salle, Ill.: Open Court, 1986), 156.

39. Gibson, *Enlightened Empiricism,* 116.

40. Quine, *Word and Object,* 24.

41. Ibid.

42. Ibid.

43. Ibid.

44. Ibid., 24–25.

45. Ibid., 22. Italics added. By this point, it should be clear that purposiveness will be an essential element in my argument for the plurality of actual worlds.

Chapter 3. The Fundamental Ontological Idea

1. Immanuel Kant, *Kant: Philosophical Correspondence, 1759–1799,* edited and translated by Arnulf Zweig (Chicago: University of Chicago Press, 1967), 252.

2. Nelson Goodman and Catherine Z. Elgin, *Reconceptions in Philosophy and Other Arts and Sciences* (Indianapolis: Hackett, 1988), 50.

3. Nelson Goodman, *Ways of Worldmaking* (Indianapolis: Hackett, 1978), 12.

4. Ibid., 2.

5. Kant, *Critique of Pure Reason*, 533, A644 = B672. Cf. 300, A298 = B354.

6. Goodman, *Ways of Worldmaking*, 2–3.

7. G. S. Kirk, J. E. Raven, and M. Schofield, *The Presocratic Philosophers*, 2nd ed. (Cambridge: Cambridge University Press, 1983), 245.

8. Richard D. Wolff and Stephen A. Resnick, *Economics: Marxian versus Neoclassical* (Baltimore: Johns Hopkins University Press, 1987).

9. Ibid., 15. Italics added.

10. Ibid., 19.

11. Ibid., 17–18.

12. Ibid. Note that theories do not observe; people observe.

13. There is a formal difference between a Kantian antinomy and Goodman's enigma. Let R be the thesis of realism, transcendental or metaphysical. In the case of the Kantian antinomy, then, there is statement, S, which is such that (1) if S and R, then not-S, and (2) if not-S and R, then S. Kant resolves an antinomy by rejecting R, whatever its specifics may be. Now, let F be Goodman's pair of truths about frames of reference. In the case of Goodman's enigma, it seems that: if R and F, then not-R. Holding F constant, Goodman's conclusion is: not-R.

14. Goodman, *Ways of Worldmaking*, 3.

15. Ibid., 20.

16. Ibid., 93.

17. Ibid., 3.

18. Ibid., 93.

19. In a radically different idiom, if there were a dialectic that appeared able to sublate all opposing framework relative representations, then it would be necessary to ask: how much opposition could the dialectic sublate, if the dialectic could sublate opposition?

20. Goodman, *Ways of Worldmaking*, 5.

21. Ibid., 3.

22. Ibid.

23. Nelson Goodman, *Of Mind and Other Matters* (Cambridge, Mass.: Harvard University Press, 1984), 31.

24. Goodman and Elgin, *Reconceptions in Philosophy,* 50.

25. Cf. ibid.

26. Ibid., 51.

27. Ibid.

28. Goodman, *Of Mind and Other Matters,* 31.

29. Goodman, *Ways of Worldmaking,* 120. Does Goodman's critique of worldmaking presuppose the ontology of sets and sets of sets that Tarski's account of truth presupposes? It is tempting to take Goodman to be asserting that truth is primary, and that the objects, the sets and sets of sets, which make up the ontologies of the manifold of actual worlds, are derivative. Goodman is, however, a nominalist. He believes that there are only individuals, and that a well-made world is such that if there are k basic entities, or atoms, there are at most 2^k-1 entities that can be constructed from them. The principal nominalist principle is that "if we start from any two distinct entities and break each of them down as far as we like (by taking parts, parts of parts, and so on), we always arrive at some original entity that is contained in one but not the other of our two original entities" (Nelson Goodman, "A World of Individuals," in *Problems and Projects* [Indianapolis: Bobbs-Merrill, 1972], 159). In other words: "For a nominalistic system, no two distinct things have the same atoms; only from different atoms can different things be generated; all non-identities between things are reducible to non-identities between their atoms" (Ibid., 161). Ontologies that violate this principle are not well made, and so the ontology of sets and sets of sets, which is clearly presupposed by Tarski's account of truth, is not well made. It is important to note that it is not that sets per se are bad, instead it is sets of sets that are the source of trouble. Goodman writes: "One may use the sign '$\in$' and speak of classes and yet have a nominalistic system if severe restrictions upon the admitted classes are observed" (Ibid., 171). The aforementioned trouble arises because of the possibility, which nominalism rules out, of there being different entities that are composed of the same entities. For example, imagine an ontology according to which there are four atoms: a, b, c, and d. And, imagine that there are two sets, K and L. Let $K=\{\{a,b\},\{c,d\}\}$ and let $L=\{\{a,c\},\{b,d\}\}$. According to standard set

theoretic principles, *K* and *L* are two things. Since *K* and *L* are composed of the same atoms, they should not, on nominalist scruples, count as two, and so any ontology according to which they do count as two is a defective ontology. This could be a reason for doubting the veracity of Tarski's account of truth. Putting this issue aside, however, Goodman's critique of worldmaking should not depend on an account of truth that presupposes an ontology that is, by its own standards, badly made. Moreover, if Goodman's critique of worldmaking is, in some manner, committed to the ontology of Tarski's conception of truth, it cannot provide an impartial analysis of an actual world where this ontology doesn't obtain. Goodman's critique of worldmaking would then seem to be incapable of accounting for the nominalist ontologies that he himself favors. If, however, that Goodman's critique of worldmaking presupposes his form of nominalism, Platonistic ontologies would then be badly made. So, if Goodman's account of worldmaking presupposes either nominalism or Platonism, one or the other will be ruled out, in a less than fair manner, as ill made, and so it will be incapable of accounting for worlds that are clearly actual. Thus, an analysis of worldmaking that presupposes Goodman's nominalism rules out Platonistic ontologies on the ground that they contain too many entities, and an analysis of worldmaking that presupposes Platonism rules out nominalist ontologies on the ground that they contain too few entities. This is, I think, why Goodman writes: "in this general discussion of worldmaking I do not impose nominalistic restrictions, for I want to allow for some difference of opinion as to what actual worlds there are" (*Ways of Worldmaking*, 95). Goodman's critique of worldmaking must not presuppose nominalism, since this would beg the question against Platonism; and it must not presuppose the Platonism that is presupposed by Tarski's account of truth. So, Goodman's investigation of worldmaking should not invoke Tarski here or anywhere. And, so, one should resist the temptation to write that Goodman thinks that truth is primary, and that the objects, the sets and the sets of sets, et cetera, which constitute the ontologies of the manifold of actual worlds, are derivative. One should say that Goodman thinks that: truth is primary, and that ontology—of whatever strain, nominalist or Platonist—is derivative. If Goodman cannot invoke Tarski, however, how are we to understand his use of 'true'? Moreover, how are we to understand his invocation of Tarski's *T sentences*? These sorts of questions fall far beyond the scope of this work, and so I will bracket them here.

30. Israel Scheffler, "The Wonderful Worlds of Goodman," *Synthése* 45 (1980): 201.

31. Goodman, *Ways of Worldmaking*, 4.

32. Ibid., 7.

33. Scheffler, "Wonderful Worlds of Goodman," 201.

34. Goodman, *Ways of Worldmaking*, 94.

35. Nelson Goodman, "On Starmaking," *Synthése* 45 (1980): 212.

36. Ibid.

37. Ibid.

38. Wittgenstein, *Tractatus Logico-Philosophicus*, 115, sect. 5.6.

39. Thomas Nagel, *The View from Nowhere* (New York: Oxford University Press, 1986), 90.

40. Ibid., 91.

41. G. H. Merrill, "The Model-Theoretic Argument against Realism," *Philosophy of Science* 47 (1980): 72.

42. David Lewis, "Putnam's Paradox," *Australasian Journal of Philosophy* 62 (1984): 228.

43. Goodman, *Ways of Worldmaking*, x.

44. Immanuel Kant, *Prolegomena to Any Future Metaphysics That Will Be Able to Come Forward as Science,* translated by Paul Carus, extensively revised by James W. Ellington (Indianapolis: Hackett, 1977), 5.

45. Cf. Putnam, *Reason, Truth and History,* chapter 1.

46. I will ask my reader to disregard putative counterexamples such as representations, which are both part of the world, and yet not representation-independent. There is, after all, a way—into the nature of which I shall not here inquire—in which representations are representation-dependent.

47. Putnam, "A Defense of Internal Realism," 30. Cf. Putnam, *Reason, Truth and History,* 49.

48. Putnam, *Reason, Truth and History,* 49.

49. Cf. Hilary Putnam, "Truth and Convention: On Davidson's Refutation of Conceptual Relativism," *Dialectica* 41 (1987): 69–77 and *The Many Faces of Realism: The Paul Carus Lectures* (LaSalle, Ill.: Open Court, 1987), 18–20. For an introductory discussion of mereology, see Henry S. Leonard and Nelson Goodman, "The Calculus of Individuals and Its

Uses," *Journal of Symbolic Logic,* 5 (1940): 45–55. In addition, see Nelson Goodman, *The Structure of Appearance,* 3rd ed., with an introduction by Geoffrey Hellman (Boston: Reidel, 1977), 33–40.

50. I will ignore such tacit presuppositions as: for all i and j, $x_i + x_j = x_j + x_i$.

51. Putnam, "Truth and Convention," 70–71.

52. Putnam, *Reason, Truth and History,* 49.

53. Ibid.

54. René Descartes, *Meditations on First Philosophy,* translated from the Latin by Donald A. Cress (Indianapolis: Hackett, 1979), 16.

55. Putnam, *Reason, Truth and History,* 15. Cf. p. 8.

56. Gary Iseminger, "Putnam's Miraculous Argument," *Analysis* 48 (1988): 191n2.

57. Jane MacIntyre, "Putnam's Brains," *Analysis* 44 (1984): 59–61. This is essentially MacIntyre's reconstruction. Note that this version of the argument employs a modalized version of the *consequentia mirabilis;* an argument whose premise has this form: *it must be that if p, then not-p,* and whose conclusion has this form: *it must be that not-p,* is valid. This form of inference is justified by the intuition that if a proposition of the form *if p, then not-p* is true in all possible worlds, then a proposition of the form *not-p* is also true in all possible worlds.

58. Cf. Devitt, *Realism and Truth,* 5, 27, 111, and 149. It must be noted, however, that Michael Devitt and Kim Sterelny have attempted to more fully spell out the content of the causal theory of reference. Compare their *Language and Reality: An Introduction to the Philosophy of Language* (Cambridge, Mass.: MIT Press, 1987). I will here bracket their attempt.

59. Putnam, *Reason, Truth and History,* 14.

60. MacIntyre, "Putnam's Brains," 60.

61. Carol A. Van Kirk, "Kant's Reply to Putnam," *Idealistic Studies* 14 (1984): 14.

62. Thomas Tymoczko, "In Defense of Putnam's Brains," *Philosophical Studies* 57 (1989): 293.

63. Putnam, *Reason, Truth and History,* 15.

64. Ibid.

65. Ibid., 14.

66. It seems obvious that in some worlds, reference is a causal relation, and in others, it is not. So the causal theory of reference is clearly contingent. Consequently, it is unclear how it could be the pivotal reason why it must be that if all of us are bevatted, *All of us are bevatted* is false. I will ignore this sort of problem here.

67. In this account, I more or less follow the excellent exposition provided by Geoffrey Hunter in his *Metalogic: An Introduction to the Metatheory of Standard First Order Logic* (Berkeley, Calif.: University of California Press, 1973). One notable exception is that I omit function symbols from Q. I have also drawn much from Elliott Mendelson, *Introduction to Mathematical Logic*, 3rd ed. (Pacific Grove, Calif.: Wadsworth & Brooks/Cole Advanced Books and Software, 1987).

68. Note that this is a formal exposition of the intuition that lies behind the string theory of truth, and that strings are the metaphorical representatives of the relations that constitute Tarski's interpretation function.

69. Cf. Alfred Tarski, "The Concept of Truth in Formalized Languages," in *Logic, Semantics, Metamathematics,* 2nd ed., edited and introduced by John Corcoran, translated by J. H. Woodger (Indianapolis: Hackett, 1983), 195.

70. Cf. ibid., 187–88.

71. Cf. MacIntyre, "Putnam's Brains."

72. Note that strings are metaphorical substitutes for the relations that correspond to the interpretation function of Tarski's account of truth. If it seems ludicrous to account for truth in terms of something as physical as string, it is a wonder why it does not seem as ludicrous to account for truth, even if it is truth relative to a formal language, in terms of something as abstract, and therefore as intangible, as a function. I have wondered why the string theory of truth doesn't constitute, therefore, a *reductio ad absurdum* of Tarski's semantic conception of truth, but this is yet another question that I will leave aside in this work.

73. Putnam, *Reason, Truth and History,* 49.

74. Putnam, "Truth and Convention," 70–71. But how could a fact about a question be relevant to the representation dependency or otherwise of objects?

75. Descartes, *Meditations on First Philosophy,* 16.

76. One might object that objects are not evidence, because sentences are evidence for other sentences, or something of this sort. Moreover, one might object that objects do not cohere, because coherence is only defined for sentences. It is evident that I mean something like this: an object is evidence for some world picture just when a sentence about this object is evidence for the picture in question. Moreover, it should also be evident that I mean something such as this: some set of objects is coherent just when some set of sentences about them is coherent. Et cetera.

77. Hume, *Enquiries Concerning the Human Understanding,* 35.

78. Ibid.

79. Ibid.

80. Kant, *Critique of Pure Reason,* 132, A100–101.

Chapter 4. Why There Are Many Actual Worlds

1. Richard Rorty, "The World Well Lost," *Journal of Philosophy* 69 (1972): 649–50. Italics added. Compare A. C. Genova, "Kant and Alternative Conceptual Frameworks," in *Akten des 4. Internationalen Kant-Kongresses* 2, (1974): 834–41. Also cf. Patrick Gardiner, "German Philosophy and the Rise of Relativism," *The Monist* 64 (1981): 138–54.

2. Ibid., 650.

3. Aristotle, *De Generatione et Corruptione,* translated by Harold H. Joachim, in *The Basic Works of Aristotle,* edited with an introduction by Richard McKeon (New York: Random House, 1941), 485, 320a1–2 (book I, chapter 4).

4. Aristotle, *Metaphysica,* translated by W. D. Ross, in *The Basic Works of Aristotle,* edited with an introduction by Richard McKeon (New York: Random House, 1941), 785, 1029a11–26 (book VII, chapter 3). Italics added.

5. George Berkeley, *The Principles of Human Knowledge,* in *The Works of George Berkeley: Bishop of Cloyne,* vol. 2, edited by A. A. Luce and T. E. Jessop (London: Thomas Nelson and Sons, 1949), 47 (sect. 16).

6. Ibid., 75 (sect. 80).

7. Rorty, "The World Well Lost," 650.

8. Kant, *Critique of Pure Reason,* 41, A1. Italics added.

9. Ibid. Italics added.

10. Theodore W. Schick, "Rorty and Davidson on Alternate Conceptual Schemes," *Journal of Speculative Philosophy* 1 (1987): 291–303.

11. Ibid., 295. Italics added.

12. Ibid., 296.

13. Kant, *Critique of Pure Reason,* 151, B129.

14. Rorty, "The World Well Lost," 651. Italics added.

15. Quine, "Two Dogmas of Empiricism," 43.

16. Plato, *Theaetetus,* 66–67, 184e9–185a3.

17. Ibid., 67–68, 185a7-e4. Italics added.

18. Perhaps the following remarks are in order. My discussion of Protagoras has depended heavily on Plato's text. Now, not only have I avoided the immensely complicated problems of its interpretation, but I have also avoided the equally complicated problem of extracting Plato's views from his account of Protagoras. Plato is hardly a disinterested reporter of the Protagorean vision. It is difficult to forget that Plato maintains that some untruths are necessary. Compare Plato, *Republic,* translated by G. M. A. Grube (Indianapolis: Hackett, 1974), 82, 414c. So, it might be that Plato's presentation of Protagoras is twisted, and that he thought that this misrepresentation is just one of a number of necessary untruths. I do not wish to deny that philosophically interesting readings may sometimes depend on certain twists of the text, and I would note that a philosophically important reconstruction of the Protagorean thing may itself require a certain metatwisting of the Platonic texts. Indeed, my readings of Whorf, et alia, have been, so to speak, systematically misleading readings, but this has been in the service of the development of both a philosophically interesting reading, and the development of my own views. I will not enter into these issues here.

19. Franz Brentano, *Psychology from an Empirical Standpoint,* edited by Oskar Kraus, English edition edited by Linda L. McAlister, translated by Antos C. Rancurello, D. B. Terrell, and Linda L. McAlister (New York: Humanities Press, 1973), 159.

20. Ibid.

21. Ibid.

22. William James, *The Principles of Psychology,* vol. 1, (New York: Dover, 1950), 160. Cf. Norman Kemp-Smith, *A Commentary to Kant's "Critique of Pure Reason,"* 2nd ed., revised and enlarged (New York: Macmillan, 1979), 459n1. Also cf. Robert Paul Wolff, in his *Kant's Theory of Mental Activity: A Commentary on the Transcendental Analytic of the Critique of Pure Reason* (Cambridge, Mass.: Harvard University Press, 1963), 105–9.

23. Cf. Kant, *Critique of Pure Reason,* 111, A77 = B102. Also cf. p. 131, A99.

24. Ibid., 135, A105.

25. Ibid., 151, B129.

26. Maurice Merleau-Ponty, *Phenomenology of Perception,* translated by Colin Smith (New York: Humanities Press, 1962), 229.

27. Compare Kant, *Critique of Pure Reason,* 140, A114.

28. Immanuel Kant, *"On the Form and Principles of the Sensible and the Intelligible World (Inaugural Dissertation),"* in *Kant's Latin Writings,* edited and translated by Lewis White Beck et al. (New York: Peter Lang, 1986), 174.

29. Plato, *Theaetetus,* 19, 154a.

30. Kant, *Critique of Pure Reason,* 134, A104.

31. Ibid., 219, B234–35 = A189–90.

32. Ibid., 22, Bxvi–xvii. Italics added.

33. Kant, *Prolegomena,* 38.

34. The project of articulating Kant's account of what it is to be an object could be immense. To avoid the obvious problems, not only will I focus on an account that can be found in the above-mentioned texts, but I will work, more or less without question, within the framework of the reading provided by Robert Paul Wolff in his *Kant's Theory of Mental Activity.* Cf. pp. 100–134, 154–64, and 260–80.

35. Kant, *Critique of Pure Reason,* 140, A113–14.

36. Ibid., 218, A189.

37. Cf. *A Commentary to Kant's "Critique of Pure Reason,"* 202–34.

38. Kant, *Critique of Pure Reason,* 137, A108.

39. Wolff, *Kant's Theory of Mental Activity,* 109.

40. There is a problem with this, however. An essential Kantian thesis is that the manifold possesses the unity illustrated by James's thought experiment because its elements are subsumable under rules. If the distinction between an objective and a subjective representation is the distinction between a representation that can and one that cannot be subsumed under rules that connect it with other representations, then only a fragment, that is, a proper subset, of the elements of the manifold is subsumable under rules, else all representations are objective. So the explanation of the unity of consciousness cannot be that the elements of the manifold are subsumable under rules. I am not sure what to say about this, and so I will, in this work, suspend the questions that it raises.

41. Wolff, *Kant's Theory of Mental Activity,* 112–13.

42. Kant, *Critique of Pure Reason,* 134, A104.

43. To avoid the repetitive use of the prolix phrase *unique, distinct, and representation-independent object,* or any one of a number of equally prolix phrases, I shall often make use of much more compact phrases such as *unique object, distinct object, utterly distinct object, independent object,* and so on.

44. Kant, *Critique of Pure Reason,* 134, A104.

45. Ibid.

46. Ludwig Wittgenstein, *Philosophical Investigations,* the English text of the third edition, translated by G. E. M. Anscombe (New York: Macmillan, 1958), p. 95e, sect. 271.

47. Kant, *Critique of Pure Reason,* 134, A104.

48. Ibid., 135, A105.

49. Ibid.

50. Ralph Barton Perry, "The Ego-Centric Predicament," *Journal of Philosophy, Psychology and Scientific Methods* 7 (1910): 8.

51. Henry E. Allison, *Kant's Transcendental Idealism: An Interpretation and Defense* (New Haven: Yale University Press, 1983), 10.

52. Kant, *Critique of Pure Reason,* 125–26, A92 = B125.

53. It is doubtful whether Kant's most thought-out position is that it can be known *a priori* that the structure of space is Euclidean. It is true that Kant writes as if it is his aim to show that certain geometric principles, for example, "there . . . [is] . . . only one straight line between two points,"

are strictly universal and necessary (ibid., 69, A24). However, it is only in the first edition of the *Critique* that Kant proffers the argument that geometry is *a priori* because such principles are necessary. It is as if Kant realized that such an argument goes further than transcendental reflection is permitted to go, and that the truly critical doctrine only shows how there can be *a priori* knowledge of space, not that some specific geometric principle is an instance of such knowledge. Similarly, Kant only intends to show that every event follows another event according to a rule, not that this event follows that event according to this specific rule. He doesn't think that it is possible to show, for example, that lung cancer follows smoking according to a rule that is far beyond my ability to state. In *The Transcendental Exposition of the Concept of Space*, Kant writes as if his only aim is to show how there can be strictly universal and necessary truths about space. He wrote that the concept or *a priori* intuition of space is "a principle from which the possibility of other *a priori* synthetic knowledge can be understood" (ibid., 70, B40). I will ignore this issue here.

54. H. J. Paton, *Kant's Metaphysic of Experience*, vol. 1 (New York: Humanities Press, 1936), 166.

55. A. C. Ewing, *A Short Commentary on Kant's* Critique of Pure Reason (Chicago: University of Chicago Press, 1938), 30. Cf. Richard E. Aquila, *Representational Mind: A Study of Kant's Theory of Knowledge* (Bloomington: Indiana University Press, 1983), 68–69. It is remarkable that Wolff nowhere mentions the metaphor of the blue tinted spectacles, given his unequivocal remark: "A serious philosophical argument cannot be based on a metaphorical premise" (*Kant's Theory of Mental Activity*, 101.

56. Paton, *Kant's Metaphysic of Experience*, 169.

57. Immanuel Kant, *Metaphysical Foundations of Natural Science*, translated James W. Ellington (Indianapolis: Hackett, 1985), 3. Italics added. Note well that this is not the same as saying that a world is a sum of actually represented objects.

58. Kant, *Critique of Pure Reason*, 134–35, A104–5. Italics added.

59. Ibid., 224, A197 = B242–43. It might make better sense here to translate *Bedeutung* as "reference."

60. Ibid., 129, A95.

61. Ibid., 135, A106.

62. Wolff, *Kant's Theory of Mental Activity,* 123. Italics added. It seems to be that the notions of belonging together and being set off are as vague as the notion of the unity of consciousness that Kant wishes to explain, but I will not pursue this issue here.

63. Kant, *Critique of Pure Reason,* 140, A113–14.

64. Kant, *Prolegomena,* 38.

65. Wolff, *Kant's Theory of Mental Activity,* 133–34.

66. Kant, *Critique of Pure Reason,* 224, A197.

67. Bas C. Van Fraassen, *An Introduction to the Philosophy of Time and Space* (New York: Columbia University Press, 1985), 89.

68. Ibid., 92.

69. Ibid., 93.

70. W. Dilthey, *Selected Writings,* edited, translated, and introduced by H. P. Rickman (Cambridge: Cambridge University Press, 1976), 209. Quoted by Wolff, "Narrative Time," 216.

71. This is not my idea, rather it is an idea articulated by Wolff in his "Narrative Time." I add an argument for the conclusion that the premise that purposes impose an anisotropic structure on human time in conjunction with the Kantian account of what it is to be a world implies that there are many actual worlds.

Chapter 5. Turning to the Social Theoretic

1. This asymmetry is the same as the anisotropy of a world's time. It might be that the time of the world of science is isotropic, but this would be an artifact of the shared aim of the members of the scientific community to systematically remove all reference to their aims from their collectively produced representation of what they take to be the one and only world. If the time of science is isotropic, this is because the scientist aims at aimlessness, and so the world of science is, paradoxically, quite mysterious.

2. Peter L. Berger and Thomas Luckmann, *The Social Construction of Reality: A Treatise in the Sociology of Knowledge* (New York: Anchor Books, Doubleday, 1966), 21–22. Berger and Luckmann use the first person singular to indicate or to stand for "ordinary self-consciousness in everyday life." Cf. p. 20.

3. This problem rests on the merely tacit assumption that social constructs must be experienced for what they are, that is, constructs. I presume that one might say this because one believes that since we construct the representations that constitute the objects, then nothing of these objects should be hidden from us, and this includes their being constructs. One might just object to this assumption on the grounds that the social theoretic case is its counterexample, but I would not pursue this here.

4. Ibid., 1.

5. Ibid., 61.

6. The innocence of Berger and Luckmann's account of the social construction of reality is really quite remarkable. On the one hand, this is clearly the result of a methodological abstraction, and in this context, it is somewhat understandable. On the other hand, this abstraction hides the vicissitudes of the origins of institutions, and in this context, their account strains credibility. Foucault put it well: "What is found at the historical beginning of things is not the inviolable identity of their origin; it is the dissension of other things. It is disparity" (Michel Foucault, "Nietzsche, Genealogy, History," in *Language, Counter-Memory, Practice: Selected Essays and Interviews,* edited with an introduction by Donald F. Bouchard, translated from the French by Donald F. Bouchard and Sherry Simon [Ithaca, N.Y.: Cornell University Press, 1977], 142.)

7. Berger and Luckmann, *Social Construction of Reality,* 58–59.

8. Ibid., 59.

9. Ibid., 60.

10. Noam Chomsky, *Cartesian Linguistics: A Chapter in the History of Rationalist Thought* (New York: Harper & Row, 1966), 3.

11. Berger and Luckmann, *Social Construction of Reality,* p. 52.

12. There is one good reason to think that social objects are constructed: if there were no social subjects, there would be no social objects.

13. Plato, *Phaedrus*, translated, with an introduction and notes, by Alexander Nehamas and Paul Woodruff, with a selection of early Greek poems and fragments about love, translated by Paul Woodruff (Indianapolis: Hackett, 1995), 64, 265d.

14. Ibid., 265e.

15. Cf. "On the Individuation of Attributes," in *Theories and Things* (Cambridge, Mass.: Belknap Press of Harvard University Press, 1981), 100–112, especially 102: "There is no entity without identity."

16. Michel Foucault, *The Order of Things: An Archaeology of the Human Sciences* (New York: Vintage Books, 1994). My discussion of Foucault includes much that I have ascertained from Gary Gutting's informative and lucid *Michel Foucault: Archaeology of Scientific Reason* (Cambridge: Cambridge University Press, 1989). The following have been similarly helpful: Hubert L. Dreyfus and Paul Rabinow, *Michel Foucault: Beyond Structuralism and Hermeneutics*, 2nd ed., with an afterword by and an interview with Michel Foucault (Chicago: University of Chicago Press, 1983); Alan Sheridan, *Michel Foucault: The Will to Truth* (London and New York: Tavistock Publications, 1980).

17. I think that *object* is ambiguous between (1) a concrete or physical thing that can be perceived by means of the senses, and (2) anything about which one can form a judgment. Clearly, I intend the second in this context. Moreover, anything that is an object in the first sense is an object in the second sense, and in both senses, although perhaps more obviously in the second, an object is what an ideally completable manifold of objective representations represents.

18. Foucault, *Order of Things*, 39.

19. Quoted by Foucault, ibid.

20. Kant seems to have thought that modal concepts are rules for making the rules that synthesize our representations, but I have here assumed that modality is a kind of object, namely, not only something about which it is possible to judge, as did Aldrovandi and Buffon, but also something with which one can be acquainted. It might seem that to embrace this is to abandon the Kantian perspective of this entire work, since this perspective depends on the supposition that there is a nonempty distinction between what can and cannot be perceived, and if modalities can be perceived, there is no principled way to keep this distinction nonempty. What cannot be perceived, I think, is the objectivity of a representation. The objectivity of a representation is a matter of its relation to other representations, and this relation, if it obtains, cannot be perceived, and so it must be constructed in thought, and this is, I think, all that needed to maintain the elements of the Kantian perspective that I need.

21. As Deleuze remarks: "Experiment, never interpret." Quoted by Alan D. Schrift, *Nietzsche's French Legacy: A Genealogy of Poststructuralism* (New York: Routledge, 1995), 62.

22. Quoted by Foucault, *Order of Things*, 19.

23. Quoted by Foucault, ibid., 20.

24. Ibid., 21.

25. Ibid., 22.

26. Quoted by Foucault, ibid.

27. Ibid.

28. Ibid.

29. Ibid., 23.

30. Ibid.

31. Ibid.

32. Quoted by Foucault, ibid., 24.

33. Ibid., 26.

34. Quoted by Foucault, ibid.

35. Ibid., 27. It is Crollius who is quoted.

36. Gutting, *Michel Foucault*, 143.

37. Foucault, *Order of Things*, 35.

38. Ibid., 33.

39. Quoted by Foucault, ibid., 39.

40. Ibid.

41. René Descartes, "Rules for the Direction of the Mind," in *The Philosophical Writings of Descartes*, vol. 1, translated by John Cottingham, Robert Stoothoff, and Dugald Murdoch (Cambridge: Cambridge University Press, 1985), 14. Others translate this passage in a way that makes it seem that the two sources of knowledge are intuition and induction, but this is acknowledged to be (i) the result of indecision on Descartes part, or (ii) a misprint in the Latin, or (iii) his intended meaning. For the first, cf. *Descartes: Philosophical Writings*, selected and translated by Norman Kemp Smith (New York: Modern Library, 1958), 10, note 8. For the second, cf. *Descartes: Philosophical Writings*, a selection translated and

edited by Elizabeth Anscombe and Peter Thomas Geach, with an introduction by Alexandre Koyré, (Edinburgh: Thomas Nelson and Sons, 1954), 155, note 1. For the last, cf. *The Philosophical Works of Descartes*, vol. 1, translated by Elizabeth S. Haldane and G. R. T. Ross (Cambridge: Cambridge University Press, 1911), 7.

42. Cottingham, Stoothoff, and Murdoch, *Philosophical Writings of Descartes*, 57.

43. Ibid.

44. Foucault, *Order of Things*, 57.

45. Cottingham, Stoothoff, and Murdoch, *Philosophical Writings of Descartes*, 13. I have omitted the notes.

46. Foucault, *Order of Things*, 39.

47. Ibid.

48. Gutting, *Michel Foucault*, 145.

49. Goodman, *Ways of Worldmaking*, 10–11.

50. Gutting, *Michel Foucault*, 145.

51. Michel Foucault, *The Archaeology of Knowledge & The Discourse on Language*, translated by A. M. Sheridan Smith and Rupert Sawyer (New York: Barnes & Noble Books, 1972), 7.

52. Compare Collingwood's remark that: "When a man thinks historically, he has before him certain documents or relics of the past. His business is to discover what the past was which has left these relics behind it. For example, the relics are certain written words; and in that case he has to discover what the person who wrote those words meant by them. This means discovering the thought . . . which he expressed by them. To discover what this thought was, the historian must think it again for himself." R. G. Collingwood, *The Idea of History* (London: Oxford University Press, 1946), 282–283.

53. Compare Hilbert's remark that "in my theory contentual inference [documents] is replaced by manipulation of signs [monuments] . . . according to rules [epistemes]." David Hilbert, "The Foundations of Mathematics," in *From Frege to Gödel: A Source Book in Mathematical Logic, 1879–1931*, edited by Jean van Heijenhoort (Cambridge, Mass.: Harvard University Press, 1967), 467. Given that it has been shown by Gödel that for any axiomatized system of arithmetic, A, there is a well-formed formula of A, p, such that neither p nor $\sim p$ is a theorem of A, it may be supposed

that Hilbert's theory of mathematics has been decisively discredited. Has Foucault met his Gödel? Could it have been Lacan? Is the Lacanian Real the Gödelian undecidable formula of Foucaultian archaeology? Is Gödel's undecidable formula the Lacanian Real of Hilbertian arithmetic? I will leave these sorts of questions aside.

54. Foucault, *Archaeology of Knowledge,* 55.

55. Ibid.

56. There is another problem with the modified account that Gutting might impute to Foucault. Namely, since it rests on the premise that the Renaissance episteme, for example, itself distributes some sort of weights over the manifold of possible Renaissance statements, it is necessary to be clear about the relation between the set of possible statements, the conjectured weighting function and what it is that makes a statement possible. However, the distribution of such weights cannot account for the modality of these statements, to wit, their possibility. The possible statements must be identifiable independently of the weighting function, because the weighting function maps the possible statements onto various weights. If the domain of the conjectured weighting function is a set of possible statements, it cannot be that these statements are made possible by this function. What are the possible statements? Are they the statements that *could* be made in the context of the some episteme? Then the possibility of a statement is not determined by the supposed weighting function. Are they all the possible statements *simpliciter?* Are they all the statements that can be made in the context of any episteme? Foucault seems to be committed to the idea that modality is relative to some episteme, and so it is not the former; he does not address the latter, but even so, what we are dealing with here is a pair of statements whose modalities are relative to the Renaissance and the classical epistemes, and if this is so, they are not to be counted among the possible statements *simpliciter.*

57. Compare Thomas Nagel, "What Is It Like to Be a Bat?," and "Subjective and Objective," in *Mortal Questions* (Cambridge: Cambridge University Press, 1979), 165–80 and 196–213 respectively.

Bibliography

Allison, Henry E. *Kant's Transcendental Idealism: An Interpretation and Defense.* New Haven: Yale University Press, 1983.

Aquila, Richard E. *Representational Mind: A Study of Kant's Theory of Knowledge.* Bloomington: Indiana University Press, 1983.

Aristotle. *De Generatione et Corruptione.* Translated by Harold H. Joachim. In *The Basic Works of Aristotle,* edited by Richard McKeon, 470–531. New York: Random House, 1941.

———. *Metaphysica.* Translated by W. D. Ross. In *The Basic Works of Aristotle,* edited by Richard McKeon, 681–926. New York: Random House, 1941.

Bennett, Jonathan. "Review of J. L. Mackie. Self-Refutation—A Formal Analysis." *Journal of Symbolic Logic* 30 (1965): 365–66.

Berger, Peter L., and Thomas Luckmann. *The Social Construction of Reality: A Treatise in the Sociology of Knowledge.* New York: Anchor Books, Doubleday, 1966.

Berkeley, George. *The Principles of Human Knowledge.* In *The Works of George Berkeley: Bishop of Cloyne,* vol. 2, edited by A. A. Luce and T. E. Jessop, 19–113. London: Thomas Nelson and Sons, 1949.

Brentano, Franz. *Psychology from an Empirical Standpoint.* Edited by Oskar Kraus. English edition edited by Linda L. McAlister, translated by

Antos C. Rancurello, D. B. Terrell, and Linda L. McAlister. New York: Humanities Press, 1973.

Bringsjord, Selmer. "Are There Set-Theoretic Possible Worlds?" *Analysis* 45 (1985): 64.

Burnyeat, M. F. "Protagoras and Self-Refutation in Plato's Theaetetus." *Philosophical Review* 85 (1976): 172–95.

Carroll, John B. Introduction in Benjamin Lee Whorf, *Language, Thought, and Reality,* edited by John B. Carroll. Cambridge, Mass.: M.I.T. Press, 1956.

Chomsky, Noam. *Cartesian Linguistics: A Chapter in the History of Rationalist Thought.* New York: Harper & Row, 1966.

Collingwood, R. G. *The Idea of History.* London: Oxford University Press, 1946.

Davidson, Donald. "On the Very Idea of a Conceptual Scheme." In *Inquiries into Truth and Interpretation,* 183–98. Oxford: Clarendon Press, 1986.

———. "The Method of Truth in Metaphysics." In *Inquiries into Truth and Interpretation,* 199–214. Oxford: Clarendon Press, 1986.

Davson-Galle, Peter. "Self-Refuting Propositions and Relativism." *Metaphilosophy* 22 (1991): 175–78.

de Saussure, Ferdinand. *Course in General Linguistics.* Edited by Charles Bally and Albert Sechechaye with the collaboration of Albert Riedlinger. Translated and annotated by Roy Harris. La Salle, Ill.: Open Court, 1986.

Descartes, René. "Rules for the Direction of the Mind." In *The Philosophical Writings of Descartes,* vol. 1, translated by John Cottingham, Robert Stoothoff, and Dugald Murdoch, 7–76. Cambridge: Cambridge University Press, 1985.

———. *Meditations on First Philosophy.* Translated from the Latin by Donald A. Cress. Indianapolis: Hackett, 1979.

Devitt, Michael. *Realism and Truth.* Princeton: Princeton University Press, 1984.

Devitt, Michael, and Kim Sterelny. *Language and Reality: An Introduction to the Philosophy of Language.* Cambridge, Mass.: M.I.T. Press, 1987.

Dilthey, W. *Selected Writings.* Edited, translated, and introduced by H. P. Rickman. Cambridge: Cambridge University Press, 1976.

Dreyfus, Hubert L., and Paul Rabinow. *Michel Foucault: Beyond Structuralism and Hermeneutics.* 2nd ed. With an afterword by and an interview with Michel Foucault. Chicago: University of Chicago Press, 1983.

Ewing, A. C. *A Short Commentary on Kant's* Critique of Pure Reason. Chicago: University of Chicago Press, 1938.

Feyerabend, Paul. *Against Method: Outline of an Anarchist Theory of Knowledge.* New York: Schocken Books, 1975.

Field, Hartry. "Realism and Relativism." *Journal of Philosophy* 79 (1982): 553–67.

Fine, Arthur. "The Natural Ontological Attitude." In *Scientific Realism,* edited by Jarrett Leplin, 83–107. Berkeley: University of California Press, 1984.

Foucault, Michel. *The Archaeology of Knowledge & The Discourse on Language.* Translated by A. M. Sheridan Smith and Rupert Sawyer. New York: Barnes & Noble Books, 1972.

———. *Language, Counter-Memory, Practice: Selected Essays and Interviews.* Edited by Donald F. Bouchard. Translated from the French by Donald F. Bouchard and Sherry Simon. Ithaca, N.Y.: Cornell University Press, 1977.

———. "Nietzsche, Genealogy, History." In *Language, Counter-Memory, Practice: Selected Essays and Interviews,* edited by Donald F. Bouchard, translated from the French by Donald F. Bouchard and Sherry Simon, 139–64. Ithaca, N.Y.: Cornell University Press, 1977.

———. *The Order of Things: An Archaeology of the Human Sciences.* Translated by Alan Sheridan. New York: Vintage Books Edition, 1994.

Galilei, Galileo. *Dialogue Concerning the Two Chief World Systems—Ptolemaic and Copernican.* Translated by Stillman Drake. Foreword by Albert Einstein. Berkeley: University of California Press, 1962 (1953).

Gardiner, Patrick. "German Philosophy and the Rise of Relativism." *The Monist* 64 (1981): 138–54.

Genova, A. C. "Kant and Alternative Conceptual Frameworks." In *Akten des 4. Internationalen Kant-Kongresses* 2 (1974): 834–41.

Gibson, Roger F., Jr. *Enlightened Empiricism: An Examination of W. V. Quine's Theory of Knowledge*. Tampa: University of South Florida Press, 1988.

Goodman, Nelson. *The Structure of Appearance*, 3rd ed. Boston: Reidel, 1977.

———. *Ways of Worldmaking*. Indianapolis: Hackett, 1978.

———. "On Starmaking." *Synthése* 45 (1980): 211–15.

———. "The New Riddle of Induction." In *Fact, Fiction, and Forecast*, 4th ed., 59–83. Cambridge, Mass.: Harvard University Press, 1983.

———. *Of Mind and Other Matters*. Cambridge, Mass.: Harvard University Press, 1984.

Goodman, Nelson, and Catherine Z. Elgin. *Reconceptions in Philosophy and Other Arts and Sciences*. Indianapolis: Hackett, 1988.

Grim, Patrick. "There Is No Set of All Truths." *Analysis* 44 (1984): 206–8.

———. "On Sets and Worlds: A Reply to Menzel." *Analysis* 46 (1986): 186–91.

Gutting, Gary. *Michel Foucault: Archaeology of Scientific Reason*. Cambridge: Cambridge University Press, 1989.

Haack, Susan. *Deviant Logic: Some Philosophical Issues*. London: Cambridge University Press, 1974.

———. *Philosophy of Logics*. Cambridge: Cambridge University Press, 1978.

Hacking, Ian. "Michel Foucault's Immature Science." *Noûs* 13 (1979): 39–51.

———. "The Archaeology of Foucault." In *Foucault: A Critical Reader*, edited by David Couzens Hoy, 27–40. New York: Basil Blackwell, 1986.

Hemple, Carl G. *Philosophy of Natural Science*. Englewood Cliffs, N.J.: Prentice Hall, 1966.

Hilbert, David. "The Foundations of Mathematics." In *From Frege to Gödel: A Source Book in Mathematical Logic, 1879–1931*, edited by Jean van Heijenhoort, 465–79. Cambridge, Mass.: Harvard University Press, 1967.

Hobbes, Thomas. "Elements of Philosophy." In *The English Works of Thomas Hobbes of Malmesbury*, first collected and edited by Sir William Molesworth, Bart., vol. 1, reprint of the edition of 1839. London: Scientia Aalen, 1962.

Hoy, David Couzens, ed. *Foucault: A Critical Reader.* New York: Basil Blackwell, 1986.

Hume, David. *Enquiries Concerning the Human Understanding and Concerning the Principles of Morals.* Edited by L. A. Selby-Bigge. 2nd ed. Oxford: Clarendon Press, 1902.

Hunter, Geoffrey. *Metalogic: An Introduction to the Metatheory of Standard First Order Logic.* Berkeley: University of California Press, 1973.

Iseminger, Gary. "Putnam's Miraculous Argument." *Analysis* 48 (1988): 190–95.

James, William. *The Principles of Psychology.* Vol. 1. New York: Dover, 1950.

Kant, Immanuel. *Critique of Pure Reason.* Translated by Norman Kemp Smith. New York: St. Martin's Press, 1965.

———. *Metaphysical Foundations of Natural Science.* Translated by James W. Ellington. Indianapolis: Hackett, 1985.

———. "On the Form and Principles of the Sensible and the Intelligible World (Inaugural Dissertation)." In *Kant's Latin Writings,* edited and translated by Lewis White Beck et al., 135–92. New York: Peter Lang, 1986.

———. *Kant: Philosophical Correspondence, 1759–1799.* Edited and translated by Arnulf Zweig. Chicago: University of Chicago Press, 1967.

———. *Prolegomena to Any Future Metaphysics That Will Be Able to Come Forward as Science.* Translated by Paul Carus, extensively revised by James W. Ellington. Indianapolis: Hackett, 1977.

Kemp-Smith, Norman. *A Commentary to Kant's "Critique of Pure Reason."* 2nd ed., revised and enlarged. London: Macmillan, 1979.

Kirk, G. S., J. E. Raven, and M. Schofield. *The Presocratic Philosophers.* 2nd ed. Cambridge: Cambridge University Press, 1983.

Lakoff, George. *Women, Fire, and Dangerous Things: What Categories Reveal about the Mind.* Chicago: University of Chicago Press, 1987.

Leonard, Henry S., and Nelson Goodman. "The Calculus of Individuals and Its Uses." *Journal of Symbolic Logic* 5 (1940): 45–55.

Lewis, David. "Putnam's Paradox." *Australasian Journal of Philosophy* 62 (1984): 221–36.

MacIntyre, Jane. "Putnam's Brains." *Analysis* 44 (1984): 59–61.

Mackie, J. L. "Self-Refutation—A Formal Analysis." *Philosophical Quarterly* 14 (1964): 193–203.

Marlowe, Christopher. *Doctor Faustus*. Edited by Sylvan Barnet. New York: Signet, 1969.

Martin, Laura. " 'Eskimo Words for Snow': A Case Study in the Genesis and Decay of an Anthropological Example." *American Anthropologist* 88 (1986): 418–23.

Matthen, Mohan. "Perception, Relativism, and Truth: Reflections on Plato's *Theaetetus* 152–160." *Dialogue* 24 (1985): 33–58.

Meiland, Jack W. "Is Protagorean Relativism Self-Refuting?" *Grazer Philosophische Studien* 9 (1979): 51–68.

Mendelson, Elliott. *Introduction to Mathematical Logic*. 3rd ed. Pacific Grove, Calif.: Wadsworth & Brooks/Cole Advanced Books and Software, 1987.

Menzel, Christopher. "On Set-Theoretic Possible Worlds." *Analysis* 46 (1986): 68–72.

Merleau-Ponty, Maurice. *Phenomenology of Perception*. Translated by Colin Smith. New York: Humanities Press, 1962.

Merrill, G. H. "The Model-Theoretic Argument against Realism." *Philosophy of Science* 47 (1980): 69–81.

Murray, Stephen O. "Snowing Canonical Texts." *American Anthropologist* 89 (1987): 443–44.

Nagel, Thomas. "Subjective and Objective." In *Mortal Questions*, 196–213. Cambridge: Cambridge University Press, 1979.

———. "What Is It Like to Be a Bat?" In *Mortal Questions*, 165–180. Cambridge: Cambridge University Press, 1979.

———. *The View from Nowhere*. New York: Oxford University Press, 1986.

Neurath, Otto. "Protocol Sentences." In *Logical Positivism*, edited by A. J. Ayer, 199–208. Glencoe, Ill.: Free Press, 1959.

Nietzsche, Friedrich. *Twilight of the Idols or, How One Philosophizes with a Hammer*. In *The Portable Nietzsche*, translated by Walter Kaufmann, 463–563. New York: Viking Press, 1954.

O'Connor, D. J. *The Correspondence Theory of Truth*. London: Hutchinson University Library, 1975.

Passmore, John. *Philosophical Reasoning.* New York: Basic Books, 1969.

Paton, H. J. *Kant's Metaphysic of Experience.* Volume 1. New York: Humanities Press, 1936.

Peirce, Charles Sanders. "The Fixation of Belief." In *Philosophical Writings of Peirce,* selected and edited by Justus Buchler, 5–22. New York: Dover, 1955.

Perry, Ralph Barton. "The Ego-Centric Predicament." *Journal of Philosophy, Psychology and Scientific Methods* 7 (1910): 5–14.

Plato. *Theaetetus.* Translated with notes by John McDowell. Oxford: Clarendon Press, 1973.

———. *Republic.* Translated by G. M. A. Grube. Indianapolis: Hackett, 1974.

Pullum, Geoffrey K. "The Great Eskimo Vocabulary Hoax." In *The Great Eskimo Vocabulary Hoax and Other Irreverent Essays on the Study of Language,* 159–71. Chicago: University of Chicago Press, 1991.

Putnam, Hilary. "Realism and Reason." *Proceedings and Addresses of the American Philosophical Association* 50 (1977): 483–97.

———. "Models and Reality." *Journal of Symbolic Logic* 45 (1980): 464–82.

———. *Reason, Truth and History.* Cambridge: Cambridge University Press, 1981.

———. *The Many Faces of Realism: The Paul Carus Lectures.* LaSalle, Ill.: Open Court, 1987.

———. "Truth and Convention: On Davidson's Refutation of Conceptual Relativism." *Dialectica* 41 (1987): 69–77.

———. "Model Theory and the 'Factuality' of Semantics." In *Reflections on Chomsky,* edited by Alexander George, 213–32. Oxford: Basil Blackwell, 1989.

———. "A Defense of Internal Realism." In *Realism with a Human Face,* edited by James Conant, 30–42. Cambridge, Mass.: Harvard University Press, 1990.

Quine, Willard Van Orman. *Word and Object.* Cambridge, Mass.: M.I.T. Press, 1960.

———. "Epistemology Naturalized." In *Ontological Relativity and Other Essays,* 69–90. New York: Columbia University Press, 1969.

———. "To Chomsky." In *Words and Objections: Essays on the Work of W. V. Quine*, 302–11. Dordrecht, North Holland: Reidel, 1969.

———. "On the Reasons for Indeterminacy of Translation." *Journal of Philosophy* 67 (1970): 179–83.

———. "On Empirically Equivalent Systems of the World." *Erkenntnis* 9 (1975): 313–28.

———. "On What There Is." In *From a Logical Point of View: Nine Logico-Philosophical Essays*, 2nd ed., revised, 1–19. Cambridge, Mass.: Harvard University Press, 1980.

———. "Two Dogmas of Empiricism." In *From a Logical Point of View: Nine Logico-Philosophical Essays*, 2nd ed., revised, 20–46. Cambridge, Mass.: Harvard University Press, 1980.

———. "Empirical Content." In *Theories and Things*, 24–30. Cambridge, Mass.: Harvard University Press, 1981.

———. "Things and Their Place in Theories." In *Theories and Things*, 1–23. Cambridge, Mass.: Harvard University Press, 1981.

———. "Reply to Roger F. Gibson, Jr." In *The Philosophy of W. V. Quine*, edited by Lewis Edwin Hahn and Paul Arthur Schilpp, 155–57. LaSalle, Ill.: Open Court, 1986.

Racevskis, Karlis. *Michel Foucault and the Subversion of Intellect*. Ithaca, N.Y.: Cornell University Press, 1983.

Rorty, Richard. "The World Well Lost." *Journal of Philosophy* 69 (1972): 649–65.

———. "Foucault and Epistemology." In *Foucault: A Critical Reader*, edited by David Couzens Hoy, 41–49. New York: Basil Blackwell, 1986.

Scheffler, Israel. "The Wonderful Worlds of Goodman." *Synthése* 45 (1980): 201–9.

Schick, Theodore W. "Rorty and Davidson on Alternate Conceptual Schemes." *Journal of Speculative Philosophy* 1 (1987): 291–303.

Schultz, Emily A. *Dialogue at the Margins: Whorf, Bakhtin, and Linguistic Relativity*. Madison: University of Wisconsin Press, 1990.

Sheridan, Alan. *Michel Foucault: The Will to Truth*. London: Tavistock, 1980.

Tarski, Alfred. "The Concept of Truth in Formalized Languages." In *Logic, Semantics, Metamathematics*, 2nd ed., edited by John Corcoran, translated by J. H. Woodger, 152–278. Indianapolis: Hackett, 1983.

Trigg, Roger. *Reason and Commitment.* Cambridge: Cambridge University Press, 1973.

Tymoczko, Thomas. "In Defense of Putnam's Brains." *Philosophical Studies* 57 (1989): 281–97.

Van Fraassen, Bas C. *An Introduction to the Philosophy of Time and Space.* New York: Columbia University Press, 1985.

Van Kirk, Carol A. "Kant's Reply to Putnam." *Idealistic Studies* 14 (1984): 13–23.

Wartenberg, Thomas E. "Foucault's Archeological Method: A Response to Hacking and Rorty." *Philosophical Forum* 15 (1984): 345–64.

White, F. C. "Self-Refuting Propositions and Relativism." *Metaphilosophy* 20 (1989): 84–92.

Whorf, Benjamin Lee. "An American Indian Model of the Universe." In *Language, Thought, and Reality,* edited by John B. Carroll, 57–64. Cambridge, Mass.: M.I.T. Press, 1956.

———. "Gestalt Technique of Stem Composition in Shawnee." In *Language, Thought, and Reality,* edited by John B. Carroll, 160–72. Cambridge, Mass.: M.I.T. Press, 1956.

———. "Languages and Logic." In *Language, Thought, and Reality,* edited by John B. Carroll, 233–45. Cambridge, Mass.: M.I.T. Press, 1956.

———. "Science and Linguistics." In *Language, Thought, and Reality,* edited by John B. Carroll, 207–19. Cambridge, Mass.: M.I.T. Press, 1956.

———. "The Punctual and Segmentative Aspects of Verbs in Hopi." In *Language, Thought, and Reality,* edited by John B. Carroll, 51–56. Cambridge, Mass.: M.I.T. Press, 1956.

Wittgenstein, Ludwig. *Philosophical Investigations.* English text of the 3rd ed., translated by G. E. M. Anscombe. New York: Macmillan, 1958.

Wittgenstein, Ludwig. *Tractatus Logico-Philosophicus.* Translated by D. F. Pears and B. F. McGuinness. London: Routledge & Kegan Paul, 1961.

Wolff, Robert Paul. *Kant's Theory of Mental Activity: A Commentary on the Transcendental Analytic of the* Critique of Pure Reason. Cambridge, Mass.: Harvard University Press, 1963.

———. "Narrative Time: The Inherently Perspectival Structure of the Human World." In *Midwest Studies in Philosophy,* volume 15: *The Philoso-*

phy of the Human Sciences, edited by Peter A. French, Theodore E. Uehling Jr., and Howard K. Wettstein, 210–33. Notre Dame, Ind.: University of Notre Dame Press, 1990.

Wolff, Richard D., and Stephen A. Resnick. *Economics: Marxian versus Neoclassical.* Baltimore: Johns Hopkins University Press, 1987.

Index